Donatian

D0120143

600069902

FAREWELL BRITANNIA

Also by Simon Young

A.D.500

FAREWELL BRITANNIA

*A Family Saga
of Roman Britain*

SIMON YOUNG

Weidenfeld & Nicolson
LONDON

First published in Great Britain in 2007
by Weidenfeld & Nicolson

1 3 5 7 9 10 8 6 4 2

© 2007 Simon Young

A CIP catalogue record for this book
is available from the British Library.

ISBN-13   978 0 297 852261
ISBN-10   0 297 85226 4

Typeset by Input Data Services Ltd, Frome

Printed in Great Britain by Butler and Tanner Ltd, Frome and London

Weidenfeld & Nicolson

The Orion Publishing Group Ltd
Orion House
5 Upper Saint Martin's Lane
London, WC2H 9EA

The Orion Publishing Group's policy is to use papers that are natural,
renewable and recyclable products and made from wood grown in
sustainable forests. The logging and manufacturing processes are
expected to conform to the environmental regulations
of the country of origin.

w.orionbooks.co.uk

'Old men ought to be explorers'
East Coker

Illustrator: Lawrie Robertson
(Portraits are based on Roman and Romano-British works of art)

CONTENTS

CONTENTS

PREFACE

The impressive remains of Roman Britain are all around us. For the last two hundred years, tourists have been walking along the ragged juts of Hadrian's Wall. Campers can put up a tent on the high bank of a fort in Scotland that a Roman legion dug on a summer afternoon almost two millennia ago. And there is a cricket ground in what was once the Roman coastal castle at Porchester, with its extraordinary fortifications; fortifications that have proved so durable that they also served as a prisoner-of-war camp in the early nineteenth century and part of Britain's Second World War defences in the twentieth. But, in as much as these Imperial edifices take our breath away and give us a sense of solidity and connection with the past, they deceive. Roman Britain lies infinitely further away from us today than the sixteen hundred years that separate our present from theirs; for the single most important thing about Roman Britain is that it was utterly, utterly destroyed.

Indeed, in the fifth century, as the walls came tumbling down throughout the western half of the Roman Empire, Britain was not only separated from the rest of Graeco-Roman civilisation, but was torn up into confetti-sized pieces. The Romano-British economy collapsed, towns emptied, long-distance trade broke down, learning and technical know-how vanished, and into this confusion came a riot of different barbarians – above all, the Anglo-Saxons, the ancestors of the modern English – who completely conquered the south and east of the island, while destabilising the north and the west. There is nothing in British history to compare with this trauma. Indeed, there is little in European history, for, with some very few exceptions, significant elements of Roman life survived in every other part of the collapsing Empire. In fact, elsewhere there was clear continuity between the Roman and the medieval period: so much so that there are fierce debates about in which century the transition between these two periods took place. In Britain, on the other hand, so sudden and unmistakable is the break that we argue not about centuries, not even decades, but about years, with scholars facing off over whether the end came in 407, 410 or 411. History descended on the island like a blade.

Modern Britons owe a great deal to the barbarian successors of the Romano-British, the Anglo-Saxons: we have the dominant language of the isles, English; a good part of our political institutions; and the borders of Scotland, England and Wales from them. We also owe much to the Celts who antedated and, in the west, survived Rome: our strong sense of insularity; the spread of Christianity; not to mention the interaction between periphery and centre in British history. But to the Romano-British we owe nothing. Though their civilisation was, at least to our eyes, more impressive than what went before and that which came after, it also proved more perishable. The result is that when we walk around a reconstituted mud hut at a West Stow open day, where an Anglo-Saxon village was once to be found, or climb onto the magnificent heights of South Cadbury hill-fort, which the British Celts inhabited long before the Romans came, we are touching a part of our history that is still alive and buzzing today. But Roman Britain is, in a very real sense, not part of our history at all. It is a ghost. One that haunts the island and was already doing so when, three centuries after the Empire's demise, an Anglo-Saxon poet composed a work describing the ruins of a Roman city as a 'Metropolis of Giants', the implication being that it belonged to some strange non-human past. What modern Britons have of Rome was imported through the Church or, self-consciously, by Renaissance humanists. It was not handed down from generation to generation in the language and culture of the people as was the case in, say, France.

Yet, paradoxically, for all that Britannia, as the Romans called their most northerly province, is insulated from us, it is far more similar to the modern island than the more important, historically speaking, Celtic or Anglo-Saxon (or Norman or Plantagenet) versions of Britain. So the Romans had, for example, a professional standing army, such as the island would not have again for well over a millennium. The Romano-British economy was potent with factories, mines and workshops; not until the Tudors would Britain know anything like it. It was governed by a unitary, efficient state in a way that could not be said of England until the sixteenth century, and perhaps not even then. Its infrastructure of roads and plumbing was not matched till the eighteenth century. The range of foreign residents was mind-boggling – we are speaking here not just of Italians, but Germans, Gauls, Syrians, Egyptians, Arabs, Ethiopians ... – and would only be equalled in the early nineteenth century, when the British Empire was close to its height. Indeed, to look at Roman Britain is to be confronted with a world that has more in common with our own than with the tribal societies that preceded and proceeded from it. It is to look, in fact, in a mirror: a fairground distorting mirror perhaps, but a mirror nonetheless.

In *Farewell Britannia* I have moulded the story of this surprisingly familiar but impossibly distant world into the saga of a single fictional family; the members of whom were real Romano-Britons, appropriated by the present author – some belonging to the royal dynasty of a tribe named the Atrebates in southern Britain. (Atrebates is, in fact, the name I give to this family.) Other named individuals in the following pages are all also attested in Romano-British or Roman sources, often in the very roles that they take up here, while the customs of day-to-day life, many objects and 'moments' are borrowed from the extraordinary archive on Britannia put together by historians, linguists and archaeologists over the last one hundred and fifty years. For further outlines see the Historical Background section at the end of each chapter; for some words on approach, references and 'curiosities' see, instead, the Notes at the end of the book.

The Atrebates family tree was hammered, screwed and nailed into place by the author with the help of a number of friends, relations and colleagues. Here I must record my gratitude to Benjamin Buchan, Salvatore Costanza, Michelle Gallagher, Linari House, Linden Lawson, Andrew Lownie, Droo Ray, Lawrie Robertson, Judith Round, Maria del Sasso, Stuart Spencer, Don and Ali Stubbs, Stephen Young, Gosia and Przem Zysk and, above all, my loving wife Valentina. It is dedicated to the memory of Tony Young (†1984) 'qui solus forte Romanae gentis superfuit'.

Simon Young
Santa Brigida
October 2006

THE ATREBATES FAMILY

Numbers indicate chapters in which the family member appears

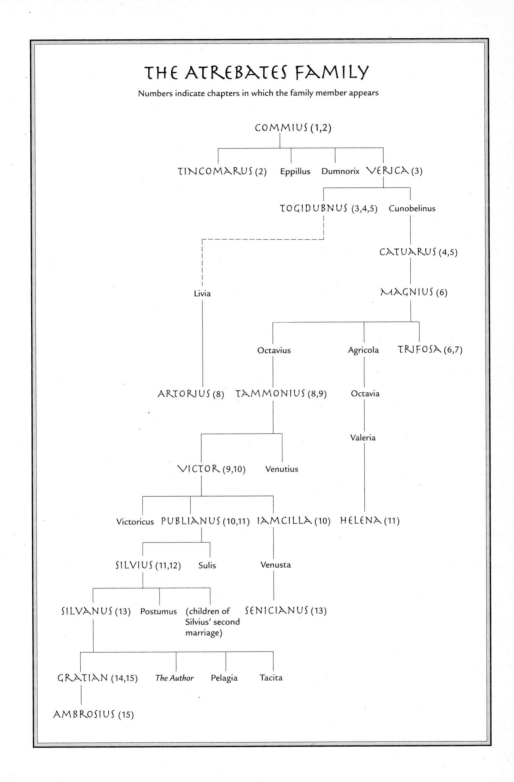

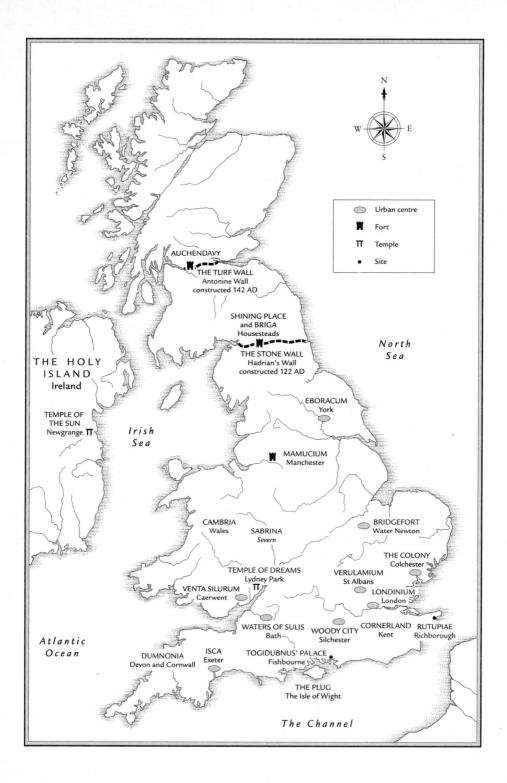

N
W   E
S

Urban centre
Fort
Temple
Site

AUCHENDAVY
THE TURF WALL
Antonine Wall
constructed 142 AD

SHINING PLACE
and BRIGA
Housesteads
THE STONE WALL
Hadrian's Wall
constructed 122 AD

North
Sea

THE HOLY
ISLAND
Ireland

EBORACUM
York

TEMPLE OF
THE SUN
Newgrange

Irish
Sea

MAMUCIUM
Manchester

CAMBRIA
Wales

SABRINA
Severn

BRIDGEFORT
Water Newton

THE COLONY
Colchester

TEMPLE OF DREAMS
Lydney Park

VERULAMIUM
St Albans

VENTA SILURUM
Caerwent

LONDINIUM
London

WATERS OF SULIS
Bath

WOODY CITY
Silchester

CORNERLAND
Kent

RUTUPIAE
Richborough

Atlantic
Ocean

DUMNONIA
Devon and Cornwall

ISCA
Exeter

TOGIDUBNUS' PALACE
Fishbourne

THE PLUG
The Isle of Wight

The Channel

INTRODUCTION

A Funeral Twenty Years after the End of Roman Britain, 430 AD

The villa had been burnt the year before in one of the Saxon raids and so my father died away from his home. He was laid out in the mud-walled fort on the ridge nearby, where all in the area had fled when the attacks had become intolerable. But his last wish was that his pyre should be built in those gardens and buildings that our family, the Atrebates, had held through the generations; in the place he had played as a child and had grown old. And it was to honour this last wish that, on the appointed day, we set out to where his vines had once stood, past the ravaged statues of nymphs and goddesses and waited with guards and lookouts posted around.

None from the Woody City [Silchester] were able to come – the roads were no longer safe; though many from that depopulated, wrecked place would have wished to pay their respects to a man who had been, in the last decades of Roman rule, a magistrate there. The road to Londinium [London] was closed entirely and even the news of my father's death will not perhaps reach his colleagues in that place until many months from now and then only through merchants running the Thames blockade. But there was still a respectable number who waited next to his corpse on the day of the funeral. And, as they came through the meadows, dozens of freed slaves, tenants, his children and grandchildren took their place and carried, as the old ways dictate, the remnants and symbols of the Atrebates.

I had heard, of course, of the March of the Ancestors often enough, but I had never seen it. And, in truth, no words could have prepared me for that carnival of silent ghosts. Many of our ancestors had had wax impressions of their faces fashioned while on their death beds, and these masks were now attached to those in the procession who were believed to have resembled them. Thus, in the twilight I saw those that I had only ever heard of before in family tales and reminiscences. So here was the scheming, unfaithful Claudia from the northern frontier, more beautiful than I had ever imagined her; while the great king Togidubnus, from four centuries back, strode serene and invincible, pushing aside my brother Gratian, as if to show that the dead are no longer prisoners of time.

Then, where no face masks were to be found, there were those who carried artefacts of their forebears' earthly existence. As the most senior of the Atrebates I had been given the golden torque that the head of our line, the Gaul Commius, first brought to Britain. There walked beside me my niece with the certificate of sale that had, long ago, been tied to the neck of the slave Trifosa, who had also shared our blood. While a cousin carried a head on a pole to represent the adventures of Trifosa's grandfather, Catuarus at the Colony [Colchester], three hundred and fifty years ago, in the revolt of the mangy lioness Boudicca. And, as the light began to be driven from the hilltops, our ancestors (for by then these representations seemed the very spirits of the departed) took the firing torches and lit the faggots and logs on which my father lay.

And it was only at that moment that I realised that the Romans had gone from among us and would never return. Over twenty years have passed since the writ went out that Rome no longer ruled the island and that Britain would have to defend itself from the fast-approaching barbarian storm: a writ causing panic in the streets and alleys of the cities. And, in that time, we have told ourselves over and over again that soon the Emperor will bring order, that Roman officials and soldiers will disembark on Britain's shores and drive away the Picts, the discontented peasants, the oily Saxons, the tyrant warlords and the Gael pirates. But we have told ourselves lies and peddled delusions.

Already I have seen the decline in the younger of our family, who never speak Latin, luxuriating in the Celtic dialect that, when my father came of age, none but workers on the land would have spoken. Few study, any more, the ancient authors – for how many books and rolls survived after the libraries were destroyed? How many can even read? I have nephews who have never seen a newly minted coin or a recently baked pot – the factories and workplaces are deserted and have been for most or all of these young men's lives. Indeed, they marvel at my descriptions of Roman aqueducts and heated floors, believing that I am speaking of a far-off magical land. It is as if the Empire had never been and that we Britons are returning to the world of tribes and primitives that was ours before the Romans walked among us.

And it was, in fact, as the fire started to tear apart the shroud of my father, revealing for the last time his face, that I decided that it fell to me, before it was too late, to preserve what I could of the history of our family and its noble origins. And, to give myself courage in this task, I remembered the adage that my father had always offered to the young Atrebates before he told his stories. Namely, that the greatest adventurer is not the hero who travels to places beyond the seas or into the forests and mountains of monsters. But rather he is the one who descends into the cellar or opens the chest where his family keeps its heirlooms; for that traveller is doubly-blessed, discovering not only unknown things, but unknown things that are already a part of him.

PART I

*Invasions
and
Settlement*

CHAPTER ONE

Discovering Britain, 55 BC

Commius, progenitor: a warlord from northern Gaul

Apart from the twisted golden torque of the founder of my family, salvaged from our burning villa, and the portrait offered here I have nothing of the brave Gaul Commius ... Nothing that is except the story of the mission to then undiscovered Britain, undertaken at the bidding of the Roman Julius Caesar before his invasion of the island.

The horizon was the most terrifying that any had ever seen for it devoured everything that touched it. At noon it had swallowed the Carthaginian tin trader that they had been vaguely following north, but whose tall mast and leather sails had proved better suited to the ocean than theirs. Afterwards, it had swallowed the coast of Gaul behind them, causing some of the men to mutter imprecations and prayers. And, for the last hour, it had been pulling down the little light that the clouds and the winds had granted them: the red sun being dragged into a red sea. For most of the day they had been rowing hard – 'Row! Row you fools! If we drift we are lost' – and by that time their hands were more blisters than skin, stinging with the salt water; and where their calves and legs had continuously touched the bench there were sores. And, though there came no order, by those common urges that sometimes seize hold of men who have suffered together, the twelve Romans brought up the oars and leant back looking about them. Nor did their tribune Volusenus try and scream them on as he had for the previous hours, for he too stared. And all around, on every side in the dimming light, they saw nothing but the Atlantic to where the limits of the sky touched the limits of the water.

It was a sight that no Roman had ever seen before and one that none on board had wished to see; for they knew that such sacrilegious venturing into the margins of the world could bring nothing but death. And the rowers bent and prayed again. One threw a gold coin that melted immediately into the foam. A Syrian centurion heard the voice of an elderly aunt in his ears warning him, as she had twenty years before, of the offspring of Neptune, the cruellest of all the gods. While a third recalled to himself how when he had first come to Gaul an officer had told him that the Romans might conquer India, Asia and Africa, but that they would never master the islands of the ocean. For those islands, the aged cavalry officer had insisted, were protected by divine writ, by the beasts of the sea and by tempests that they had never imagined on the gentle Mediterranean.

Behind them in the stern of the ship – there were a mere forty feet between the boat's extremities – stood the piles of supplies. Little had been brought, for they had been told that the crossing to the island of Britain – 'a simple reconnaissance' – would take only a day. And in and among this inadequate store were the three Celts of northern Gaul. Two were merchants who, it was rumoured, had had contacts with the Britons in the past; though from their mewling – they had tried to hide themselves in and among the sacks – it was obvious that they had never been on the longer ocean routes. Then besides them was another Celt. The tattoos visible on his uncovered arms announced him as one of the allied tribes in the newly conquered territories in northern Gaul. The torque twisted around his neck showed that he was of royalty. And, whereas the merchants crouched and cowered, Conmius, for that was his name, stood and held onto the boat's broad pine sides. He did not speak, though he evidently wished to; he was worried by the lack of activity. And his face only softened when the Romans were bullied into taking up their oars again.

Then it became dark surprisingly quickly. The sky caved in and stars were everywhere: more stars than the crew had seen in Italy, in Gaul, in Spain, in the Persian desert for those who had served in the east. And there came the cold too, burning the raw hands of the rowers. Yet they continued to pull in and pull out, for their tribune continued to scream. Then when he became breathless he spoke instead: couldn't they hear Caesar's voice, he said, congratulating them for being the Romans who discovered the lost isle of Britain? And, in between screaming and encouraging the men, he shouted at the Gauls, ordering them to pull out the tinder and light the lamps. And he continued shouting intermittently for almost an hour, calling the Gauls dogs, trouser-wearers, fungi, wretches and slaves; stopping only when the one called Commius shouted back at him to find his own tinder, for it was the Romans that had loaded the ship. There was none there; there were lamps and torches but nothing to light them with. And at that the men put down their oars once more and, though the tribune roared at them, they risked his displeasure, so even when he pulled out the long rods that he used to beat his charges they ignored him, moaning like lunatics as they writhed on their benches, their steaming breath but not the agony on their faces illuminated by the moon- and star-light. And, sensing mutiny, the tribune relented. He said that they would wait for an hour and then they would row again; though there would be no sleeping, mind! No answer from the benches, but the clack-clack of the oars being dropped. And after a furious conference with the Gaulish prince, who warned him once more of the danger of drifting, the tribune collapsed onto the deck whispering profanities that all could hear.

Gaius Volusenus Quadratus, head of the Twelfth Legion's cavalry and Caesar's choice as scout ahead of his British adventure, cursed the sea, the tribune cursed Commius and he cursed, for the first and last time in his life, Caesar. How, he asked, his voice rising again, could men invade the ocean? What was it that their general wanted? Was it so very important to bring these natives, his ambassadors to the unconquered, across the great waters to lands that may or may not exist? And then his voice fell off again into whispers that were drowned out by the glug of the water from the skins. No one was careful, as they had been before, to ration. There was some joy in the savage drinking and rule-breaking after so long and so fixedly pushing forward. But the rowers were careful in standing and moving. They warned their neighbours before they got up, stretching after taking a few steps. They were cautious, for the boat was not a natural ocean-runner and was inclined to tip. Its mast had been placed too centrally while its sail was of cloth and had been torn to the point of uselessness by the winds: the Romans had still not learnt, at that time, to build ships equal to the tide and gale-driven ocean. And, as the minutes passed, the men fell away from their drinking into listlessness. Already they were praying that one hour might become two – for how would their tribune know the difference: hadn't the horizon sucked away time with the land and the light and everything else?

Then, very slowly, the exhausted ones started to mutter, the voices rising between the benches; for many of the men had laid out as best they could, knowing that they would not be able to sleep later. They asked few questions and received few answers. Then, seeing that the tribune did not tell them to be quiet, as he had all that day, they began to talk aloud to all and to none. At first there were sentences and unconnected thoughts. But a Spaniard started and could not stop his mouth. He spoke of an uncle who had worked all his life on the boats. This one from a southern port had started his maritime profession in the secret Atlantic sardine grounds, on the fishing lanes: passing through the Pillars of Hercules [Straits of Gibraltar], out to where the whales spoke in echoes. Later, this same man had worked with a slave trader heading south along the coast of Africa towards the Isles of the Blessed [Canaries], to shores where volcano fumes crested the jungles. And there, after mute trades with tribes who spoke no language but their own, they had run from the sun, returning with gold and gorilla pelts and chained men. Then, on the death of the Spaniard's grandfather, a little money had come rolling into the outstretched hands of his uncle, who had bought half a ship, foolishly spending a decade shivering his way into the Baltic for amber – a useless occupation that had lost him three toes and part of his lower lip to frostbite. From a voyage five years ago he had not returned.

And had this uncle spoken of Britain, they asked, the island that

General Caesar wished them to find? The Spaniard said that certainly he had not heard of it, though his uncle was no fool and would never leave the land behind as they had done, but rather had hugged the coast on his voyages – this comment was greeted with murmurs. However, his uncle had talked of the islands of the ocean, yes: Thule the Far, the Holy Isle Where the Cannibals Live, the Little Pigs, the Dangerous Isle and even the Island of Magic, Albion. But of Britain he had never heard a thing. Then a voice came from outside of the circle of Romans. It was the Gaulish prince, the ambassador of General Caesar, who was speaking now in his imperfect, curious Latin, claiming that Albion and Britain were the same. But the Romans laughed at him. Tell the native to shut up – it was an appeal to their tribune Volusenus, who, it was well known, detested the Gauls. The fool was ignorant! Albion, the Magic Isle was where the druids went.

The Twelfth Legion, to which all belonged, had attacked one of the Gauls' forts the year before and out of it, after the surrender, like wasps from a nest, had come a line of druids with their half-shaved heads and their ragged white cloaks and these had been going to Albion for their schooling as all druids did. Albion was Britain, indeed! The Gauls could not open their mouths without lying. And this Gaul was doubly cursed, for it was said that it was to suit his purposes that they had been sent on the long crossing to this Brit-whatever-it-was-called place, as Caesar's ambassadors had to be brought to certain tribes who lived the furthest from Gaul. Commius though, used to the Romans insulting his people, was only half-listening. It was true that the tribes with whom he had been instructed to negotiate lived far along the coast of Britain; but why couldn't they have crossed at the narrow point and followed the British coast along, as he had argued, instead of risking the open sea? Because this fool of a tribune would never listen to his advice. He looked at the waves that were growing larger; the brine splashed constantly into the faces of the resting crew. And as the men had been speaking the wind had risen, and now clouds came over the sky like a sheet being pulled across a child's bed. And the moon and the stars vanished, and in the space of what seemed only minutes, the little light they had been granted disappeared from them.

But strangely the darkness did not bring with it fear. It came as a kind of blessing. For, as the waves now became more regular, the black plunged down on them and freed them from the chains of rank and race, depriving them of even their shadows. And the Romans spoke in a different way. It was as if they were at the feast of the gods on one of the mountains of Greece, drinking wine and eating peacock, merrily incoherent and excited; though truly they had bloated themselves with nothing more than stale water and some chicken haunches passed greasily from hand to hand. The first to start with this new voice was a north Italian legionary who spoke of dolphins rescuing men; before it had been he who had insulted the Gaul. Another, his brother, who had been holding the rudder, told a tale – he insisted it was a true tale – of a Greek man who, blown out into the great ocean, like a second Odysseus, had come to an island where beasts with the tails of horses lived, beasts who had abused him pitilessly. A well-read centurion tried to speak of the Atlantis of Plato and the measurements of the sacred city, but he was almost imperceptibly hushed. Then, unexpectedly, came the voice of the tribune Volusenus. To his men, to Commius, the tribune never spoke unless it was to shout. But now, in the dark, he talked in a short, calm, almost gentle voice of how, when a boy, he had been taken to Rome to see the strange red people, who had been washed up out of ocean, onto the shores of Gaul. No one knew from which land. Some said that they had passed over the globe from India itself, others that they were from the antipodes of the world.

And then, finally, into the ears of all came Commius' voice again and this time there were no protests as he spoke. He talked of the sea lung, an aquatic monster that sped along the currents and other beasts in the ocean to the south of Britain; nervous faces turned towards the sounding waters. He told them of the sea mist, when sea and fog became of the same substance, a substance that was frequently encountered by those who travelled into the north. Then he remembered, for himself as much as for them, what was said of the Britons and their strange rafts made of stretched bull hides and wickerwork that a bee sting could sink, but against which a warship would never prevail. He spoke of the druids once more, for he had not been lying before – Britain was also known as Albion, the Isle of Druid Magic; the Carthaginians who traded tin there called it, instead, the Cassiterides. Then, as an end, he talked of the Celtic gods, who walked across the ocean leaving trails of white flowers behind them.

The Romans listened in awe, after asking questions, questions that seemed never to end. Had he been there? Was it true that the Britons were dangerous? Was it true that they all lived to one hundred and twenty? Were there Celts like him – was it true that they spoke the same language as the Gauls? But Commius had said enough and did not answer. And with his refusal to respond, the conversation died out, the men casting further furtive glances into the pitching liquid around them. For some minutes more, they remained in silence in this way and it fell to Volusenus, awaking first from out of the spell, to bring his crew to order. Standing, he reminded them yet again that if they drifted they were lost; while if, instead, they returned, they would be rewarded by Caesar. He afterwards rationed what remained of the night into small blocks in which the men could sleep. But, though the first shift tried to close their eyes, none managed it, for it was so cold that in the end they chose activity, paddling weakly – some in an almost token fashion – kicking their legs against the chill breezes that wrapped around them.

In the morning, when the sun broke across the sea, there was a moment when it seemed that the horizon would regurgitate not only light but also hope. As the first rays appeared, they talked again and scanned the water on all sides. But it soon became clear that they were faced with the same bleak sight that they had seen at twilight the evening before: water on every side to the sky edge, no birds and no other sign of life. And the divisions between the crew that had dissolved during the night now returned. Fiercely, one of the legionaries interrogated Commius and the tribune Volusenus did nothing to silence him. How far was it to Britain? The Celt was hesitant, talking of perhaps another day. It all depended where they hit the coast. If they came to the east of the island called Vectis or the Plug [Wight], then there was some hope that they would arrive that very afternoon. If they were going to the west, it would be tomorrow or maybe the day after.

This news was taken badly. Didn't the Celt know everything about Britain? Commius insisted he had never been to the island; he knew that some Celts related to his people had settled there, but nothing more. So he knew nothing, stated another of the soldiers, to general approval. The Celt was speaking like an ass. They could be adrift for three days before they arrived. Or six and then they would be dead – who knew how vast was the ocean where no Roman had ever been before? Commius though was furious with lack of sleep and he had, in any case, his own recriminations, for, if they had listened to his counsels, they would have crossed to Britain at the narrow point, instead of taking this insane ocean route. But their commander, he gestured at Volusenus, who stood at the front of the ship, knew only of war not of navigation. In his tribe, he almost spat now, there were those who constantly begged Commius to return and make war on the Romans. Well, he was no fool and would not do so. But that oaf, their leader, was the best argument for revolt he had yet heard. The men looked down at their tribune, who had remained strangely quiet through this speech. And they looked past him and understood why. Beyond Volusenus a series of rocks were breaking out of the horizon, and beyond those rocks a strip of gold and the first hints of vegetation. Father Ocean had spared them. Britain awaited.

In the long night, Volusenus had decided that if they were lucky enough to arrive safely, then he would come close to the shore and there let his men sleep off their exhaustion. He had also intended to have proper bearings made and align himself with landmarks. But, as they came nearer and nearer, the island hypnotised them all. Above the beach was a large massif covered in the most powerful green that they had ever seen, greener than the spring in Gaul. And the noise of sea birds was deafening, until what had at first been an invitation became an imperative. Then, the waves pushed them towards the beach and it was only with an effort that they managed to steady the ship and prevent it running against the shore. They had lost their chance to scout for a gentler harbour and so there, in the shallows, they resisted the waves and stared with nervous amazement at what was before them . . . Britain, the Isle of Druid Magic, the Cassiterides, Albion. The name no longer mattered. It astounded them.

The events that followed were never clear in Volusenus' mind; nor, indeed, in the minds of his men, though all agreed afterwards that it had had the quality and the inevitability of a dream. He remembered that Commius and his two companions had begun to collect their belongings to disembark, when, from one of the surrounding cliffs, a subtle, low sound came. On the high rocks off to their left there stood a man, a naked man with a long, narrow tube of wood or bronze. And slowly the noise was answered by others further inland – here from a creek, there from a valley, and there, finally, from a hilltop where smoke suggested human habitation. Commius said something about a welcoming and he and the merchants, Caesar's envoys, turned to the side. No one wished them luck. But none of the three seemed frightened. Even the traders were dazed rather than scared. Pushing into the water they paddled for a few yards, holding bags above their heads with one arm, until their feet reached the sand, when they set off wading ashore.

Then it happened. As the three emerged onto the beach, from out of the trees above the sand came men. They carried with them shields made of highly polished metal that caught the sun and, for all that the Romans tried to shade their eyes, they could still not see past them to faces or expressions. These figures walked halfway down the beach. There were perhaps half a dozen, perhaps a dozen times that number and Caesar's ambassadors moved towards them. There was no noise. But the blinding sun again dazzled the crew on board the boat and when they looked back their sailing companions had disappeared into the shields and the men who carried these shields vanished moments after. On the cliff above, where there had been the trumpeter, no man now stood and no smoke rose from the hilltop where they had suspected the presence of a village. Volusenus shook himself. They were to move along, he shouted, trying to rouse his men. And, silently, he swore the most sacred of oaths that, until they had returned to a friendly harbour, no one else would leave the boat.

⟿ Historical Background ⟿

This chapter was written not to illustrate Caesar's two British expeditions of 55 BC and 54 BC – expeditions that were, at least by the great general's standards, failures. Rather, I was interested in the 'discovery of Britain': an event that might seem remote today, but that provoked in ancient Rome emotions not dissimilar to those excited by man's first walk on the moon, two thousand years later. The existence of the island had been rumoured – and sometimes denied – for centuries in the Greek and Roman Mediterranean. But it was only as the Romans fought their way into northern Gaul in these years that Britain became something tangible as opposed to a legend or a remote source of tin: the Romans were not even sure whether it was a peninsula or an island at this time.

Caesar tells us that he gave to two of his most trusted men, the task of preparing the way for his attack: the tribune Gaius Volusenus Quadratus, who was responsible for searching out a suitable harbour; and the Celtic prince Commius from Gaul, who was to take care of diplomatic relations with the southern British tribes. (We do not know whether they travelled together; that much is a fictional presumption.) The hostility between the two men is hinted at by our sources. Certainly, after his British adventures, where Commius was held hostage for several weeks, the Gaul returned to his homeland and got enmeshed in a revolt against the Romans. Volusenus took it upon himself to attempt to slay Commius on two occasions, botching both attempts and, the second time, almost getting himself killed. Then, in the end, with a nasty scar that Volusenus had given him on the head, Commius escaped back to Britain, using a ruse (described in Chapter Two) with a sailing boat, establishing his own kingdom there, possibly founding the Atrebates tribe of that island.

After Caesar the next important contact between Britain and Rome came a generation later when Tincomarus (who was actually the son of Commius) was driven from the still-unconquered island to Roman Gaul ...

CHAPTER TWO

A Briton in Rome, 9 AD

*Tincomarus, son of Commius: the first of our line to be born
in Britain, an exile from his homeland*

Even today, in these times of decline and disaster, when the name
of Rome has vanished from our lives, it is well known among
my kin that Commius founded a tribe in Britain, the Atrebates,
one from which our family takes its name. His eldest son and
first-born in the island was Tincomarus, later driven to Gaul by
jealous brothers and made, in those distant centuries, to endure
a hateful exile among the Romans, an exile that we have undertaken to recount...

The news came to the mansion in Rome in spring and was greeted by Gnaeus Sentius Saturninus and his wife with the horror normally reserved for violent death. The senator, the letter stated, had been chosen for a very great honour: it was his household that would host a visitor, a king who had been driven in exile from unconquered Britain. Sentius Saturninus had a long and varied experience of the barbarians. He had known, of course, the garden vegetable types, the Gauls and the Syrians, who were endlessly, tirelessly, traipsing through the city. He had also seen some of the more exotic species present in Rome as hostages or ambassadors from afar – the silk-covered Chinese of the Seres Plains, the bejewelled Parthians with their troops of sycophantic courtiers, the holy Ethiopians from the Land of the Two Kingdoms, Indians who had bathed in Ganges mud and who were the first to see the sun every morning as it rose in the east. But a Briton … Were they mad? A Briton in his house, at his table, at the theatre … Sitting down, he quickly shook off his slaves and penned a response himself – he usually dictated; and though the tone was polite, its message was unmistakable. His eldest was to come of age that year; his wife was confined awaiting another child – they hoped for a boy; the mosaics were being pieced out in the new hall; they had just bought some Jewish slaves, whom he would prefer not to unsettle; there was that trouble at the country villa that took up much of his time; then there were others who would leap at the opportunity and the advancement that it promised. A Briton as a guest, what a thrill.

Best wishes and try to take care on the dangerous northern campaigns.

He sent his reply back with the messenger who had delivered the letter and, within two days, the matter had been relegated to an itching worry, within a week, it was a hazy memory, and, within a month, it had been utterly forgotten. Indeed, when the same messenger arrived, at the beginning of spring, Sentius did not recognise him. 'I have come from the Rhine, my Lord.' The senator simply took the letter and smiled; what news now from the northern wars: discoveries, battles, ambushes – how he missed the life of camp. He opened the seal and then, slowly, the smile subsided. 'Shall I wait for your reply, honoured one?' He waved the messenger down the corridor and walked, instead, through the hall. At the end, he turned rapidly and shouted for secretaries, for parchment, quills, for ink. The impudence of it: had he ever read such a letter? Reasons of state for having a Briton in Rome! Then, why could they not put the Briton in a cage at the coliseum? He had been chosen as the perfect host; well, they would have to find a less perfect host! There was a precedent, Cicero had feasted with a druid in his house: and look what had happened to Cicero, gibbeted by their present leader no less! There were also excellent military reasons – the Emperor hoped to turn to Britain next year and planning for the invasion was already under way. Here the senator began to scrumple the letter up. He had listened to descriptions of Caesar's raids on that damned island: a lack of silver, a lack of gold and a surfeit of savages.

He had just settled down to writing a letter to close the matter, this time jettisoning polite formality for sterner cadences, when a knocking came at the door. It was his Greek butler. 'A messenger, Lord. Not the one from the Rhine, but a second.' 'Tell him to wait!' said the senator, barely troubling to look up. 'I think it is urgent. It seems the Briton has arrived. He is outside the city with an escort.' Sentius was speechless for a moment and then started angrily, but the slave pre-empted him. 'My Lord, the messenger carries the seal of the

Emperor.' Even in private, rage against the First Citizen, against Augustus, could be misunderstood, twisted, misreported. Only a minute ago, he had remembered Cicero's unpleasant end, the hands nailed to the gate of the city, the old man's head lolling on a lance: had he not seen it in his youth? Aware that his every action would now be judged, the senator addressed his scribe, telling him to destroy the half-composed letter to the Rhine and replace it with one of thanks – he himself wrote in the first line. Meanwhile, he would receive the Briton. But – anything to win himself some time – it would be better after dark. It was well known that barbarians, on first coming to Rome, were sometimes almost paralysed by the city's extraordinary dimensions.

His panic allayed by the sound of scurrying feet and activity, he turned to think for the first time of what it would mean to have a Briton in his mansion. He would have to send some of his household to the country immediately: the last thing he wanted was the female slaves giving birth to little savages nine months from now. He would also borrow some bulky Germans from his friends. He would have to secure the store rooms: the Celts everywhere loved to drink. In fact, he would send out for some Greek salt wine – that would keep the Briton from getting too boozed-up. It would be best, too, to prepare a first-floor apartment with no easy access to the garden: he could do without nocturnal adventures. Then, there was the question of ablutions: did the barbarian know how to use the baths or a toilet? Well, he would have to be taught. And his family? He had forgotten that they did not yet know. He would keep them in private quarters for a couple of days. At least, until he had assured himself that the Briton was manageable.

The afternoon passed in a fever of activity. But then, in the early evening, came further news. Not only was the Briton to stay in his house, but that very night a party of fellow-senators would come to dine with the monarch and question him on the hopes for an invasion of his island. New orders, screaming fits with the cook, instructions to bring in extra chairs from the back houses, an appalling, appalled interview with his darling wife. Then, in the midst of this confusion, the Roman guests began to arrive. An overweight equestrian – one from that social class second only to the senatorial in prestige – waddled to the door and made adverse comments on Sentius' roses. A party of two senators conspired to creep in by the rear entrance so as to see his much lauded murals and another three turned up with slaves pulling a wild Umbrian swine, it transpired the Briton's favourite meal: the menu would have to be changed again. Sentius, red in the face, trooped off towards the kitchen to give yet more screamed instructions, while above him in the courtyard he could hear the other senators greet each other and make sarcastic comments about the decor in a typically Roman *sotto voce*.

Exhausted and demoralised by the wait and his peers, it was perhaps not surprising that when, in the second hour of the evening, the word came that a group of horses and accompanying litter had drawn up at the gate, the senator felt a certain relief. The relief perhaps that the prisoner feels when he, finally, hears the executioner passing down the steps in the palace cellar. Straightening himself up, he walked towards the entrance and strutted out into the reception area. Sure enough, there were the riders and there was the litter, though the red curtains failed to move. Vigour. Vigour. That was the action that the barbarian appreciated most in the Roman. Without hesitation he strode across the compound, thrust open the curtains and was faced with ... nothing – the litter was empty. For a second, he stood incredulous and then began – the Emperor had personally trusted him with this task – to turn over the brocaded cushions, his long fingers trembling. It was only after this useless faffing that, from behind him, a voice broke in. 'Senator! Excuse us, but he always insists on riding.'

Sentius, aware that in choosing vigour he had sacrificed something of his dignity, turned to face his nemesis. And, as soon as he had seen Commius' son, he wondered how he could ever have missed him.

Tincomarus sat on the smallest horse in the party and yet towered almost a full head in height above the tallest of the cavalry assigned to him. His body was not strong, it was elongated, while the hooded coat wrapped around this body was multicoloured. The senator would have lingered a little longer on these features if he had not caught sight of something hanging from the horse's mane. They were globular shapes attached, below where a great sword wrapped in cloth had been fastened to the steed. Drinking bottles maybe. Then, the shapes started to resolve themselves into artificial faces. Ethnic pottery, gifts even? And then, with a gasp that he only just managed to contain, the senator realised that they were human heads.

The melancholy eyes of the king's victims stared out at him, wanting, it seemed, to communicate something important to the senator. But their message, if there had been one, was lost as the rider flicked his chin, letting down his hood and, for the first time, the Roman saw the face of his guest. It was not the bleached white hair moulded with animal fat into something resembling a cock's comb that first struck him, nor the twisted golden torque wound around his neck, nor the shining teeth, staging a smile. No. It was the blue tattoos that snaked from his shoulders up over his face in concentric circles and horrible lines. They covered his eyelids too in a ghastly mauve. But, under all these distractions, it was certain that the man was no longer young: perhaps sixty. About the age, in fact, of the senator.

Another awkward silence and then the Briton turned to his escort and, speaking in execrable but understandable Latin, asked: 'My welcoming party, where is it? Where are the princes of Rome?' The party of guards, who had been tamed by the Briton on their long ride south, looked with embarrassment in any direction but that of Sentius. However, the Roman's natural arrogance had returned, the poor quality of the barbarian's Latin reminding him of who was the master here and who the brute. 'Majesty,' he intoned, 'I am your welcoming party. But a group of the princes of Rome, who are more important than either you or I, are awaiting your arrival within. So if you would please make your way down from that horse we will go inside.' Again the Briton stared at him, turned once more to his riders: 'I expected him taller', his perturbing consideration on Roman manhood. Then, kicking the leg of the leader of the escort, he pointed in the direction of the senator with what was, clearly, a prearranged signal. The man shyly coughed and spoke: 'I present his Majesty Tincomarus or, as we would say in Latin, Great Tench, chieftain of the British Atrebates, son of Commius and Lord of the Woody City [Silchester], driven unjustly from his tribe. He is here among his friends the Romans as an honoured guest, knowing well that they will help him to retake his throne in that island that we know as Britannia, but whose true name is Prytain.'

It may have been the hour, it may have been the stresses of the day. But, for a moment, the senator had to stifle a desire to do something absurd and unroman: kiss the Briton's hand or bow. Instead, he waited for his guest to dismount and then walked back towards the mansion, trusting that he would not need to comment on the architecture that must have been far superior to anything that this Tincomarus had in his own land. But the Briton was notably unconcerned with his surroundings. He did manage a nod in the direction of the high balconies as if to say 'I have several like this in Britain'. And, once at the main door, he tested the breadth of the wood with his enormous hands, turning to the senator with an it-satisfies-me expression. In the reception hall, the king was escorted towards the dining room by the bulkiest slaves that Sentius Saturninus had been able to find. Though, even then, at the very end of the welcoming ceremony, there was a slight altercation when an attempt was made to confiscate Tincomarus' sword; for it was illegal to carry weapons within the bounds of the Empire. But the attempt having failed, the senator quickly walked ahead of the Briton, who had now attached three of the heads to his belt, and tried to show the way into the dining room. Yet Tincomarus was having none of that and, allowing the senator to open the door before him, pushed his way past the guards, past his host and took the lead into the bright space that had been prepared for his arrival.

As the king went ahead of those who should have flanked him, Sentius' spouse, his eldest son – who shared his father's name – six senators and two equestrians rose to their feet. The Briton beamed around him, stared with special appreciation at the lady of the house and then strode into the middle of the room sitting, not lying, on the couch usually reserved for the senator himself. Taking this as a cue – and ignoring the bewildered remonstrances of their master – the slaves entered, laying the food out. And the swine that had been specially chosen for him was critically appraised with a knife from the Briton's belt. All held their breath as the monarch tasted the flesh. And they applauded when Tincomarus gracefully announced that, though in the Woody City the meat was of better quality, this met with his satisfaction. Relieved and, in some strange manner, honoured by this mild praise, the senator also stretched out his knife, only to have his hand slapped by the king. A moment of stunned silence followed, while the Briton explained that the cutting must be left to the greatest warrior in the room, an insult that the senator was going to contest. But then the fish with vinegar arrived, and guests and host alike were distracted by another northern dish, prepared for the special delectation of the newcomer.

For a while they ate and bantered harmlessly. The king was disgusted by the use of olive oil on everything – slug's slime, he called it. He also made fun of the Romans' reclining position; at home, he boasted, his people knelt on straw on the floor to eat their meals. But the real pains began when the king asked the room where the Roman women were. Sentius explained their absence: his friends were unaccompanied because they wished to speak, after the meal, of freeing Tincomarus' kingdom. Hardly a subject this for the gentler sex: smirks rippled through the room. But Tincomarus shook his head impatiently, and pointed at the senator's wife, the only female present. He wanted to know where the senator's other wives were. Now the eldest son had stopped eating, the guests looked up at each other and the slaves responsible for bringing away the dishes hovered at the door with their trays to hear Sentius' reply. The Roman sighed as audibly as possible: 'In Rome, Majesty, we have only one wife.' Another silence from the king, this time more considered: 'Only one wife ... So you share your wives between brothers?'

This could have been an innocent anthropological question. But a hint of desire in the Briton's eyes warned Sentius that the conversation might, instead, be moving in an intolerable direction. It was, though, the senator's son who brought the matter to a head, inquiring with unwanted precocity: 'So how many wives do you have in Britain, your Majesty?' 'Just for me, seven; but of course, we, in the Woody City, swap ... '. The senator's wife shouted for desert *repeatedly* and, with some urgent questions about British agriculture, the younger of the two equestrians managed to get the conversation back to a more civilised tenor. And there it remained for the best part of a half-hour before a rumble of carts, typical of those that charged through Rome after dark, sent the king to his feet, posturing with his sword as if it were a dragon rolling by on the cobbles outside.

After Tincomarus was calmed, wife and son absented themselves, the former ignoring Tincomarus' enthusiastic salutations; and Sentius inwardly groaned, anticipating some sharp sentences later. But this leave-taking served, at least, as a signal for the men gathered there. They stood and pushed their couches closer to the Briton; and called for scribes and a translator, who had, until then, waited in the hall. For, though Tincomarus seemed unaware of this, the festive dinner was about to become an earnest meeting dedicated to Imperial strategy. The king continued to chew on the bone of the Umbrian swine, while all eyes signalled the most elderly senator; for it had been planned that he would begin the assault.

The man coughed a little and set off – how could it be otherwise? – with some dalliances into sycophancy to get the monarch's attention:

something that was easily, smilingly done. Then, after reflecting, for long minutes, on the king's noble bearing and royal airs, he slipped in a question. Britain could only hold one man of the quality of Tincomarus, surely he was the island's only king. Yet the tattooed monarch shook his head sadly at this, admitting, with occasional help from an interpreter, that while a predominant king, maybe the mightiest king in the island, he did have some brother rulers. All feigned shock and the questioner started again. He found it difficult to believe that these three or four kings were Tincomarus' equal. But again Tincomarus stopped him. There were not three or four kings, stated the Briton, but numberless kings, each with their own tribe. He then reeled off a list that the scribes, sat in the corner, caught only partially, many of the difficult Celtic names escaping them. But all the Romans present had gathered that there were between fifteen and twenty tribal federations in the island. That was an awful lot of hill forts to storm and the Romans glanced thoughtfully at each other.

One of the guests, an ancient and much respected Roman equestrian, now offered his question. He began, too, palming flattery on the guest like mortar on bricks, paying special attention to Tincomarus' kingly stature, then artfully turning to the subject of the Britons' arms. Did they, for example, still use the chariot – these were important considerations if the Romans were to win Tincomarus back his lands as they would very much like to? The king gave what was, for him, a stately smile and then said, in his hesitant Latin, that he would answer that question with special frankness because the equestrian's and Tincomarus' father had been such firm friends. At first, the company did not understand, thinking that the Briton had become confused in the language, which was not his own, or expressed himself badly. But Tincomarus repeated more forthrightly that his father had known the equestrian's father in the Gaulish campaigns of sixty years before, this time naming Gaius Volusenus Quadratus. The equestrian's mouth opened, for the barbarian did, against all expectations, know his father's name. Tincomarus spoke once more: had Volusenus

The Tribes of
Pre-Roman Britain

N

W · E

S

NORTHERN BRITISH TRIBES
(later the PICTS)

DUMNONII OF
THE NORTH

VOTADINI

SELGOVAE

NOVANTAE

North
Sea

IRISH
TRIBES

BRIGANTES

Irish
Sea

PARISI

DECEANGLI

ORDOVICES

CORITANI

CORNOVII

ICENI

DEMETAE

CATUVELLAUNI

DOBUNNI

TRINOVANTES

SILURES

ATREBATES

CANTIACI

DUROTRIGES

Atlantic
Ocean

DUMNONII OF
THE SOUTH

The Channel

never mentioned Tincomarus' father Commius? The equestrian's reaction on hearing 'Commius' was further shock, the elderly man nearly tipping off his couch.

Tincomarus, seeing the mystification of the other Romans, stood up joyfully; for speaking about their fathers' brave deeds had always been a favourite pastime of the Celts. His *pater* Commius, he told the small assembly, taking on the pose and the hand movements of a practised storyteller, had been born in Gaul and, as a young man, had been an ally of the Romans in their conquests there. And Volusenus, he gestured at the equestrian, and his father had been firm friends, even sharing an important mission to Britain together; their affection being assured from the first moment they met. Volusenus had returned to bring intelligence on British harbours, while Commius was imprisoned in Britain, only escaping back to Gaul at a later date. However, a subsequent war in Gaul between Commius' people and the Romans had meant that the two friends had reluctantly become enemies. Volusenus – why deny the burden of the soldier? – had tried to kill his father on numerous occasions. There had been the time when Volusenus had brained his father with a Roman sword, in a parley between the two sides – a good trick that and one that had left a long scar on his father's forehead. But Commius had managed to get away. There was the other time in the Belgian forests when Commius had been ambushed by Volusenus, this time on horseback, but – Tincomarus had to stifle laughter – Commius had ridden the Roman down and wounded him in the thigh. Then, finally, there was Commius' escape to Britain.

What, had they never heard of Commius' escape to Britain!? Well, he Tincomarus, Commius' son, would tell them of the chase – 'a warrior's day' he called it, when the assembled host showed gentle and embarrassed disapproval. Tincomarus then spoke with pride of how the Romans had almost caught his parent and there he pointed enthusiastically at the equestrian, for Volusenus had been part of the chase. But Commius, in desperate straits and facing almost certain capture, had seen a sailing boat perched high on a beach. The Celt could in no way push it towards the sea, for it was too heavy and the tide was still a long way from the boat. Thus – and here Tincomarus lapsed into British Celtic so ecstatic was he, waving at the translator to continue for him – this brave Commius had leapt into the vessel, raising the sail and letting the wind billow into it. The pursuing Volusenus and his men had just rounded the headland, a mile away, when the sails went up and, assuming that the game was over, and their enemy escaping into the ocean, pushed off back home. By evening, the tide had become favourable and Commius was in Britain in a matter of hours. And, within a year, he had made himself king of one of the federations there; for his skill in war had been honed by long experience with the Romans and none of the neighbouring British-Celtic warlords had proved a match for him.

Sentius' admiration for Tincomarus rose considerably as the king so efficiently reduced one of the Empire's most senior and respected nobles to a corpse-white and trembling lump – Volusenus' son was extremely unhappy. The senator could not, though, allow the awkward recriminations that might have followed such a story and, quickly, launched into another of the questions that they had prepared beforehand. Tincomarus' father was, doubtless, a great man, he stated. But was it normal for the Gauls to come to Britain in this way? Were the two people really on such friendly terms? The king answered this as if it was the most obvious thing in the world: the Celts of Gaul were a strong people, whose only fault had been to cede their territory to the Romans – it was evidently inconceivable to Tincomarus that the Romans would ever rule in Britain. These Gauls made good druids and spoke the same language as the Britons.

Sentius, immediately, queried this last assertion, saying that he had heard Gaulish and it sounded nothing like the language that the king spoke. But the exile, who was rarely contradicted, looked archly across the room and claimed that he had spoken to the Gaulish slave in charge of the senator's wardrobe without any recourse to Latin in the reception hall. Now Sentius Saturninus had, indeed, sent his Gaul into the fray to lay hands on the sword of the king, so the two had met and perhaps exchanged words. Nevertheless, he, at first, put the claim down to barbarian boasting and summoned the slave in question to make a fool of his guest. But the Romans listened, instead, fascinated as the two men babbled their strange tongues together. And, while it would have been untrue to say that they were speaking the same language, the two tongues were apparently close enough to allow much understanding.

By this time they were all rather tired – Volusenus' son, especially remained in a speechless stupor on his couch. So they left it to the most senior among them, a confidant of Augustus the Emperor no less, to ask the last question, the one about Caesar's invasions of a generation before. Had the brilliant general made an impression on the simpering British? Had the name of Rome thus become a word to create fear in the Britons? All this, of course, was phrased rather more diplomatically. But here they had yet another surprise. Tincomarus did not seem to know anything about Caesar's campaigns against the Britons. Now, all joining in, they repeated the general's name in various ways, described 'the big Roman honcho', 'the one who whipped you Britons'. Sentius even sent a slave running to find a bust. But all to no effect. The king had heard nothing of this man, save for some vague references of his father to the wars in Gaul. Indeed, they were just about to conclude that Caesar's adventures in the island had been more of a failure than had been rumoured, when a light came into Tincomarus' eyes – it was a chance reference to the burning of the Britons' crops that did the trick.

Were the Romans, asked the British king, tense with interest, speaking about the oppression from across the sea? Not quite knowing where this was going, the assembled host nodded. The Briton then set off on the most extraordinary story of the 'danger that came to Britain' that destroyed the wheat and barley in the fields there. At first, the Romans thought that this was just blather – and in some respects it was. But, from the details Tincomarus let slip, it was clear that he was describing, albeit in a fantastic and absurd fashion, Caesar's attack. The iron stakes, for example, at a river crossing that Caesar described in his works and that had caused the general severe problems, became a Celtic King Cassivellaunus, dressed in an invisible cloak slaying his enemies. While the capture of a British noble by the Romans became an episode about the hanging of a mouse on a fairy hill.

It was just too much for the Romans' more historical minds. And, following some minutes of this kind of nonsense, they escaped from the king and retreated for private conversations into the garden, while the Briton contented himself with calling for more wine and luring an Illyrian slave girl towards his table. Gnaeus Sentius Saturninus stood there among the half-closed flowers, the moon and the stars, and words and phrases of the past two hours returned to him: 'wife-swapping', 'slug slime', 'fairy hill'. Then glimpses: the hand-slapping episode; the sword jerked out of the scabbard as the carts had passed; the savage but irresistible face of his guest . . . He was woken from his reverie only by the equestrian, the son of Volusenus, who spoke to him in a voice that Sentius had never heard him use before. In fact, his gentle comrade of more than half a lifetime whispered poisonously that, if ever Tincomarus should be 'past use', then he would gladly arrange his disposal. But, as the senator knew all too well – he refused politely – his association with Tincomarus was only just beginning.

⸗⸗ Historical Background ⸗⸗

This chapter tells the story of the visit to Rome of a British king, Tincomarus – who was, historians believe, the son of Commius – and the resulting explosion as the Celtic and Roman worlds collide. (For many years, it was believed that Commius' son was actually called Tincommius. A recent coin find in Britain has shown, instead, the correct form.) Now, barbarian kings and nobles were regularly sent to the capital of the Empire in this period as hostages or guests. We do not know whether Tincomarus also came to Rome. But we do know that he was driven from Britain by his brothers, picked up by the Romans when he arrived in Gaul and that his safekeeping is mentioned by Augustus in the Emperor's list of achievements, the *Res Gestae*. Wherever he was kept, Roman hospitality was by no means selfless or neighbourly as, in this period, the Empire was seriously considering an invasion of Britain: an invasion only given up with the changed priorities following the catastrophic Varus Revolt in 9 AD, when three legions were lost in the German forests. The senator Gnaeus Sentius Saturninus is included as a prelude to his son's part in Claudius' invasion of Britain – for which see the next chapter. He was an important Roman in his day, commanding the legions on the Rhine some few years before the events described here.

Roman interest in Britain waxed and waned. It was not until 43 AD that the Emperor Claudius finally determined to absorb the island into the Empire.

CHAPTER THREE

Invasion, 43 AD

Togidubnus, nephew of Tincomarus: a British youth
of great promise, educated in Rome

Of Tincomarus' end I have been able to ascertain nothing; for
the family archives were dispersed when the barbarian attacks
began. I know only that the Emperor Augustus abandoned his
plans to take our homeland. It fell, instead, thirty years later, to
another Atrebates in exile, the youth Togidubnus, to board the
invasion barge and restore his family's fortunes in a territory
that, without the protection of Roman arms, the Atrebates still
inhabit to this day. And yes, even now, when Rome has been
forgotten in the island, we, in our tales, follow young Togidubnus, who had been forced to leave his homeland at the
tender age of five, to the Channel ports, where almost a thousand
sails have been gathered for that long-awaited event, the conquest of Britain . . .

Two hours before sunrise, the fires were lit and, minutes later, many of the boats were already making their way onto the open sea. There, they congregated by torchlight into the prearranged squadrons, corresponding to the three legions and the various barbarian auxiliaries in the force – German skirmishers, Sardinian slingshots, Syrian archers . . . Boats approached too from the north and the south, from secondary harbours, where the horses had been loaded into carefully prepared floating stables. A strict injunction to silence had been given. But, with this long wait, there were sometimes hints of discipline breaking down: a man weeping, an officer barking at his legionaries to shut up with mutinous talking. There was, even, a cohort that refused to board, for it was well known, they said, that the ocean would never forgive trespassers. But they were threatened with immediate decimation and huffily walked up the gangways, whispering about what they would do to their centurions when they were in Britain, *if* the gods allowed them to get that far.

Then, as those last rebellious stragglers were incorporated too into the force, and daylight dulled the lustre of the fires, a small craft that had been racing up and down between the columns came to a standstill. A slave walked across the deck to where a man sat gazing at the dark west, seemingly unconscious of the vast fleet behind him. The slave spoke: would General Aulus Plautius please note that the nine-hundredth-and-seventy-fifth vessel had now joined the convoy, all forty thousand men were embarked and in position. The general barked at an official he had brought with him. This man lifted the *cornu,* the Roman bugle, and let out, repeatedly, long, mournful blasts. From the head ships of the squadrons, these were answered by other similarly long blasts. And, nervously, the ships started forwards, towards the place beyond the clouds, beyond the horizons where they had been assured that Britain lay. Angry shouts came as the waves crashed; boats collided into each other and, in some cases, oars were broken, while one sail collapsed on the huddled legionaries below it. But the minutes passed and the boats spaced out, the invasion force settling into place, the distance between the vessels increasing. Then, up in the heavens, an omen. The moon was still hanging in the spring sky and close to it came a fiery breath of light such as those that normally occur at night. The shooting star had pointed from the Gaulish shore to Britain: the holocaust of cows and other animals the day before had served and the gods had blessed the enterprise. It had taken the Romans a hundred years to get round to invading Britain after Caesar's failures; but they had planned the enterprise to the last detail.

However, for the herdsmen watching from the cliffs, astounded by a dawn such as they had never seen and would never see again, there was one last surprise. As the invasion fleet passed from the Gaulish shore into the lap of Holy Ocean one of the watchers pointed to the left of the long line of ships, where something seemed to be happening. At first, there was just some noise and roars. But then, the western wing of the invasion fleet started to peel away from the other ships, heading not north but to the west. This operation was begun while the individual boats were still visible and, by the time these had reached the horizon, there was not one fleet but two: the first heading towards the Cornerland [Kent], with close to nine hundred vessels, the second to another destination, with forty.

Togidubnus Atrebates, the young British prince who leant against the figurehead of the second ship of this breakaway group, remained, like the legionaries, in total silence: games had been forbidden, as had conversation. The Roman scouts, who had made contact with the allies of his father, had assured him that the journey would take almost a day. And he had nothing to do but think and watch as the hours passed in the sleek but hard-built ocean-goer. The men munched on grain and bread. The centurion sitting, instead, with three whips before him had warned his charges that they would be punished if they spoke; and screams from another ship reminded the legionaries that he would carry out this threat. Then, by evening, they had come close enough to see the British shores, where already the rest of the invasion fleet would be disembarking.

In his left hand Togidubnus held the torque of royalty – his father, Verica, the son of Commius, had died in Rome several months before – and in his right the helmet that had been given him to keep his head safe. Then, as the sun settled in the west, the centurion stood up, holding the strip of parchment that contained the instructions. With the legionaries – there were almost fifty in the boat – watching, he snapped the seal, stretched the parchment and read. 'At dawn we will arrive in the territory of the Atrebates on the south coast of Britannia. At the harbour we will be met by the warriors loyal to the deposed king Verica. We will pass with them into the British interior to fight against the Bodunni, one of the clans that has opposed Roman influence in the island. Our victory will depend on speed and good order.' The legionaries looked at each other: it could be worse. The centurion offered a few more considerations of his own, rather rabid and unco-ordinated.

Togidubnus decided to close his eyes and sleep. The boat was lit well with a dozen lanterns and he could hear now the legionaries using the shadows to exchange, in low almost inaudible tones, sentences and news, some of which drifted through the gloom towards the Briton. One talked of how, ten years ago, another invasion had been planned by the mad Emperor Gaius Caligula but had ended in farce. The legionaries – he had been one of them – had been forced to collect seashells on the shore as a victory over Ocean. Then, as the centurion began to snore, the prince too passed out of consciousness knowing that the next day, whatever its outcome, would be the most extraordinary of his life.

The weak sun behind them did not wake most of the men. It was the yells of the pilot in the leading boat. They had now steered towards the shore to find the rendezvous and almost immediately they had been spotted. Togidubnus scratched at his face and stared over the side of the ship. There, not half a mile away, was the British shore, wooded and uninviting, and, on the edge of the beach, where a rudimentary road led across the dunes and rocky inlets, five or six mounted men were riding; they were naked and carried spears. Even from that distance the war cries came to the Romans and the centurion shuffled over towards the prince. 'Majesty, what is it they say?' 'The name of my grandfather's people: they are shouting "Atrebates".' 'Are they allies?' Togidubnus shook his head. This could bode badly for the mission. Hostile riders from the enemy clans so close to the landing ground. Still, they had always known that this was a danger. They would have to fight their way to land and men would die. But, unless there was a gathering of all the Atrebates clans, unless all the negotiations with his father's followers had been a subterfuge, they would still manage. Of course, they would have to build a fort quickly and seize grain. But he was sure that they could do it – they had planned for every eventuality.

However, as they came closer and closer to the harbour, which had been identified weeks before by Roman sailors, the horsemen held off. And, as they started to round the headland where the pilot told him that the rendezvous had been arranged, the words of their pursuers changed and were directed not towards the Romans, but towards the rocky heights that coruscated the shore there, for tens of Britons lined the cliffs. Then, as the first ship turned towards the beaching place, now only yards away, screams went up from every direction: 'The King! The King! The King!' Naked warriors with the shields of Togidubnus' clan – the dancing horse – swarmed from out of the trees and greenery. 'The King! The King! The King!' The exile reached into his toga and pulled out Commius' torque from where he had left it the night before. This was the moment. And slowly, painfully, for it was too small for his large frame, pinned it to his neck. He had only the vaguest memories of Britain; he had left when he was five. But none of those memories corresponded to the smells, the noises, the things he was seeing. 'The King! The King! The King!' 'What are they saying, Majesty?' 'They say that their king has returned.' The centurion nodded. 'Could it be a trick?' Togidubnus replied that it was not and the centurion rose to his feet and shouted instructions. Shields were to be prepared, they were to line the sides of the ship. They must at all times keep silent. They were not like these savages.

The first ship came towards the land and the almost naked Britons ran down to meet it. They hugged at the bow of the boat, as if to drag it forwards from the waters. When Sentius Saturninus, son of the man who had, years before, hosted Tincomarus in Rome and now tribune in charge of the mission, appeared at the front they cheered, some even called him the king. The second ship was less enthusiastically welcomed. But Togidubnus stood as straight as possible, leaning his hand against the figurehead. Perhaps it was his height that first attracted the attention of those on the shore. But it was the torque that set them off, clearly visible and hanging down over his toga. 'Commius' torque, Commius' torque! Commius' heir has returned to rule us!' The Britons left the first boat and crowded around the stern of the second; some passed up their hands. His master in Rome had told him that he might recognise faces. But he saw no one that he knew; nor, indeed, anyone that he would want to know. Instead, he hovered, looking down at the thirty or forty men, naked apart from shields, war paint already liberally applied; none had beards, all were moustached, all were delirious with joy.

His people had been under pressure for as long as anyone could remember and, since his father had been driven out, they had suffered humiliation after humiliation at the hands of other Atrebates clans.

Well, the king had returned and justice would be done! From behind him, the centurion pushed at his back and the taller of the natives clutched at a low part of his toga. Then he was falling through space, dragged into the monster of outstretched arms, brought to the ground and embraced and kissed on every side. Men held him and sentences came about his younger days. At Rome he had only ever spoken British with his maid – a slave from further to the north in the island — and so did not always understand the madly happy words of his fellow-countrymen. But they either did not notice or did not care. And, by almost universal consent, they tore at his clothing; for they wanted him as their king, a true Briton ready for war, naked and woaded-up.

Ten minutes had passed and Togidubnus, more familiar with the sun on the Tiber than this freezing British shoreline, was now nude, his body goose-bumped from head to foot; he pulled a native cloak tightly around him. The legionaries, who had disembarked, were lining up above the beach. The artillery men had set themselves apart and were preparing the weapons; they would be ready for moving soon. A Roman surveyor had taken a group of men up the slope before him, where it had already been decided that the fort would be built. Indeed, the legion's architect stood with a pole and the balances of his trade hanging from it. On the far beaches, the horses were being led off the ships; the British whooped with pleasure at these large animals, so much more impressive than their diminutive steeds. And, still hanging out in the bay beyond, stood the vessel that the Romans had decided to keep to the last as their 'surprise'. Covered in canvas and with Egyptians running around on the webbing, it attracted little attention – though occasionally strange noises echoed from out of it, as if musicians were practising within.

'Your Majesty,' the senator Sentius Saturninus did not look directly at the Briton, but rather surveyed the activity around him. 'I understand that your people are celebrating. But we agreed that we would move within an hour. We will take scouts. You too saw the riders

41

when we were coming in. They', he gestured at the Britons, 'will just get in the way if they come with us.' Togidubnus diplomatically translated the instructions to the senior men of his sept, men who had identified themselves as uncles and cousins. 'They acknowledge your plans, Senator. They are only sorry that they cannot join us. But they wish to warn you that the other clans of the Atrebates tribe know already.' 'All the more reason to move quickly. Do they know anything of the opposition?' 'The main gathering is at the stronghold of which we have been told, five miles to the north-west of here – according to my kinsmen it has been heavily defended.' Sentius sighed: in hostile territory over rising land five miles was a long way and yet he had sworn *at all costs* to have it in his hands by nightfall.

Within half an hour, ten minutes more than the senator would have wished, the cohort was ready. Three hundred of the men, almost a third, had been given the responsibility of preparing the camp. They had removed the carefully cut stakes from their belts and were digging frantically for their own preservation and against the cold. The rest of the troops had discarded their heavy packs, which lay in a huge pyramid, at the centre of the grounds of the future stronghold; while the mounted scouts had returned, confirming what the natives had already told them – the roads were free of menace. And so, with care, Sentius had the men who were not working on the fort get into marching order and, guarding both his front and rear with cavalry, set off into the interior. But, before leaving the harbour where their ships had moored, he told the centurions once more that they would have to take the enemy fort by nightfall if there were to be any hope of breaking resistance in the area.

After only ten minutes it became apparent that the primitive trackway that they were using left a great deal to be desired and was not as had been described by the spies in their reports. The studded sandals of the legionaries allowed them, for the most part, not to slip in the mud, but, as more and more passed, the earth churned. It was also narrower than they had been led to believe and, at parts, the line of men had to press into each other only five wide. There were enough horror stories of apparently friendly natives leading their Roman masters into ambushes in the German forests to make not only the commanding officers, but also the men behind them, anxious. Then, as they passed towards the river, a scout returned, slipping through the cavalry, to the prince and the senator. There was a concentration of Britons on their side of the bank. He had not seen exactly how many. But he would guess close to a thousand. The senator nodded: so the Britons had come out to meet them. In many ways it would be better to fall upon them now rather than at the fort. He called for a horse and the men started to break through the undergrowth to form into larger units as they approached the river meadows.

Sentius mounted his horse, pulled Togidubnus up onto it, and went back through the ranks shouting instructions and, most of all, encouragement. Then, as he came towards the back of the line, there broke out a hubbub of screaming that was clearly not Roman. Togidubnus felt his stomach shrink within him, while to his left the faces of even seasoned legionaries became serious. But the senator was having none of it: 'On at them! You will be able to do better than these savages. You saw those *Britunculi* [wretched Britons] at the landing ground – they are naked and virtually without arms.' Then, urging the horse round, he pushed back down towards the vanguard. As he and Togidubnus emerged onto the open fields by the river bank they were immediately confronted with a long, thick line of screaming, naked natives, many painted in the traditional colours of war. The estimate had been wrong. There were perhaps two thousand, that would make the odds four to one. 'And these, Majesty, are your relatives?' 'Another clan of my tribe, but, yes, these are my people.'

However, for all their insults and the occasional slingstone or axe blade that raced through the air at the Roman side, the Britons had not taken advantage of the invaders as they emerged disorganised from the wood; this boded well for the battle. They had also shown

43

unwarranted arrogance in crossing the river rather than defending its far banks. The cohort had already started to form into blocks, each three men deep. Another unit was kept back behind with the cavalry – Sentius Saturninus had ordered that these would be used only if the situation got out of hand or for pursuit. He simply did not consider the possibility of defeat and looked over his men now with a real pleasure. The centurions were in place and behind each unit stood the *optifer* with his long stick for holding the line, ready to beat or poke at any man who wavered. The senator, taking a shield, rode towards the back of these solid blocks and began to scream – the legionaries as their custom, were completely silent. 'Look at them! Most of them are weeping women! Remember your lines of battles. Listen to your commands and *nothing* can go wrong!'

Then, on the other side, spurred on by the senator's instructions, the whooping ceased and a huge barrel-shaped man emerged from the centre of the British lines and screamed across the fields at the Romans. Togidubnus spoke up: 'He is asking for a challenge, Senator. He wants to fight you before battle begins.' 'How kind! The horn, Centurion!' Off to the left a blast came, for Sentius was in no way going to fight that beast, a custom the Roman army had long since given up. And his men locked shields marching forwards in perfect order. For a moment the Britons were shocked by this failure to duel, and the strange, mechanical stomping of the Romans. They were made uneasy too by the quiet of the Roman ranks, which after a few steps became eerie and, for the first time, panic flickered through them. But then their cries rose again, more brutal, more horrible and, as the British war horns responded, the crowd took off, to race at the Roman lines and overwhelm them.

Togidubnus had never seen a battle before. But he had heard, from slaves and from retired dignitaries, of the effect of the Roman *pilum* throw. The steadily approaching Romans were locked to prepare for the approaching mass. Then, as the Britons came within range, they broke for a moment and the first and second line threw their heavy black lances towards the barbarians. The missiles with their iron heads travelled high and sank precipitously into the moving crowd. The nude and painted Britons had nothing to defend them from this devilry. None wore helmets and even those few who carried shields were as good as undefended, for the sharpened Roman spears sank through the wood or metal casing into the flesh behind, breaking off at the deliberately weakened iron necks.

The Britons tripped over each other, but somehow – perhaps by sheer momentum – in the confusion and screaming they continued their charge, the front now raising swords and spears. However, the Romans had retreated back into line after hurling, their shields tensed. Then, as swords and sprinting bodies rebounded on the shield wall, the Roman line opened again. British spearmen were half decapitated by the sharp edges of Roman shields rammed upwards. British swordsmen were stabbed at as they lifted their arms to strike once more – the Romans with their much shorter swords floated in under the attackers' arms, at unguarded torsos or into the faces of the oncomers, sending still more to the ground. Then, too, the third rank of Romans let loose their *pilum* high but short and these crashed down into the natives gathering and urging behind and war cries married with the screams of the unfortunate.

The senator turned to the cavalry and gave a signal, and these worked around towards the flanks. They would be there to chase the Britons once the rout had begun. Now, it was only a matter of time. 'You will understand your Majesty that on this first encounter it will be good to kill as many as possible: we are teaching those who drove your father from his kingdom a much needed lesson!' Togidubnus acknowledged this from above the rage – it sounded as if a thousand blacksmiths were banging on their anvils simultaneously. But he could not help wondering how many of the Atrebates would be left to be ruled. There were rumours that Sentius still nursed a grudge against the Britons for an insult that Togidubnus' uncle Tincomarus had served up to the senator's mother thirty years before in Rome.

A litter of dead and dying lay in the meadow behind the line but, if the Britons had suffered in their first encounter with the Romans, there seemed to be no desire to retreat yet. In fact the two lines, for the moment, shuffled apart and the Britons pushed their shield carriers to the front. Togidubnus could also see British chieftains and warriors stretching out their swords before them – swords two or three times the size of Roman weapons – and trying to straighten the weak, inferior blades that had bent on impact against Roman armour. 'They must continue the attack!' The senator waved at the bugler who let off some short blasts and the Romans, reluctant and exhausted, moved forwards. The Britons too started to yell and the two forces were preparing to close again, when the Roman horn was met by another greater horn behind them, a furious, angry horn.

Togidubnus turned and saw that 'the surprise' had arrived. The handlers had evidently had difficulties with it on the muddy road. But now it had reached the meadow and bad-temperedly, with its man-carrier strapped to its back, a man-carrier from which two fearful Greek bowmen peeped, it strutted zigzaggedly across the field. The senator watched its progress nervously: the history books were full of elephants who had stampeded through the ranks of friendly troops. But his worries here were entirely misplaced. The elephant let off another mammoth blast on its trumpet and the rear line of the British who could see the beast, a beast that they could only assimilate to a giant cow, began to turn, stumble, those who could do so running towards the safety of the river. The senator roared again his commands at the cavalry. But here, too, there was no need. Tensed and ready for this moment, the horses broke forward and javelins flew towards the retreating Britons. For the first time too the Roman lines screamed and charged at the front rank, all that was left of the British army.

It was estimated afterwards that half of the British force was slaughtered before they got to the river. Those who did reach its banks jumped into the water or made their way across three crowded bridges. But here they were deceived, for Sentius had also brought with him a body of Batvians, Germanic auxiliaries who served in the Roman army. And they had swum the wide river one hundred yards up and, as the British tore terrified through the trees, came screaming through the woods upon the enemy. The cavalry too forced its way over the river and only the infantry were instructed to give up the chase and finish, instead, the wounded Britons groaning in the field and retrieve any unbroken Roman *pilum*. There had been deaths on the Roman side, but few. For the most part, there were injuries. Legs slashed at by Britons who had already been thrown to the ground, some slingstones had found marks on faces, a spear had broken off in an arm or leg. The wounded, in any case, were quickly herded into a group and the two cohort doctors sent to look at them. Those who could not walk would be escorted back by a group of cavalry – stretchers were unrolled. But it must be done quickly. The army had only covered half the distance to the fortress of the enemy and the senator was anxious to finish the job by nightfall.

Togidubnus was sent to the other side of the river: Sentius stressed yet again the need for all to hurry forwards. And there the Briton attached himself to the first century of the cohort that had, by now, been ordered to move forwards in formation. The Romans were encouraged by their victory and by the trotting hooves of friendly cavalry ahead of them on the road. However, as the hundred men left the river meadows and moved into the trees, the gloom depressed them. And, while they passed deeper into the forest and the oaks broke up their lines, they reminded each other of the danger they were in – was it not in the forests that the druids dwelt? What if this was a trap? Hadn't their victory been too easy? For the best part of an hour, they moved on in this way as the woods became denser. Off to their left and off to their right they could hear, but not see, the other centuries. Then, as the group made its way across a wooded glade, came a low blast on the horn. They were to form and remain still. On horseback a man trotted behind them; he had a feather tied to his spear, the sign of an official messenger, and shouted that there was danger, a counter-attack. They must break the attack and then move forwards for they had to be within the enemy fort by sundown.

The men prepared. They could see no sign of activity. But there was, now they listened, a distant, rusty wheezing coming from across the glade, as if some of the locals were fetching water out of a well. Loath to relax in an area where there were Britons, the centurion removed a long piece of wood from his belt and knelt, placing the wood between the ground and his right ear. And Togidubnus saw immediately from the centurion's face that there was something that confused him. 'From that direction horses, but also something else, perhaps a siege engine?' Togidubnus almost laughed at this, for he knew his people quite incapable of that kind of sophistication. But something certainly was coming and, too late to warn anyone, just as the squeaking, metallic noises became properly audible, the prince realised . . .

Birds and a boar came out of the undergrowth, as frightened as the Romans now. Then, like monsters from a nightmare, the enemy emerged screaming through the fronds. First the horses, with peaked caps, then the long, painted axles and the painted drivers roaring with war anger. So astounded were the Romans by this sight – chariots had long been forgotten by the barbarian peoples of the Empire and none of the men with Togidubnus had ever seen them – that their reactions were numbed, their shields were not as well bolted together as they should have been and to Togidubnus' left, the centurion fell over his buckler with a British javelin through his throat. In fact, a considerable number of these weapons cruised through the air, the rest crumpling harmlessly against shields or into the ground. On having let fly this first attack the twenty or so chariots veered suddenly to the right across the glade and the javelin throwers behind the drivers let loose another, and then another round. Togidubnus, kneeling behind a shield, felt fear; but he also could not help feeling a little pride at what the hostile members of his tribe had achieved.

However, the Britons' ascendancy ended quickly. Thinking that these extraordinary fighters would, disappear back into the woods, the legionaries were astounded to see the javelin men dismount and try to take advantage of the invaders' shocked state, sprinting towards them with swords and cutters. The century surged forwards, locking their shields, determined to take the barbarians while they were vulnerable. A couple were caught in this way and brought down; but the others, sensing defeat, ran towards their vehicles and span their steeds away. Having now routed the chariot-riders, the Romans broke out of rank to revenge their centurion. But it proved impossible. One of the Britons rode his chariot across a steep bank, leaving two of the legionaries flat on their faces. Then, the second death in the party came. A legionary, a man unknown to the prince, chased a chariot and tried to grab hold of the horse's mane to prevent the rider escaping and to give some time for his companions to surround the Briton. But his strategy went disastrously wrong. The rider, with the horse already in motion, glided up the yoke and buried a blade through Roman mail and on into the soldier's lower back.

As they stood recovering in the wood, the voice of the senator came from behind them. Sentius Saturninus mounted, looked down at the century, a sixth of his men moving towards the fort. It was twice, he told them, that they had defeated the Britons. Now, they were less than an hour's march from the fortress. It *would* be theirs by night. It *must* be theirs by night. And, after having arranged for the two dead to be carried back, the century did as they had been commanded, setting off into an open space strewn with abandoned chariots, sometimes, ahead of them, hearing shouts that were not Roman. They stopped again and were allowed to take turns in eating a little bread, observing that the sun was now descending in the sky. Then, once more, they set off up the folds of the valley until finally they crested the top of the rise. The view was not a spectacular one – the river snaked ugly behind them. But they could at least see, reassuringly, two of the other centuries and, ahead of them, their objective, the hill fort, the fort of the hostile clan. It was less than a mile away across a series of low fields; the going now was quick. And, off to the left, the century using the track had actually arrived within striking distance of the first barricades.

As they began to form once more into an army across the fields by the river, they watched the Britons appear on the battlements with their weapons. But the Britons, for all their yelling and bad manners, were surprised. None had believed that the Romans could arrive so quickly and, from this position, the Romans could also see a line of warriors, perhaps the victims of the morning's encounter, heading away from the stronghold, escaping into the interior. No orders were given to chase them, for it was good that some witnesses to the effectiveness of Roman arms got out to spread the word among neighbouring tribes. And Togidubnus remembered what his father had told him before his death. Namely, that the best advantage the Romans would have was that they would not stop after a victory, as the Britons did, to celebrate and get drunk for a day or two. They would keep on marching, keep killing, keep destroying until the objective was met.

The soldiers formed up, looking towards the heights. They were excited: the first to enter the stormed fort would be awarded the mural crown, one of the greatest honours a Roman soldier could hope for. And there were only three or four hundred warriors above them there. True, their position was better. But the Britons were now actually outnumbered. In front of them, on the plain, the giant cross-bows or *ballista* were being set up; carts had been brought rapidly in behind the approaching army, whips having been applied cruelly to bleeding donkeys. And, as the Britons watched dumbfounded and Togidubnus cringed, knowing what was to be done to what would, after all, become his fort, the Romans opened fire.

The *ballista* were first. The long arrows were aimed at the top of the confines where the round thatch huts of the tribal leaders stood, the Britons screaming their dismay as the missiles thudded into the ground there. Then there was also a sprung catapult. Winding this catapult with grimaces and pants, the legionaries assigned to it let a boulder, collected from the river, fly; it span through the air towards the fort and took off the top half of one of the chieftain's halls, before sinking out of sight on the hill behind them. Again commotion among the Britons, who had never seen throwing machines. Some legionaries jeered, while another group rolled a stone up for a second go. The catapult kicked hard like a wild ass; and the stone descended on target. It slipped through the air and then bounced into the compound, where the chieftain's huts stood. The screams, this time, were of women – and poultry and pigs exploded from out of a wrecked circular hall.

Then, as the third load was being prepared, Togidubnus saw that there was movement at the bottom of the fort. The gates were thrown open and the warrior who earlier that day had challenged the senator in the river meadows, emerged with his long sword. He threw the weapon before him and knelt and then lay, family members and other warriors pouring out after him. Togidubnus Atrebates looked around: Verica, son of Commius, had been avenged. It would make, he thought, an excellent site for a town.

⁓ Historical Background ⁓

The Roman invasion of Britain had many false starts. As was mentioned in the notes for Chapter Two, Augustus' plans were put off after a military disaster in Germany. And, a generation later, the Emperor Caligula also thought about invading the island; though, as is recorded in this chapter, the 'invasion' ended in farce when his legionaries were instructed to collect shells on a Gaulish beach and so declare a victory over the sea. However, in 43 AD Caligula's successor, the Emperor Claudius, finally sent the legions in. His excuse for an invasion was that one of the tribal kings of southern Britain, Verica – historians believe the son of Commius and the brother of

Tincomarus – had been driven from his kingdom. We know almost nothing of this Verica, who seems to have died just before or in the years immediately after the invasion took place. However, we do know that a certain Togidubnus (thought by many to be Verica's son, sometimes called 'Cogidubnus') became a Roman client king in the conquered island and remained so until his death at the end of the first century. There is no proof that Togidubnus was educated in Rome, but it is a distinct possibility, given the Roman practice of 'adopting' royal children from beyond the Empire's borders.

Likewise, the splitting of the fleet into two parts – one for a landing in Kent, one sent to liberate Verica's kingdom – is not mentioned directly by any source, but has been suggested by some experts, e.g. Christopher Hawkes. The battle, the skirmish and the short siege in this chapter never took place. They serve simply to show what our sources tell us war between the British Celts and the Romans was like. Gnaeus Sentius Saturninus, the son of the homonymous senator Sentius Saturninus in the last chapter, was one of the commanders of Claudius' invasion of Britain.

Rome gradually took control of southern Britain over the next years, installing puppet rulers such as Togidubnus in friendly tribes, ruling directly in hostile areas and banning weapons everywhere. By 61 AD, as the legions and the Governor were pacifying northern Wales, however, revolt was brewing in the Fens . . .

CHAPTER FOUR

Boudicca's Revolt, **61 AD**

Catuarus, nephew of Togidubnus and messenger to the Iceni

After the invasion Togidubnus was installed as a native ruler in the conquered territories. And among his most trusted counsellors was the young Catuarus, a nephew, the most able Atrebates of that generation. And even today, in the burnt-out remains of Britannia when so much is forgotten, my family still tell the tales of the courage and dashing of this one, most of all his mission to the Fen tribes on the eve of Boudicca's revolt . . .

'Tiberius! Tiberius!' The voice of King Togidubnus' slaves echoed through the compound and the British princeling walked reluctantly from the stables towards the building. When they tediously shouted his Roman name Catuarus knew that visitors from overseas or from the garrison were on their way. The modest reception area of the tiny villa that Briton and Roman alike called 'the palace' would be swept. The tribal elders who lolled half-naked and tattooed on the tessellated floor chased away with the dancing girls. The shrunken, decapitated heads removed from their pegs. Enormous beer and mead horns replaced by fragile wine glasses. The furs taken down from the walls; and the Celtic they habitually spoke in the presence of his uncle, the king, would give way to mincing Latin – Latin that their guests might or might not see fit to correct.

But, as Catuarus approached the open doors of the room – 'the throne room', as they termed it – he was surprised to find a guest already seated with his uncle. The preparations to clean out barbarity had been seen to prior to his arrival. And the man was not a Roman. He wore the dress of the Greeks, his square robe wrapped tightly around him in a room that, even with their elaborate heating meas-ures, he evidently still found cold. The king waved his kinsman across the floor and briefly presented Catuarus to their guest, an agent of Lord Seneca, minister and adviser to the Emperor, returning from business among the Fen Britons and the Colony [Colchester]. Then, stopping only to lard some compliments on his visitor, he informed his nephew that their new friend had had an unpleasant experience.

Catuarus sat down on one of the couches that had been rushed into the room to make the Greek feel more at home – the Briton always felt uncomfortable reposing – and listened as the newcomer spoke with a pained voice. He had been, it transpired, setting out for the return journey from the Fens ('a savage and barbarous place') when he and his small escort had come upon a body laid out, face down, beside the route, only a few minutes ride from the Colony. A corpse! Hardly a rare event in Britain, considered Catuarus, though it would be best not to confide this to the agent of an Imperial minister. And had his uncle really brought him from important tasks to hear such nonsense? But then, instead, came details that were worth hearing. The victim, a young man, barely thirty, had been pushed down into the marsh, his back stabbed and trampled on. The Greek's bodyguard had pulled the murdered one up and the dead man's face was blue from suffocation; a twine was caught around his neck, a bloodied knife lying in the water nearby.

The king looked straight ahead ignoring his nephew. Yet, notwithstanding this lack of communication between them, Catuarus understood that this was the reason that he had been summoned. The Greek had stumbled, quite unknowingly, upon the remains of a forbidden druidic ceremony. It was the threefold death – the victim would have been throttled, cut into and then pushed downwards, drowned as the elders stamped his body into the swamp there. It was one of the strongest British magics. The twine was made with hazel, the tree of suffering and, if the Greek had looked carefully at the face, he would have seen what the Celts called 'cure-all' [mistletoe] smeared onto the man's mouth. The threefold death on the very outskirts of the Colony, next to a Roman road! If a clan in Togidubnus' kingdom searched out a slave to die for a good harvest or success in an illegal raid, they were at least careful to do it with little fuss and certainly they made sure that no Roman ever saw the body.

'Yet, Catuarus, our Greek friend brought us not only *news,*' the king stressed the last word, 'but also a present from the Fens.' The prince followed his uncle's hand and saw, to the left of the throne, a half-open sack, its neck coloured red. At the king's nod, and as the Greek apologised, the young Briton knelt, separated the folds and found himself looking at a hare, with its throat cut. It was not a conventional gift: the hare was the animal that augured war. He had never seen the ceremony. But he had often heard of how it was performed from the old-timers, who had fought each other and even the Romans before he was born. When a tribe wished to start a campaign they would release this animal from out of the skirt of a well-born woman; if the hare ran to the right then weapons were summoned, if to the left then peace was kept. In this case, the hare had run to the right. 'Forgive my curiosity, dear friend. But it came, you said, from the Fen Britons. Perhaps one of their clans or the king?'

Catuarus understood that his uncle's lapse was deliberate. He was testing his visitor's knowledge. 'Quite impossible, Majesty. The monarch of the Fen Britons died five months ago – a man called Pran ... Prius' ('Prasutagus' supplied the two Atrebates). 'Indeed. The death of this man was one of the reasons that the Lord Seneca sent me to Britain – a question of debts you understand; though I should not talk of that. But, yes, in a manner of speaking, this ghastly thing came from the Briton you mentioned, for it was from his family, from a woman: a sister or a wife I believe. I apologise again. But I thought that it was something precious. They wrapped it so the blood was not visible. I was also advised by the Imperial slaves in the Colony that it was best not to anger the Britons. There were already a good few difficulties ...'. But the king was satisfied. 'Of course, of course. I ask only because it would be polite to send a gift in return. Yes, for this trifle! In fact, my nephew Catuarus has himself business in the Colony.' Catuarus had been well-schooled never to show surprise in front of outsiders and poked at the hare with a finger. 'He plans to leave tonight. Now we must send a gift with him. I wonder what gift we shall send?'

Catuarus' journey began an hour later, as the sun was already colluding with the hills in the west. The gift from his uncle was secured on the side of the horse, his instructions memorised and he had put on his most Roman clothes to avoid problems with any patrols. It was three days' ride to the Colony and yet he had been instructed to make the trip in half that time; there would be no luxury of starting his ride the next morning. He burst out of the gates at a gallop, mainly to impress the sentries. Then, as he passed out of sight, he went more cautiously over the road that was bumped and holed in places; until, after an hour of careful riding, picking out his way with the very last of the light, he came to the good road built only five years before by the Romans, where, even in the dark, he could trust his horse to trot.

By dawn, he had passed out of the lands of Togidubnus and into the territory of the Cantiaci [the men of Kent], the enemies of his people in the times before the Romans. And then, as dawn lit the hills and the broad valley of the Thames, he continued to make good progress, for the way was practically empty. The Governor, his uncle had taken care to remind him, was away, campaigning in the Cambrian mountains with half of the British garrison. And only a solitary mule train with some westward-bound reinforcements slowed him down as he approached the wide river. He could also console himself that his crossing took almost no time now that the bridge had been built. And, mimicking the custom of the locals, he removed a coin from his belt and tossed it into the water, a small tribute to the spirits of the river.

On the far side of the bridge stood the recently constructed mart of Londinium [London] – having the same age as the British prince. There had been no true cities in Britain before the conquest, just agglomerations of huts on hilltops and even those that had been built in the last years disappointed. Yet Londinium was the exception and Catuarus usually enjoyed his stays in this strange world of foreigners and the long-travelled into which few Britons strayed. After only a minute of entering the city gate, he had seen a merchant with the dark skin of the Arabs, a party of Sardinian sailors and a man with the purple-edged robe of a senator, who strolled under Imperial arches. But, with his urgent commission, the settlement, for once, left Catuarus cold; so even the tavern next to the Temple of Isis with its swinging jars of wine in the doorway failed to tempt him.

Only as he was passing along the river bank with his tired horse did he look with curiosity at a crowd gathering there. A divine sign had excited them. One woman swore that the night before she had seen houses in the depths of the river; while another, a Roman official, claimed instead that the phantasm buildings had been floating on the water and that they had been burning. The crowd of street sellers and low craftsmen enjoyed the babble and one chanted 'omen' repeatedly, until a Frisian slaver insisted that he had seen the ocean turn blood-red on the crossing from his homeland. A disaster perhaps for the Emperor or losses on the Welsh campaign, thought the prince, or more probably just the hysteria of ne'er-do-wells; Catuarus would later consider it strange he had not thought of the trouble brewing in the north. And, already bored, he pushed through the mob and moved on to the reddish granite mansion that was the property of his uncle and where a number of horses were kept. He entered and then, after some minutes of conversation with a groom, emerged on a fresh mount.

To reach the Colony by nightfall he would have to ride faster than the goddess Epona with the fairies pulling at her mane. But first he must change. His uncle had warned him to arrive before any fighting broke out – for the Fen tribes were certainly going to rise. Yet, to travel alone in Roman dress through a rebellious province was suicide. So, making use of a cluster of trees to the north of the city, he removed his Roman clothes, which he tied next to the gift on the side of his mount. He then pulled on the leather trousers used by the natives and wrapped his woollen shirt in a British *birrus,* or cloak. For a moment he considered, too, daubing woad on his face – but that would be a provocation to any Romans he might meet. Then, satisfied with the extent of his transformation, he mounted, passing into the lands where his uncle had warned him that danger would lie. And how he felt the difference! After only a hundred yards a peasant working in a ditch hissed at him the name of Andate, the divine force of Victory and Sacrifice, the goddess always invoked by the Britons against the Romans. Passing a resting band of workers, he saw men who had barely troubled to hide weapons – spears and a sword – all illegal. Even the road towards the Colony was cursed: it jarred against the hooves, cold and unwelcoming under him.

For four hours he made good time. But then his horse began to tire; and he, in truth, was exhausted, having not slept the night before. The hypnotic pulse of his mare *might* still have pushed him ahead to the Colony, not before dark, but at least before midnight; however, a strange meeting delayed him – and, as he sometimes later considered, perhaps saved his life. Usually the Romans took care to clear the country around the roads for a hundred yards on either side, to prevent ambushes and other misunderstandings. But, as he came down from the low hills there, onto the vast plains that opened into the Fens, he passed a place where brambles and other plants had grown to intolerable levels. He was determining to make a report of this at the Colony on his arrival, when a voice came from out of these green shadows. The word *amicus* or 'friend' was said quietly in Latin, almost as if a wood goblin had whispered it. Catuarus knew little about wood goblins, but he was sure that they did not speak Latin and so slowed his horse and trotted back. From the leaves, a fat head and double chin protruded; then, this face seeing Catuarus' good intentions, a portly body followed and a small British horse was dragged from the briars.

The river of words came immediately. Had the young fellow not heard the news? There were some brigands ahead, a nasty business! Catuarus tried to calm the stranger down, deducing from the tense, heavily accented Latin that here was not a Roman but a Romanised

Briton, rare in this part of the world. A few more gentle sentences revealed that his name was Faustinus and after this the river became a waterfall. Had Catuarus never heard of Faustinus? Incredulous at the ignorance of youth, the man boasted of his origins. He was of the Fen Britons, an Iceni no less of the Horse Clan. He was not only a Briton, but also a Roman – a citizen indeed. He was one of the few of his people who spoke Latin. Was Catuarus sure that he had never heard his name – not even at the highest tables in Londinium? He was famous on the northern road to the coast for serving food to all who travelled there. Why, his villa was legendary for its hospitality to Briton and Roman alike; for, yes, he had made a little money, he was not ashamed of that, and had friends on the Governor's staff. Certainly, he knew Togidubnus, for they had met often at the annual Meeting of the Council of Britain in the Colony, sponsored by the Roman authorities. He also had mining interests in the south ... and had travelled abroad, he would not deny it. And why was he hiding in the brambles? He had met a group of five or six insubordinate tribesmen. Had Catuarus not heard their shouts? Discontent among the natives. Best to be careful. He had thought that he was followed. Maybe he had been!

Catuarus could see nothing on the road, which stretched a good league across the plain before rising up to the horizon, and advised Faustinus only that he should set out to Londinium. Yet, the man fumbled and procrastinated. He wished not to travel alone with savages on the loose and no protection. There was a lot of anger on account of the recent outrages, though he would not dishonour his Roman friends by recounting these. Would Catuarus not escort him back towards Londinium? He could pay well. And, besides, the young man must not go to the Colony for there was trouble there.

Catuarus was attempting to make his excuses, without admitting the mission for his uncle, when something caught the midday sun away to his left; something metallic, with glints of iron and bronze, had appeared to the north. By great good fortune, his conversation

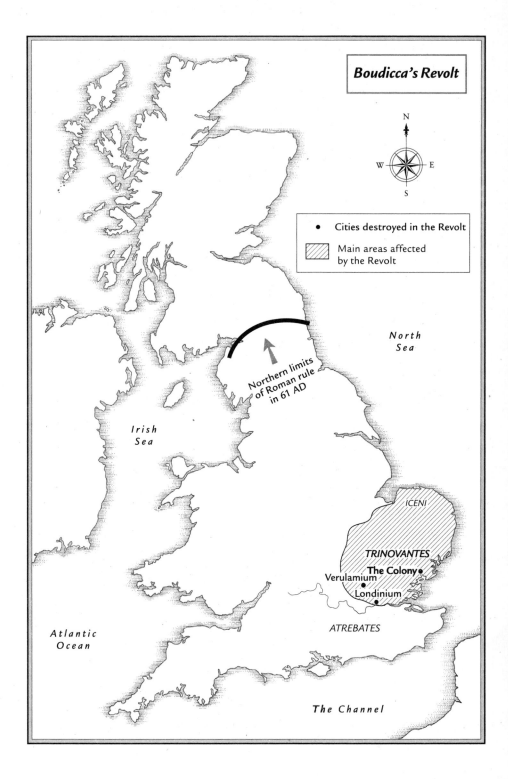

Boudicca's Revolt

N
W E
S

• Cities destroyed in the Revolt

▨ Main areas affected by the Revolt

North Sea

Northern limits of Roman rule in 61 AD

Irish Sea

ICENI

TRINOVANTES

The Colony •

Verulamium •
• Londinium

ATREBATES

Atlantic Ocean

The Channel

with the villa owner had taken place off the track, on the siding; and, urgently, he caught the man by his arm and pulled him back towards the undergrowth. Knowing that there were only minutes before the war party he had spotted would arrive – it was at most two miles down the road – he tore at the nettles and thorns with his stick and infiltrated the greenery, thrashing out a path beyond, where the two horses could be tied, afterwards making his way back to the road and a vantage point. Five minutes had passed and already the outriders were approaching, and the singing and shouting of a crowd of men behind them was now just audible. They were too disordered to be Roman, too irregular. The little man was right. They were in danger.

Catuarus returned to the tree and assured himself that Faustinus was safe and their mounts silenced; seized the gift of his uncle, for he wanted no prying hands; and returned to watch the procession as it drew close. The horses were already in sight, British warriors with javelins. They were nude and covered in woad – keen for battle. As there was the risk that they would inspect the vegetation, he ducked as they came within hailing distance and let them rattle by on the road. Then, as the sound of their hooves disappeared, he rose again, determined to make some kind of estimate of numbers and strength. He had expected one hundred or two hundred. But here there was a long snake of men, a thousand at least. There was no question of brigandage: this was the full rising of a clan, maybe of a whole tribe. He paid careful attention to the front ranks, as they walked towards him. Yet, he did not recognise their leaders, who were covered in blue paint and, in some cases, wore stolen Roman legionary helmets. However, he could see from the tattoos and the painted designs on their faces that this was a coalition of different peoples. Here there were septs of the Trinovantes, the Britons who lived beyond the hills, to the north of Londinium. But there were also the Iceni, the wild northern people of the marshes and the swamps – he caught glimpses of their signs. There was the Boar Clan, the Horse Clan – of which

Faustinus claimed membership – and the Royal Clan with its wavy lines and stars.

All the Fen Britons were involved in this enterprise, then. Nor were they poorly armed: there were slingers and bowmen, but also sword and spear carriers, bulky shields on their arms. The weapons hidden for years from the Romans in bogs and beneath the dykes in rusting packages had been retrieved. They were also blooded. There were heads and hands aloft on some spears. These did not look like the remains of soldiers. Most, judging by the skin colour and expressions, were British, the easy victims from villas along the way: natives who spoke Latin, farmers who gave passing Romans water or made money from the conquerors, selling crops to the troops. Britons, in short, like Faustinus.

It took almost an hour for the broad colunm, hemmed in by the thickets that had grown on either side of the road, to pass. By then Catuarus and with him Faustinus were long gone. Determined more than ever on the completion of his mission, the princeling had edged back to the horses. And, afterwards, he passed along the back of the green wall that separated the two fleeing men from the marauders, stumbling with the villa owner, who shivered at the screams of murder and invocations to the goddess of blood mere yards away. They moved constantly and tensely, only stopping once the shouts and footsteps receded behind them.

Catuarus said nothing as they caught their breath and wiped the sweat from their faces. But the villa owner began almost to cry. He was certain that his home was torched and the Colony overrun – for, already when he had left, there had been talk of attacking the city. It was useless to go to the north, but to the south were those beasts. He spoke of the stupidities of revolting. How the Romans would punish his brother Britons terribly, for the Romans always won. And all the fault of that Greek ... Catuarus pricked up his ears: Togidubnus had been right, then, in saying, in their last moments together, that the little foreigner was at the bottom of it all. Yes, continued Faustinus, it was all the fault of the messenger of Seneca. There had been trouble enough already. Rome had refused to allow a prince to succeed in the clans on the death of the King of the Fens, Prasutagus. The clans were also angry about being made to pay for the buildings in the Colony and some land had been stolen to settle retiring soldiers. All that would have been bearable, if it had not been for the Greek. He had arrived at the Colony ten days before. Come from Rome. News from the Emperor. He had insisted that the debts of the tribe be paid.

Catuarus knew that word 'debts' only too well. The same trick had been played in the Kingdom of his uncle: Britons had money forced on them and, later, were expected to pay back this useless coin at extortionate rates of interest. Well, Faustinus insisted, this Greek had come demanding repayment for a debt that Seneca had gifted to the Fen tribes. And the reason, the reason ... Here Faustinus' voice rose so high that his young companion had to shush him. The reason was that the Emperor was considering abandoning Britain! Catuarus could not hide his shock. But his companion continued oblivious. Of course, the Greek said it only at one select dinner party and he was drunk at the time; had complained, in fact, about the lack of revenue and the disappointment of the Cambrian silver mines. But the news spread. Then, when there was the problem of repaying Lord Seneca, the soldiers had been sent out. Among the Iceni, the Royal Clan had been humiliated: men roughed up, two of the princesses raped and one of the king's wives had been given the strap by a centurion – they had publicly whipped her. Catuarus shook his head at the stupidity of it. First the news that Rome was considering abandoning its newest province and now these absurd scenes. What would his uncle say when he learnt?

They waited almost an hour in a dell further down the road, while Faustinus spoke in a blur of despairing words, complaining and complaining about the events that had led to the revolt and the likely incineration of his Fenland property. Then, as the afternoon sun began its steep decline, the younger man stood and announced his intention of reaching the Colony. His travelling companion implored him against this, insisting that they must lie low, that it was their only chance of survival. But Catuarus quickly detached himself from the man whom he had come to see as a burden and set off. His horse had the brand of Togidubnus, and could not be used if the tribes were now in open revolt – he would be butchered in a second as a friend of the Romans. So he placed it on the road and gave it a kick towards Londinium, knowing that he would never see it again. And then, with nothing but his uncle's gift in his hands, a long knife on his thigh and woad now streaked across his cheeks, he set out north on foot, confident that he would be able to bluff his way past the rebels he was sure to meet.

The journey to the Colony took the rest of that day and the whole of the next. It was a long, hard slog even on well-laid Roman grit. And, as he continued to move to the north, the signs of desolation became more and more frequent. At first, there were just burnt buildings – the rebels had destroyed anything Roman and this included rectangular houses: only Romans or collaborators built square dwellings as opposed to the circular native ones. But then he came upon gravestones that had been passionately defaced: writing, after all, was Roman. Catuarus marvelled at the time the vandals had taken to hammer off the face of a legionary carved in rock. Milestones had been overturned. At one point of the road, he found a sack left behind by some marauding rebel with pieces of bronze statue that had been hacked from an inanimate victim, a sacrifice this to Andate. And with such confusion there were constant groups of warriors moving backwards and forwards. He had already guessed that the men he had seen before could only be the organised vanguard of a much larger army, slowly gathering itself up from out of the silted channels and wet plains of the Fens.

Catuarus reasoned, correctly, that individual horse riders would not care to stop him, being too busy on their own business, carrying messages to and fro among the clans. The bands of warriors, though, he tried to avoid. Sometimes this was possible, for these men were too intent on their own unpleasant pursuits. However, when it was not possible, he gave words of greeting. If asked to explain himself he pleaded a lame horse, urgent business to the north, speaking little and slowly so that they would not hear his quite different Celtic dialect. Only on one occasion, on the second day, were men aggressive, not recognising a Fen clan in Catuarus' spiralled woad, and insisted on seeing what he carried in his bag. For some moments the prince was fearful for his mission and his life; but the leader of this gang found nothing of interest or value in Togidubnus' gift, and handed the sack back to the young man. The interview even proved useful, for it was there that he learnt the army heading south had been sent to guard against relief arriving from Londinium. And, distracted by other passers-by, this knot of rebels soon let Catuarus return to his trek north. By then, he could see bellows of smoke on the skyline – the Colony was only an hour's walk away.

He had already determined that it would be better to arrive at the town by night, given the likely confusion of a besieging army. So he waited for dusk, in a hollow out of sight of the road, thinking carefully over what he was to do when he arrived. His uncle had been quite emphatic. He was to get there, if possible, before war broke out – well, that was now out of the question. Yet, war or no war, he was to make contact with both sides and to express enthusiastically the family's support. Togidubnus – who had also taken the liberty of sending messengers to the Governor in Cambria, to his tribal neighbours, to the Imperial government in Londinium, to the illegal sect of the druids and had even ordered out one fast boat to warn the Romans in Gaul – was taking no chances. He would play the game of artful neutrality until the very end, until indeed it was clear beyond doubt that one side or the other was going to triumph. Catuarus then *must* break through the disorganised, straggling besiegers into the Roman town and afterwards pass back through the ranks to the rebels, where he would give his uncle's gift to the leaders of the revolt.

But, as he drew near the Colony, Catuarus understood the uselessness of his plan. The Britons were in far greater numbers than he had expected and, if disorganised – many were blind drunk – then, in their thousands, it would be almost impossible to penetrate to the city beyond. The Colony itself was in flames. Warriors had already stormed the mansions and town houses, so the inhabitants who had survived – mainly ex-legionaries and administrators and their families – had retreated into the stone box of the incomplete Temple to the Divine Claudius, the liberator of Britain. The rest of the citizens of the Colony were being dealt with. As he followed the road towards the city, he saw one Roman grandmother being dragged towards the woods on the side, by her hair. And there, between the elms, there were little hellish tableaux: men belted to trees suffering taunts with knives; a young Roman virgin with her breasts cut from her, mocked and touched by a dozen Fen warriors; an ancient councillor crucified on a rapidly erected platform. Blood had spread out, so it seemed that the Britons had intended, with their ritual ecstasies, to carpet the floor of the wood with this substance; and, in the torchlight, the red took on a sickly bluish hue.

Then, turning himself from this slow carnage, he faced once more the temple ahead, surrounded by baying warriors. One of these had already reached the statue of the Emperor Claudius atop a horse in triumph, and, climbing it, had sawn off the bronze head. This was now hoisted on a pole and was being bumped up and down by the throng. He could hear little from within the temple, where the last five or six score of the Colonians survived: for the most part, silence had seized hold and the Roman silence was far, far worse than the barbarian noise. But there were some shrieks. A child complained of the heat, a woman shouted about 'mercy', a man with a harsh Gaulish accent gave out obscenities, threatening what the relief would do to the Britons when they got there. One warrior picked up this last sentence, translating it for his colleagues, who laughed. These then began, with all the art of a theatrical troupe, to imitate Roman

67

trumpets and riders arriving from afar, with straight expressions and stiff bodies. What had before been a rumour – that a relief legion had tried to break through, but had been destroyed by the rebel army on the road to the south – was now being confirmed. An ambush had been worked, and the Romans had walked straight into it. Indeed, as Catuarus watched, the insignia of a recently slaughtered centurion was being handed around to wide-eyed shield carriers – a legion defeated! Londinium was doomed, for the nearest Roman army was several hundred miles away with the Governor in the west.

Now Catuarus had to decide. Perhaps, by some miracle, he could break through the lines and link up with what remained of the Colony in the walls of the temple. But this would be a foolish way to spend his life. Those inside were already corpses: no relief could now come. His mission would, instead, involve simply making contact with the rebel leaders and so he turned away from the walls of the temple and walked back into the crowd. For some minutes, he pushed aimlessly through the churning, celebrating Britons, until at last he fell on a circle of wagons, with chariots tipped over in rows and, heavily guarded by warriors, two or three dozen clan leaders with the torques of royalty on their necks.

Almost at random, he walked up to a group. He spoke deliberately with his normal Celtic, letting them know that he was not a Fenman. There was confusion and then suspicion and then anger. What was an outsider doing among them on the night of their revenge? Did he want maybe to end like the Romans – the dismembered body of a veteran legionary lay only feet away – and, taking up this challenge, two young braves, entirely naked, rose to their feet. But Catuarus, knowing how to play a Briton among Britons, was careful to show no fear: 'I have come many miles from the mighty King Togidubnus' – a Trinovantes chief screwed up his face at the name of such a famous collaborator – 'and I have not come to speak to the Romans, but to your leader, if you have one ...' 'There is our Queen. However, no one can see her. She is kept apart now that the war has begun. She is inviolate.' It was not unheard of in wars, for the tribes to choose a woman as their head. 'Forgive me, brother, but I have never before visited your lands. What is her name?' 'Her name is Boudicca ['Victory' in British Celtic], a good name. She was beaten and her daughters raped.' Catuarus remembered the description of the stupidities of the Roman officials in trying to reclaim their debts. 'But she will soon revenge our clan on the heads of these.' He gestured in the direction of the city.

'Then I must see your Queen now. A message was sent to our King, and I am the reply. I have a gift for her here.' The warriors looked at the bag suspiciously. 'No one can see the Queen. She must be kept apart: it is the custom.' 'But she must see ...' While they spoke, a figure had strayed across the little band and, on hearing the discussion, pushed his way to face Catuarus without ceremony. He was a portly individual, who was also covered in the blue designs of the Horse Clan. Catuarus paid no attention to the newcomer until this warrior spoke, but then almost dropped the heavy object he was carrying. He knew that voice! It was the voice of Faustinus; for, transformed from nervous Roman villa owner to proud chieftain, that one stood before him again, arrogant in his new guise.

Faustinus did not smile, as acquaintances are wont to do on meeting for a second time, but clicked his lips rudely at Catuarus, mocking him. 'A guard on the road was necessary, brother. I had been set to catch Romans. One Roman can bring a legion. But you I could not catch. Of you I could not be sure. I am still not sure.' Murmurs of agreement came from the other leaders around him. 'What is your King's gift then?' It seemed a challenge. Catuarus took the sack and rolled the object out onto his palms. 'It is a gift from the Lord Togidubnus, to the Queen of the Fen Britons and the leader of our holy war for freedom. It is a sign of esteem and of brotherhood.' Faustinus reached and took the severed head by the hair. The expression of the Greek was one of mystification, not outrage, as is often found on those who share that fate: maybe because the operation had been performed quickly in the kitchens, while Catuarus' horse was being prepared. Perhaps because Seneca's agent had still been thinking of the blue face of the throttled man and the threefold death. Faustinus allowed a smile. 'You will not see our Queen. But tell your King it is a good gift. By the morning this man's head will hang with the heads of those in the Colony who die quickly! The order to storm the last confines is about to be given. After that there will be Londinium and the other cities. For the Romans the sky will fall. Britain will soon be free.'

~~~ Historical Background ~~~

This chapter looks at the initial stages of the most famous event connected with Roman Britain: Boudicca's Revolt. The revolt centred on the two East Anglian tribes, the Iceni in Norfolk and the Trinovantes in Suffolk. Three cities – London, St Albans and Colchester – were sacked, seventy thousand Romans and allies were killed, if we are to believe Tacitus, and the best part of a legion destroyed before the Roman Governor managed to put down the unrest and instigate his own savage retributions. The exact motives for the revolt included two major grievances. First the Iceni, though subject to Rome, lived in a semi-independent kingdom under their chief Prasutagus. But, after Prasutagus' death, c.60 AD, his kingdom was annexed. Second, this annexation involved or coincided with the recall of debts – partly the fault of the Imperial minister Seneca, who may have heard a rumour that the Emperor wanted to abandon Britain. And the resulting mistreatment of the Iceni included the flogging of Boudicca (Prasutagus' wife) and the rape of her daughters.

We have reason to believe that Togidubnus and 'the Kingdom', as his territory was called by the Romans, remained true to the Imperial cause. In telling the story, then, from the point of view of one of Togidubnus' kin – Catuarus is a name found on a golden ring discovered in what was probably Togidubnus' villa at Fishbourne and possibly a relative – we are looking through the eyes of an apparent Roman loyalist. The fact that Catuarus is also made to deal with the rebels is a tribute to Togidubnus' pragmatism: the king was a survivor – he may have ruled for as many as sixty years – and we know from Tacitus that some 'friends' of Rome went over to the Queen of the Iceni.

Following on from the failure of Boudicca's Revolt there were no other serious insurrections in Britain. Instead, the focus of Roman might was now the northern frontier, approximately the English-Scottish border, beyond which the unconquered Britons dwelt.

CHAPTER FIVE

Wife on the Frontier, c.100 AD

Claudia Severa, grandmother of Artorius, mother to the guardians of the frontier

Catuarus prospered in Britain after the failure of the revolt; ageing in peace and prosperity. But I turn now, instead, to Claudia Severa – we will let the story itself reveal her connection to our kin – who dwelt in the fort at Briga on the northern frontier. Today that same frontier is overrun by Picts and other enemies of the civilised, but in those times, even before the Stone Wall was built, it was held by ten thousand polished Roman helmets and swords ...

The day that the prefect Aelius Brocchus and his wife Claudia Severa arrived at Briga [Piercebridge], the fort on the high Pennine inclines that was to be their home for the next years, an uncharacteristically ferocious storm broke over the valley. And it was only natural that there were as many explanations for a tempest of such violence as there were nationalities in the valley that Briga guarded. So the German auxiliaries, mercenaries to the Romans, talked of one of their gods with his mighty thunder hammer welcoming their new commander, and confirming the man's vigour as a war leader. The legionaries, mostly Italian, jammed in eight to a room, noted gloomily that the blasts came from the west and so portended disaster – civil war, an ambush on one of the spring marches or, worse still, a failure to pay promised bonuses. The merchants from Gaul and Spain and Palestine, who kept their emporiums a stone's throw from the Roman stronghold, were more practical and ran to plug dripping holes and pin together thatch so as to protect their stock.

Meanwhile, the Britons who lived in the hollows, the caves and in huts among the trees crawled excitedly onto the thresholds of their dwellings as the thunder and lightning alternated. They did so for it was believed among the Celts of the island that the sky only ripped itself open in this fashion when a great soul passed from the world. Indeed, they had learnt as children that, just as a candle being blown out frightens those depending on its light, so, in the same way, the life of a powerful man disturbs nature when it is extinguished. And the truth of this was confirmed, for two weeks after the commander's arrival the news reached Briga that, far away in the south of Britain, Togidubnus Atrebates had passed on.

When prefect Aelius Brocchus heard this news (it had come from Eboracum [York] with the dispatches and intelligence about native movements in the unconquered zones to the north), he was already settled into the business of the fort. There were the new rotas to prepare. There were men to be disciplined – a nasty affair of a centurion who had beaten a trader. There were also supplies to be ordered and sandstone to be cut in the nearby quarries. But, still with this extraordinary quantity of difficulties to worry at him, he read and reread the brief communiqué announcing the death. Aelius was new to the island, but in his last posting in the province of Asia the name of Togidubnus had been known and celebrated. For, at the time of Boudicca's Revolt, a generation before, this Togidubnus had been the only Briton to stand shoulder to shoulder with the Romans, without hesitation, without fear. And Prefect Aelius could say with pride that, on the way to their new posting at the frontier, he and his wife had stayed in the old man's newly constructed palace, an enormous complex of gardens and villa buildings on the south coast.

Aelius had, in fact, spoken at length to the king – the last independent ruler of the Britons – whose exquisite manners and Latin made him a remarkable host, and, best of all, the venerable monarch had shown kind attentions to his dear Claudia. Now, his kingdom would be absorbed into the Empire, his treasures dispersed, his harem sold, for does not time kill ... Then Aelius' eyes fell down the lime-wood tablet on which these words had been written, and something else there caught his attention: something more pertinent and more pressing than the extinction of an old man who had, anyway, had more than his share of years. His hand started to shake, half-chewed breakfast fell from his mouth. Stumbling to his feet, he raced past the two legionaries at his door and into the adjoining room where his wife sat perfectly still, in the first months of a pregnancy, watching the rain clouds blow down from the hills through the open doorway.

Claudia had been a fourteen-year-old when Aelius, five years her senior, had promised himself to her and even then she had been forthright, determined and difficult; she had been convinced from the beginning that she had married beneath her. And it was typical that now, ten years on, her husband deranged with stupid excitement, she was the first to speak. Indeed, she pointed to the rain, noting that this was August in Britain; and asked acidly what December would be like. Usually, he would have hushed her with considerations about the slowness of promotion; the need to do time in the most challenging provinces; a reminder too about the wives of the other fort commanders in the area – she could hope to make advantageous friends with matrons and ladies of consequence. But on this occasion he just stood before her, holding out the wooden tablet. She took it from his hands and examined the words that were written there. At first, she thought that it was Togidubnus' death that had driven her husband to distraction. In fact, she felt something like relief at reading of the end of the old man: what a lecherous, devious type he had been! It was only when her husband pointed to the lines below that she understood. She read once, then twice, then a third time, then looked up. *He* was coming to the north to examine the proposals to build a wall on the frontier. And, in his trip into the frontier zone, *he* had chosen to stay at Briga. In one week's time the Governor of all Britain would be a guest in their own house.

Her husband, whose voice had returned, spoke now about the honour of it, about the surprise, about the glory. But Claudia dismissed that kind of nonsense immediately. The honour and the surprise and the glory did not interest her in the least. To facts: the Governor was one of three or four senators based in Britain who were capable, with nothing more than a letter, of having a prefect promoted. Aelius was young, he was still relatively inexperienced. But with a nod from the Governor anything was possible. Why, look at that equestrian that had just left, Haterius whatshisname. He had been born somewhere on the fringes of the African deserts and had ended in this same terrible place. But he had been noticed and shifted on to an important post in Egypt and now there was talk of him being sent to Rome as chief of the fire service there. This providential visit could be their way up and out.

Claudia knew better, of course, than to try too hard to convince her husband of this. He seemed perversely content with his frontier posting and expected – sometimes she thought that he wanted – to spend the next years there. But she would not stand for that. The Governor would be so impressed by the time he left Briga that they would be on a ship across the Channel in the space of a month. Otherwise, they could be here for years. And she would divorce her Aelius before spending half a lifetime on this unpleasant heath-land. She ignored the last fatuous comments to issue from the prefect's mouth, walking to the doorway shivering. This called for extraordinary acts of preparation and dedication. She would do what-ever it took to get her son and her unborn child back to the civilised world.

That very afternoon Aelius led a patrol to the north – he was still familiarising himself with the territory. And Claudia, left on her own, set about her plans. The first decision was whom to invite to the welcoming meal, a meal that she had decided, thanks to a felicitous coincidence of dates, to describe as her birthday party – it served her purposes admirably that no one know of the Governor's arrival. The Governor had specifically asked to meet with native leaders; this was a problem, as in her brief time in the north she had not been intro-duced to a single Briton whom she would like to invite into her dining room. An image of one of the local clan leaders straining Falernian wine through his moustache caught at and, for a moment, dragged down her concentration.

Then, there were their neighbours, the other fort commanders; here too she had difficulties. The nearest fort, the Shining Place [Housesteads], was inhabited by the dreadful Flavius Cerialis and his wife Sulpicia. The names were Roman, but both were newly made citizens from the marshes of the Germanic coast, brought to Britain to command a body of their co-nationals. Cerialis towered above her husband and Sulpicia towered above them all, while both had shocks of horrid blond hair that seemed to Claudia positively indecent. At first, she wondered whether it would be possible not to invite them: Cerialis, she knew, was desperate for a promotion; indeed, had already nagged at Aelius to write letters praising him to the provincial head-quarters in Londinium. But then she remembered their dreadful, stomping Latin and their sub-Roman manners in the dining room. No, she would have them there. Anything to put Aelius in a better light ... Bending over one of the lime tablets they used for messages, she wrote out a brief and polite invitation to be sent to the Shining Place that very afternoon. Then, going through the other com-manders in the region, she chose whom else to invite on the basis of who would and who would not impress the Governor. Aelius and Aelius alone was to be at the centre of attention.

Her invitations finished, she then set about a careful survey of the fort. The latrines would have to be re-dug, of course; and not only those of the prefect but also those of the legionaries, the smell was *appalling*. She looked too with contempt at the bath-house that the troops alone used. There were some who said baths weakened sol-diers, made them practically oriental in their foppishness, some who said that it would be better for the Empire if military baths were abolished altogether. She knew that she would not be able to convince her husband of this; some of the legionaries even wanted hot water facilities installed – unbelievable! But she would, at least, get him to have the structure re-tiled, so that it impressed. She walked now to the gate and the green banks that constituted the wall of the fort. Here too some repairs perhaps – the Governor was known to appre-ciate energy; why not make it higher all the way round? Those dogs of soldiers were all stupidity and appetite; they would have to be forced to work this week as never before. Maybe, too, she could get her husband to put up an inscription to one of his officers who had been killed by tribesmen – anything to make the surroundings seem more Roman.

She turned then into the fronting, where the shops stood. A party of British natives were bartering with the eastern merchant from Alexandria who held the largest of the shops. Pennine bear furs were spread out on the porch and a litter of puppies was also being offered up by the locals, who had only recently discovered the wonders of trade with the Empire. The merchant clearly intended to buy up all that was before him, hunting dogs from the northern hills were now one of the most successful British exports, and worth almost a purse of silver in Rome. He had called his slave to go and fetch some wine *amphorae* – the real love of the natives – and was arguing with his pidgin Celtic when he became aware of a slim, well-dressed woman wading through the mud towards him.

Claudia stood before the little crowd who, with the lascivious exception of the oriental, looked at her indifferently. She was considered a great beauty by Romans, but these oafs were unable to appreciate grace or perfection or any of her twenty-four years. They preferred their women wide-bellied and with locks down to the hips; she had seen the 'prize' British girls with the embassies that came from the nearby septs and clans on business, girls who tugged at their husbands and were aggressive and immodest. She did not enjoy talking to the natives, but the Governor had asked to meet locals and they were only a week away from the visit. She scanned the faces until she found one that she recognised. He was a man from the tribe on the forested higher ground. He had come to Aelius the previous week looking for patronage; he had come twice. Indeed, he was one of the very few Britons in the north who could speak Latin and he hoped to enter the Roman army the following year and eventually to become – Claudia felt a spasm of pain – a citizen.

'You! No, the tall one.' 'I am Brigionius ma'am.' 'I am not interested in your name, Briton.' She would, in any case, never remember it; to her all these savage words were the same. 'I demand your help if you want more of my husband's recommendations.' The Briton dipped his head. He would say anything for the prefect's letter, for he would never embark on his service under the eagle if he failed to have an *epistula* in his hands when he visited the recruiting office at Eboracum. 'In seven days an important Roman guest will come. Do you understand?' She hesitated, waiting for an affirmative. 'He wishes to meet some of your people. I will expect a gathering of Britons to greet him.' Brigionius again gave her a bow. 'Then the best-dressed and best-educated of your tribe – preferably those who, at least, understand Latin – are to be at the fort in seven days to greet this big chief.' The bow deepened until Brigionius' hair fell down and grazed the muddy floor.

Her trip had so far proved productive enough. She would now add to her success by getting the question of the ingredients for the feast out of the way; there was some urgency involved. She turned to the shopkeeper who was crouched in modesty, hoping for some crumbs of the lady's custom. In a moment, she had him by the elbow and was whisking him through into the covered section of his store, leaving the man's son, Salmanes, to haggle with the Britons. Then, as they stood in his back room, surrounded by hanging meats and bottles of imported fish sauce and other delicacies, he tried to speak. But Claudia pushed his words impatiently aside: 'Listen to me, merchant, and listen well. You have heard that we are expecting an important visitor. Well, I have urgent need of goods to feed him and his party and I need them in the next few days. You will have to send out a rider this afternoon.' The trader sighed with pleasure and opened his hands in thanks. But Claudia's hard voice jogged him out of his reverie. She started again. She did not want any of that dreadful Celtic beer that the legionaries lapped up – he was not to dare to try to sell that to her; nor was she interested in garlic paste or barley. There was too much of both in the fort stores. Her party would be one with style and she had some very particular ingredients in mind, ingredients that would have to be shipped from the south.

The merchant took up her cry: why, yes, 'style', too few attended to 'style' today. It was all British meat and British . . . She told him to be quiet. She wanted him more demure and measured in his responses. And then she began to list, kicking off with Spanish wine and olives from Italy. He reached for his stylus and tablets to write upon. And when Claudia came to some of the more difficult ingredients she was gratified to see that he did not hesitate. Indeed, when she mentioned the rarer flavourings he even asked her which of two markets in Eboracum she wanted the order to go to. He did, however, irritate her by pointing out that the little time at their disposition meant that the price would rise. He named a price. Claudia looked fiercely at the man: no one had ever complained of her ability to bargain. She had heard, she said, that a centurion had treated the merchant shamefully. The merchant's eyes fired. It had been dreadful, he had been held over a ditch and forced to say that his goods were only fit for the sewers. Claudia yet again cut him short. 'If you want justice from my husband, merchant, make sure that all these goods arrive on time and for two-thirds of the price you mentioned.' She walked out while telling the trader that he could start ordering, afterwards passing through the middle of the British tribesmen, who were loading their wine onto pack animals. She took special care not to touch any of them.

The time before the Governor's arrival passed with such bewildering speed that Claudia later had the impression that the seven days she worked had been two or at most three and certainly could not distinguish in her mind's eye between the sunlit mornings and candlelit nights she had sweated with the slaves in the kitchen. From the evening of that first day, when she passed into the confines in which food was prepared, until she emerged, a week later, on the morning of the feast, stained with sooty smoke and cinders, she never wavered from her task; only making occasional sorties to assure herself that repairs were being undertaken, the soldiers' immorality contained and that the tribespeople were preparing to come and greet 'the great chief'. Indeed, by the time she woke on the morning of the seventh day, she knew the layout of that room with the thatch roof, the doorposts blackened with ashes, the pots buried in the ground with salt and fish flavourings, on which the slaves constantly stubbed their toes, better than that of her own boudoir. But she could also, as she left, look with a certain satisfaction on the vast array of foods laid out and the dozen slaves who waved flies away from uncovered delicacies.

Of course, if she had had to depend solely on the resources of the fort and the surrounding countryside then the meal would have been a Spartan one. At best there would have been venison and beavers' testicles. Some of the heather honey found in the combs of wild bees on the edges of the mountains. Twisted bread with its creamy, peppery crust. The first of the season's puffballs – a Celtic fungus. Not to mention bog butter – the rancid British dairy concoction left to mature in the swamps around the edges of settlements and reckoned a great delicacy by the locals. And, yes, it would have been as good as the Governor would eat anywhere else on the frontier. But from the moment she had heard of his arrival she had determined that he would have so much more than that and had buried herself in the masters; her collection of cooking books and parchments lay open or unrolled all around the kitchen – Iatrocles' *On Cakes*, Simus' *Cookery* and numerous other treasures from the chefs of the past.

To meet the ingredients demanded by these culinary artists she had had to turn to her own resources. She had brought their preciously guarded collections of condiments and herbs in sealed glass containers; the slaves who worked in the kitchen had never seen glass used there and gasped with excitement. Usually it was enough to deploy pine kernels left in with the precious Indian spices, pine kernels that absorbed flavour and smell. But for the Governor she spared nothing, sprinkling actual saffron and nutmeg and cinnamon onto the dishes with abandon. She had opened up, too, their small selection of Italian wines for the cooking. Olive oil from the fields of

Lebanon had been sacrificed and she had put hunks of cheese from Dalmatia above the rafters, over the fire, to cure them in preparation for the great man's arrival. Then she had tried to convince and, finally, simply ordered her husband to break open the small colony of snails that he had brought north as a delicacy.

There had been problems, of course. Some of the British oysters she had ordered – though kept carefully in salt water – had gone rancid and had been thrown away. Part of the wine from Africa arrived as vinegar despite the new-fangled resin-sealed toppers. Then there were grain pots in the legionaries' stores. There was always the initial level of mouldy grain to dig off – that was inevitable. But some of the lower levels had been infested with beetles and she had set the slave children to separate bugs and seeds until there was a corner of the kitchen ankle-deep in insect corpses. Then, in the last hours before the feast, she had realised that they did not have enough red meat for all the party and so had had a couple of horses killed, despite the weeping protestations of two cavalry officers. It would do for the tribesmen.

However, most of her fears and nightmares were caused by the terrible wait to see if ingredients coming from the markets in the British cities to the south would arrive in time. She remembered her dance of joy when the catfish from the Nile got to Briga on the last evening, still alive in specially constructed containers – the Governor was rumoured to be driven to distraction by this food. Figs were easily bought even at the fort. But her nerves were punished again and again by the wait for the pomegranates that were, in the end, dropped off by a specially assigned rider on the fifth day. There were also so many vegetables and fruits that she had taken for granted in Aelius' previous postings, but that were only now being established in Britain. So she was relieved beyond words as marinated cabbage turned up at the entrance to the kitchen and the first of the recently planted British peach and cherry crops were brought in.

Then, at the dawn of the day she had worked towards with such fidelity, her greatest hope: the flamingos arrived. She had been so unsure as to her success in acquiring this creature that she had had the local Britons go out with nets and decoys to hunt migrating herons. But the riders had done it; they had got them to her just in time. She killed these curious pink birds as soon as they were unpacked, wringing their necks close to the body and pounding their unco-operative heads onto the stone tables of the kitchen as she did so. Then the joy of flamingo on the very edge of the world overtook her – the feast was now only hours away – and in an ecstasy she did all the jobs she would have normally assigned to slaves. She plucked. She boiled them in water with vinegar and dill. The euphoric hostess even tossed in a bouquet of British leeks and some coriander to bubble with the birds, ripping the heads off easily when their meat began to bulge in the huge pans. Then, when it was done, she threw *defrutum* on the skin to flavour it and added – after a long hour of work with the mortar – pepper, caraway, coriander, asafoetida, mint, Pennine roots and Jericho dates, while cooking liquor was mixed in a sauce with cornflour and left ready to pour over the birds on the Governor's arrival. The Governor's arrival. The Governor's imminent arrival …

She walked out to the door and saw the mumbling soldiers prepared into ranks. To the left were the awkwardly dressed British tribespeople, stuffed into togas and cloaks supplied by her husband that very morning, all men, no women strangely enough. There, as well, were the envious fort commanders and their families who had only learnt an hour before what kind of a party really awaited them – tall, blonde Sulpicia glowered from the corner mouthing the words 'happy birthday'. Claudia looked back behind her and cauterised two slave girls who were not taking the necessary precautions with a roast joint. Then it happened. The man on the guard tower turned and, before he shouted, she saw his face and knew.

This was the moment. Even on a fast palfrey the Governor would need the best part of twenty minutes to come from the ridge to the fort and she would have to be clean. As the guards formed into line, she walked out of the door to her quarters where the gown for this day of celebration had already been laid out. The hot water was all ready as she had instructed. She undressed from her filthy cooking clothes and sat on a wooden couch, while the servants worked on her skin. And then, the bustle outside became more and more audible ... A slave ran in, the Governor's face was now visible, the lines of purple on his senatorial gown had been spotted. She stood up and threw herself into the dress, uncovered her hair that had been prepared the night before, and took a flask of fermenting British beer, which doubled as a cream for the Roman women of the north, palming the foam from it onto her face. Then, as the servants dabbed the foam away, before they had properly finished, she started to walk, they scuttling along beside her.

She passed out with measured steps onto the hard stone walkway that had been cleaned to a pale white. And there, framed by the gate, was the Governor. He did not head the body of a hundred or so horses and bodyguards, but he was in the second line sitting higher and more erect than the rest, as was only proper. And she looked across at the kitchen and the rows of perfect dishes and at her husband and their jealous neighbours, also all perfect in their own way, and then at the gleaming legionaries, for whom she felt an unusually motherly and proud regard. She had done it. She had won. She had pulled off the impossible. Could anything, she thought, possibly go wrong?

Then, just as the Governor rode to the front along the road immediately before the fort, the attention of all was drawn by a musical whine and inharmonious cooing. Claudia, despite the dank earth and her fear of getting sandals or clothes dirty, strode forwards. But there was no need: the singers were coming towards the Governor from out of the shadows of the fort. She looked nervously at her husband, who walked over smiling: 'Brigionius' idea; it seems it is a British custom to honour visitors.' She had already forgotten Brigionius, the Briton at the merchant's store. But she watched now with a horror, only matched by the horror on the Governor's face, as about fifty blue naked people, entirely mauve except for patches of pubic hair, serenaded by a couple of native harp players, appeared before the eminent visitor waving their hands. They were all women, undressed and painted from head to feet with a British dye. She would make her husband pay for this imbecility and she would finish his Brigionius!

And so the day continued, for fortune once bated does not easily abate. As she was walking to meet the Governor, his horse stretched out and bit her. Afterwards, she was introduced to the Governor's principal assistant, a certain Catuarus Atrebates, nephew of the vile Togidubnus, a southern worthy whom she had slighted earlier on in her time in Britain. As they sat down, it emerged that rumour had been wrong: the Governor did not love Nile catfish. In fact, he could not even bear to have others eat it, so offensive did he find the stench. Then, the Britons who had been packed into the room got rowdy because they thought that the flamingo was a goose, a bird they held holy. Indeed, only as the sun came low in the sky, and the other fort commanders made their excuses and began to drift away, did Claudia's luck finally change.

The Governor, having listened to the complaints of these various prefects and the case for and against a wall across the frontier, turned now attentively to her. He complimented her on the food and then on her high breeding and they talked across Aelius, who was tirelessly, tiresomely reminiscing about his times in the province of Asia; for not the first time in her life she felt so much better at this game than her husband. Then, as the sun dipped down and the lamps were hurried in, the Governor asked whether the hostess might not show him the way to his quarters. She smiled and led him from the banquet, full of his roaring and, by now, half-drunk staff, out and into the quiet of the grounds, the stars all around. As they moved, she felt she should say something about the absurd accidents of the day: the misunderstandings, the naked blue women, the fish ... But she walked silently alongside him until they reached the room that had been set aside, fighting a desire to touch this extraordinary individual, the sixth or seventh most powerful in the Empire ... They passed inside; only there, out of sight, could she bring herself to speak and then she stuttered.

Her Aelius, she started, the Governor must have recognised as a remarkable man, a man of talent. Was there nothing that the Governor could do to help him on and away? Why, he had seen the dreadful savages that lived in this outpost and what they had to tolerate. A position in Londinium would do for now. The Governor smiled like a god but said nothing. How many times a day were requests of this kind made to him, she realised. He did, though, move towards her and she could almost smell his might: this was one who sentenced the guilty and sometimes the innocent to death; who had walls put up or dragged down; who wrote letters that won equestrians positions; who talked to the Emperor ... She again wanted to touch him.

But now he spoke, gently. No, he had to confess he had not noticed that Aelius was a man of talent: a natural middle-ranker, he would say. But he had been much impressed by Aelius' wife. While she watched his dangerous mouth, his fingers touched the tresses of her hair. And she had to shake herself. She had been tricked like this before. She remembered that awful man Togidubnus, the British king, the father of the child she was carrying. Why, she had thought that he would help Aelius; but he had done nothing, had simply refused when it was too late for her to refuse back – how she had hated that scaled body. She shook the Governor off her. Could he, at least, give her a promise that she and Aelius would go away from this awful island? He looked at her quizzically and then lifted his hands and spoke the most sacred words he could to the effect that in less than a year she and her family would be far from the shores of Britain.

Several minutes later, the Governor stumbled from out of the bedroom to leave the woman, whose name he had already forgotten, some time to dress and slip off into the night. Couplings in camp were always dangerous: divorces and even exiles had been known to result. But there was no danger here. His staff were talking, the cuckold husband laughing with them. And, yes, there had been that promise: he would see to it back in Londinium. A promise was a promise, but no reason not to have some fun with this Aelius and his vulgar wife, who had given him some vague pleasure and whose cooking had condemned him to indigestion. He would send them away from Britain; he smiled at the thought of it. But where? He had been much struck on his trip north to talk to a recently transferred officer who had served in Pannonia [Hungary], in the newly con-quered territories there, staring out over the infinite steppes and forests to the north, trying to deal with impossible tribespeople, prob-ably not all that unlike those that he had met today. Yes, he would send them to Pannonia, to the furthest, most distant fort listed in the itineraries of the Empire. He would personally write the com-munication. And, so as not to encounter the woman again on her trip south, he would charter a North Sea crossing, for reasons of urgency.

Then, finally satisfied with the day and the part he had played in it, the Governor of all Britain strolled across the open ground of the fort, back towards the sound of drunkenness and merrymaking.

ᜰᜰᜰ Historical Background ᜰᜰᜰ

This chapter is based overwhelmingly on one set of sources: a series of letters, the Vindolanda tablets. These letters written on wood have been dug up in the last thirty years at Housesteads, the Roman fort of Vindolanda ('the Shining Place'); Vindolanda stood on what was, at that time, the Roman frontier with the unconquered northern Britons. And these letters give us a precious glimpse into what life was like in this north-western corner of the Empire; ranging from the duties of soldiers, to relations with the natives, to the suffering of pack animals on the road. What is extraordinary about the Vindolanda tablets is not that they were written –

every Roman fort in Britain and, indeed, every fort in the Empire will have produced a similar corpus – but that they survived – this thanks to a 'damp anaerobic environment', i.e. the peculiar quality of the soil. All the characters in this chapter, with the exception of the merchant's son, Salmanes – for whom see the notes for Chapter Seven – are taken from these letters.

Claudia Severa and her husband, Aelius Brocchus, who did leave Britain for Pannonia, did not live at Housesteads, but at nearby Briga – meaning 'the fort' in Celtic – where this chapter is set: a fort that has not yet been identified. Claudia sent a birthday party invitation to Flavius Cerialis, the Prefect of Housesteads and his wife, Sulpicia Lepidina, who were both probably Batvians. Haterius (Nepos), the census officer, who is remembered by Claudia, climbed rapidly up the *cursus honorum,* the Roman career ladder, ending as Prefect of Egypt. A nameless merchant from the region was threatened by a centurion and, afterwards, sought retribution for this offence: 'he punished me all the more until I should declare my goods to be worthless or pour them down the drain'. Brigionius, a Briton, attempted, through contacts with the Romans, to find his way into the army. The story of the Governor's visit is invented, though the letters do make reference to the peculiar climate of patronage and promotion operating in the Empire as well as his office. Claudia's unseemly behaviour is, meanwhile, simple slander.

PART II

*Establishment
and
Apogee*

CHAPTER SIX

At the Waters of Sulis, c.150 AD

Magnius, son of Catuarus: an elderly Briton of noble blood

A few months afterwards Claudia left Britain for the Danube; I will return later to her and Togidubnus' grandchild, brave Artorius. Here I offer, instead, the face of Magnius, son of Catuarus. Today his smashed gravestone lines the walls of that battle-besieged place, the Waters of Sulis [Bath]; threatened by the barbarians from Ireland and the wild Britons who have crept onto the plains now the Romans are no more. But I am concerned not with the present but with the past and venerable Magnius' last trip to that city, taken, three centuries ago, in his seventy-ninth year ...

Magnius Atrebates had always enjoyed the pools at the Waters of the goddess Sulis, the place where the deep springs blew forth their health-giving vapours. In his infancy he had come once a year with his father Catuarus and watched them lifting the first blocks of stone in what had before been barren fields, dangling his feet in the holy and magical streams, while the lines of slaves carried mortar and marble around him. He had come to the Waters too as a young official riding backwards and forwards in the period when the Atrebates kingdom had been integrated into the British province and the old clans dissolved. But his visits had been fleeting and he had not always had the time to enter the still-incomplete confines that the Romans had set out. Then, he had retired after an injury received in the army and trips had become easy and leisurely. There had been residential buildings and a wall; and the great basilica and the hot rooms and the cold plunge pool had all been worked to perfection – the barren lakes with alders growing around them were just a memory – so that nothing had lacked, or so he had thought. But now that he was in his dotage – and how he enjoyed his dotage! – he recognised that something had, instead, been lacking all along: people.

Before he had been born none but the druids or their crones had been able to bathe in the Waters of Sulis. When the first bath-house had been constructed only Roman soldiers had queued up to throw themselves into the artificial lakes and ponds created there or the natural ones that persisted. The Romanised Britons of the region had felt, instead, ill at ease. After all, they and their parents had learnt, for the best part of a century, that nudity was something not to be encouraged in the Empire, and had still not understood that within a bath it was, instead, indispensable. Even his father, as Roman a man as you would ever meet, had been nervous there and had always kept two loincloths strapped conveniently around his waist to insulate him from what he thought of as barbarity. And yet, in the last years, the Britons of the southern plains, where civilisation had taken root most firmly in the island, had finally learnt the pleasures of bathing for themselves. Other baths had been built in the towns and outside some villas, where all ran naked, slipping on the tiles. And, as the spring gave way to the summer, the wealthy and those careless with their time flew to the Waters of Sulis to enjoy the steam and the gossip.

Magnius himself had persuaded his family to come for two months that summer: there had been some trouble with the Governor that he was happy to escape. And the Waters never failed to relax and entertain him. Yesterday, for example, he and his son had been driven to hysterics by the antics of one aged Briton from the north, no younger than Magnius, who was at the Waters for the first time. His tribal background had been immediately apparent because his half-naked form – he had, of course, held a towel modestly to his privates – was covered in tattoos that would have been drawn and pricked on him when he was a young warrior and the Pennine clans still had their independence. This relic of the past had eventually been persuaded to lie out on one of the massage tables by the staff of the bath and an embarrassed nephew, who had not a blue line on him and spoke a Latin so fine that it almost put Magnius to shame. All had gone well for the first minute and then a masseur had made the mistake of placing a metal scraper on the old fool's back and beginning to press. This bull of the hills had reached back in terror, thinking himself attacked, and, with one swift movement, the ancient northerner had broken the wrist of his twenty-year-old 'assailant'.

And they said that now the wall was built Britain was well on its way to civilization . . . Well, Magnius had never taken the propaganda of the Governor – that marsh-rotted sheep – too seriously. Honestly, all that nonsense about Britons worshipping the Emperor in their newly woven togas. He had served too long in Cambria and the northern marches, where the unconquered or the just-conquered peoples lived, to believe that kind of nonsense. Why, even at the Waters of Sulis it was enough to walk two miles out into the countryside and there were whole villages where they did not understand the Roman language, only Roman power; where no one could read or write and where no one had ever travelled outside the twenty miles necessary to sell or rustle cattle. But in the spa itself there were his friends. And, especially on a warm summer evening like this one, when he and some of his old colleagues met for a bath and then for a long meal afterwards, he felt that life was, despite his age, well worth living.

It was true that rumours had dogged him in the city too. Since the news had come that the Governor was displeased at his recent speech at the Council of Britain his circle of friends had shrunk. But there were still many who were proud to be seen at the table of the Atrebates – a family, after all, of noble origins. And, in the baths itself, five or six would come that very night. The slaves behind him were handed his clothes as he removed them and he saw his daughter Trifosa with her attendants, already running unclothed into the inner pools towards some of her foolish friends; well, she was only fifteen. And, once he too was undressed, he pulled on a long shawl, not for the sake of modesty, but rather warmth. And he walked towards the temple where he would meet his little dining club; they would afterwards head to the water and then retire to one of the taverns to feast.

He waited, as he always did, under the enormous temple fronting and the sculpture of the Gorgon's head painted a bright, fiery orange, a head that some in his family claimed had been based on the noble face of Magnius' grandfather Togidubnus. And there was, it was true, some vague resemblance. Its Celtic lines, in any case, outraged every

Roman visitor and perhaps for this reason he liked it. The locals, meanwhile, not really understanding what a Gorgon was, had claimed that it was an ancient king of the city who was able to fly – they believed the snakes radiating out from the face were wings. Magnius had once tried to explain to a bath attendant, who was particularly insistent on this point, that when the Waters of Sulis had had kings then the temple and city were not even dreamed of. But he knew that it was impossible to argue with such certainties and he had heard that the townspeople had now even given their flying king a name, calling him Bladud, the son of the god Nodens. Within a generation he would more likely than not be related by the storytellers to the Atrebates themselves ...

The minutes had passed while he reflected on the origins of the stone and, as none of his friends had yet appeared, he found himself returning to an episode concerning this sculpture and his boyhood years. He had been ten at the time and his father had taken him to see it lifted into place; many of the well-to-do Romano-British of the south had been invited, he remembered. It should have been a banal childhood moment: impressed into his memory because of the extraordinary pulleys and knots that had been used to perform the operation. But, instead, he had come that afternoon as close as he ever had to death. His mistake had been to push between the adults and through the guards holding back the crowd, to stand almost under the Gorgon and stare up at it. And then, as he had stood there, had come a screech and a snap and one of the supporting ropes had broken. Like a hypnotised animal in front of the swaying weasel, he had watched the vast, ton-heavy stone monster swing before him. And suddenly he had been conscious of its weight about to smash down, the final rope dissolving into broken strands. And then the miracle. From the group of artisans near the wall had leapt a tall man with a scar across his forehead and this man had pushed the child out of the way. The small Magnius had seen the face and the sword scar – for such it certainly was – and had been conscious of a great wind like a gale on the coast, afterwards falling against something hard.

And it had all been over; the room was cleared and his father had hugged him to his side, knowing how close his heir had come to being crushed. Then the questions had begun. The family had seen Magnius fall. But none had seen his saviour and they doubted his word when he insisted upon the presence of the one with the long cicatrix. They had asked among the artisans. But when all had refused knowledge of such a man the relieved family had turned to jokes. Magnius could still recall the taunting seventy years later. They had said that the man had been a daemon or a familiar spirit, Mercury sent by Jupiter, a dead ancestor from Hades come to save him or a fairy who had lost his way in the world. But, through the mocking, Magnius had remained certain then, as he, indeed, remained certain to that day, that he had seen the man and that he owed his life to him.

Almost an hour had passed. He was cold, colder than he had expected. And he broke out of his reminiscences and realised that his friends were not coming. It was best not to think of it. Of course, he had known that some would abandon him now that he was out of favour. But Lemnus, Aufidius, Julius, Lucius . . . In one case, perhaps two cases, there could be an explanation. Yet it was hardly possible that all four had been caught up in unexpected crowds or struck down with food poisoning. Magnius did not trouble with sighs. But in that moment he felt foolish and abandoned. Perhaps his speech at the Council against the Governor had been a bad idea after all. They had warned him that there would be consequences; reminded him that he had his children to think of and the reputation of a great line. Justice was not enough, they had told him in letters and private conversations. But he would hardly return to his slaves and wander the streets to his lodgings alone without at least trying the waters. That would be too much like a surrender to those dismal ex-associates of his and unbidden circumstances. And so, brooding, he wandered with his bag of toiletries into one of the hot rooms, where the water would come up to his waist, intending to sweat his preoccupations away.

The baths were almost empty; it was now dark and still a little outside high season. And he found himself alone in the small circular space with the steam. He imagined the sweat and grime on him being liberated and he concentrated on the hope of the sharp metal working its way down his body and the long-travelled oil floating over his skin. Perhaps he should apologise to the Governor, go to Londinium, write a letter. There were many ways, they said. It was best to face this problem immediately. Even his now grown-up children had noticed the cool reception from some of their old companions in the spa. Yes, it would be best. And then, to add to his discomfort, he thought he saw his friend Lemnus' face at the doorway staring quickly and then moving on. He clutched his fingers weakly into a fist and hit the brick sides.

The lights on the torches were smoking and tapering and the water, he had noticed, was dirty. It had probably been used for mud treatments that morning and a bandage from some man's wound floated by, as did several chicken legs left behind by an earlier visitor. Despite the filth, he had just determined to settle again before seeking out one of the temple slaves for his scraping, when, into the doorway, came three giggling and naked girls. And he realised with horror that he had chosen one of the rooms reserved for mixed bathing and that Lemnus had seen this. The girls, of course, ran off, screaming with laughter; they did not want his company. And Magnius looked around and noted to his side graffiti boasting of a 'conquest' paid for in bronze coins and sexual feats so incredible that, had he been in a good mood, he would have enjoyed reading them. And the girls had perhaps thought, girls that might have been his daughter's friends, that he had desired them. He was a useless old man! He would leave and go home; he would not trouble with the cold baths or the scrapers or the massages. Then, tomorrow, he would head off to Londinium and the Governor, his arthritic joints bouncing up and down on a horse ... And, as he thought of this, he realised, for the first time, that an interview might not be granted, that he might be in greater danger than he had imagined.

He was starting to his feet to leave the room, when a voice came from behind him: he had been wrong, he was not alone. The Latin was uncertain and in truth Magnius did not properly understand it. But, nevertheless, he sat back down and stared through the steam at the figure beside him, who wished to communicate something; they might say that Magnius was a traitor or a slanderer, but no one had ever accused him of being rude.

From what he could see it was an old man, quite naked like Magnius himself. Should he speak? It seemed only proper and he asked the man his name. And again the stranger spoke, while Magnius could make nothing of the words. Indeed, he wondered if perhaps the man was not speaking to him in Celtic and attempted to unplug an ear with a finger. And then, as he was doing this, the words made sense; the stranger had asked what the oldest of the Atrebates had in his bag. It was hardly a normal request, but Magnius felt at ease. This was not, he was sure, one of the bath thieves who were so infamous in the Waters. Indeed, he trusted the figure to his right. And so he undid the lace at the top and took out the items one by one. There was his scraper, a house key, the ring with a gem of Nemesis' griffin attached to it, a gift of his father from long ago. Was that all, asked the man? Magnius hesitated and stared again through the steam at the form that sat, sometimes visible, sometimes not. Didn't he perhaps recognise the man? Hadn't they been introduced, he inquired out loud? Was this stranger, whom he addressed, a friend of his family?

But the stranger did not answer. Instead, he asked once more the question: was that all there was in the bag? Magnius stared and then carefully reached into the woollen container with his hand and pulled out a small glass phial. And what was in the phial? Magnius felt uneasy now. What stranger asked so insistently after the contents of a bag? What stranger remains unnoticed in a room for an hour and then speaks? And usually, even when there were few bathers, there was noise in the baths: pleb-strongmen as they lifted the weights; the sound of the slaps of the masseurs; ball players screaming about their scores; hulks diving into the water with a whale-like splash; not to mention the screams from the vain as armpit hair was removed. But, in that moment, and the moments before and the moments after, there was no noise.

The man continued to look ahead and to ask his question. He was not cruel, was not unkind, but seemed interested only in one thing: the phial. And now Magnius was ready to reply. It was belladonna, he said simply. It was the herb of courage. The substance that had ended the Emperor Claudius' life and that men took when they knew there was no further sense in their living. Of course, there were other ways to die – the stranger in the steam had asked him nothing more, but Magnius felt obliged to continue. Some opened their veins in the bath and bound themselves up again to eat and drink, then a little more blood was washed into the water until ... But – he almost choked with a spasm of tears as he said it – he ... he hated blades.

It seemed quite unnecessary to explain to the stranger, who certainly already knew, that he carried the phial in case the Governor ordered his arrest; it had always seemed such a vague possibility though. And then the sitting man stood up. He stood up and came round to face the heir of the Atrebates and said two simple words: 'Take it!' and vanished into the steam. But Magnius had seen the sword scar across the man's forehead and recognised the ghost as the one who had saved him seventy years before. In the man's faded eyes he had seen warmth, but in the black dark of the pupils, like a scrying glass, the Governor's merciless candour and slave markets and the instruments of persuasion and confiscation and shame and ridicule and the faithlessness of friends. The old man had always been proud of being honest, at least with himself. But in these last weeks, he suddenly realised, he had failed. He had surely known all along that he had brought ruin on his family with his speech, that the Governor would never forgive him and that only one act – an apology would be worse than useless – could possibly free his children from the weight that they now carried like so many inadequate Atlases?

And absurdly, frightened by death and this guardian spirit of the Atrebates, for such he must have been, Magnius really did fall asleep and he dreamt. And he was in an ancient street in an ancient city. And though he was a foreigner a man came across the painful cobbles barefoot and begged in Magnius' language that he go in the huge building there for him. The Briton was to go out of the heat, up the stairs of the enormous palace with buttresses and turrets and he was to make his way through the portal. Magnius looked at the man to see if he were mad, but he saw only terror. So he agreed and, taking the bundle – a white towel, pollen yellow in the sun – he started up the steps. The building was packed and people walked up and down the great stairs greeting each other. Those who walked down had red faces and wet hair. Those, like Magnius, passing upwards had towels and a man at the entrance handed out keys. Magnius' key had a number and a letter: the floor and the room – he was on floor nine, at the very top, though no bath he had ever been in had had floors, nor keys with characters cut into them. He passed, nevertheless, into the confusion of people and steam and went upwards, squeezing in and out of the groups of men, mainly elderly and patrician, speaking in their own unintelligible language. Many stood naked except for the towel hanging down from their middle, others were naked altogether. And he walked past a man who seemed to be his father in his younger years, who spoke with one whose face vaguely resembled that of the Gorgon he had stood under earlier, and above him on the stairs he glimpsed a figure with a sword scar who nodded as Magnius climbed past him.

Then, when the stairs finished, he walked down the long corridor to the room signalled on his key and, after knocking, gingerly passed in. It was a room not unlike that he had been in before. And again no one was there; at least no one that he could see. However, the room was full of white, burning water vapour and his vision was limited to three or four feet in front of him. He locked the door and stripped quickly. Then, the towel tied above his hips, for here he was strangely modest, he started to fight his way through the scolding steam. But, he was interrupted. Someone was hammering frantically on the door against the wood and jamming down on the handle. Magnius turned around, disconcerted. Who could it be? The old man's pursuers? No, the knocking was frightened, hysterical. The old man himself perhaps? He moved towards the door and with one hand on his towel unsnapped the lock and sharply opened it. Nothing. Silence. He stepped out in pursuit and the cold bit his skin all over. The corridor was empty for a hundred yards on each side. Star- or moonlight sifted through windows at either end. There was no one. Neither the frightened man, nor any of the bathers who had inhabited the space minutes before. He shivered at a current of air and the door of his room slammed behind him. By an artifice that he did not understand he had been left standing almost naked at midnight, in an empty corridor.

He started walking down towards the distant window. It was while walking that he noticed the dust; there was at least a half-inch of it on the marble floor. He continued, aware that thinking would not help him now. He walked and walked and then, unable to resist the urge, looked back. Down the corridor behind him stretched a trail of footprints – his own. He was ready to go on, but froze, feeling what was almost a physical presence. Before him there were also footprints. They came from far down the corridor in front of him to where he stood. He looked at his feet. Exactly where his big toes shivered were the prints of two other feet whose toes faced his, almost touching them. And so it was over. After years and after miles of losing and finding paths, of foolishness, of speeches, of ambitions, of efforts and of failures, he had arrived. He had come to the end of himself and could reach out his hand to touch the place where the mirrors meet ... And in a distant province of a distant empire an empty phial floated on the waters and then, banging against the immobile thighs of an old man, capsized, sunk slowly into the green-black water and was sucked through the grating into the intestines of the bath.

᪲᪲᪲ Historical Background ᪲᪲᪲

In the late first and the first half of the second century, the Romans constructed some of their most monumental works in Britain. And this chapter looks at one centre where a great deal of building was carried out, namely the Romano-British spa town of Bath; showing the achievements and the limits of Romanisation not to mention Roman customs of bathing. The impulse for the story was the (probably) first-century Gorgon head from that city, one of the most famous works of Roman art in the island, and a gravestone recording a certain Magnius who buried a foster child there at the end of the first century. The name Trifosa is explained in the notes for Chapter Seven. Magnius' friends – Lemnus, Aufidius, Julius and Lucius – are all names associated with Bath gravestones in the first and second century.

In the years when Magnius was growing old the defences of Britain's dangerous northern frontier were being perfected. First Hadrian's Wall (AD 122) and after the Antonine Wall (AD 142) were built and garrisoned; the second of these stands at the centre of the next chapter.

CHAPTER SEVEN

On the Turf Wall, c.160 AD

Trifosa, daughter of Magnius, a slave in the North

The body of Magnius was found floating in the baths he loved.
But his children were not so fortunate: execution or slavery or
penury awaited them all. The annals of my family and the stories
of my father recall only one of these, Magnius' daughter Trifosa.
Indeed, by some accident of history, her certificate of purchase
sits now in my hands and tells, in the difficult-to-read cursive of
two hundred years ago, that she was sold as far as the Turf Wall
[Antonine Wall], in the time when the Roman frontier was
dragged north to enclose almost the whole of Britain. And there
she became the possession of a senior centurion, Marcus Cocceius
Firmus ...

Marcus Cocceius Firmus was almost asleep when the alarm was raised, dreaming happily about the future. There was the small villa within a stone's throw of the Black Sea, where he would take the girl when, in six weeks, his three decades of service ended. He was almost dozing when the horn blew. As the junior centurion ran down the corridor towards his quarters, he was already smelling the grass and hearing the shepherds with their flocks and their bells. Then, as the knock came on the door, he was teaching Trifosa words of his language – for, when he had left, few had spoken Latin and he was. ... The knock became louder and Cocceius sat up in bed – as the First Centurion he had the right to a room of his own – and listened to the urgent words on the other side. Quickly, he tried to assess what was happening: the officer was worried, but not panicking. It seemed unlikely that this was an all-out attack. It would be bad luck, just as it was finishing, to get one of the Picts' hooked spears through his gut.

He reached for his sword and strapped on his cuirass, walking down the corridor, now, at the side of the younger man. He understood that something had gone wrong, but the soldier was not sufficiently coherent. There was no sign of a raid. That much, at least, was clear. As he passed into the yard, the light of the torches flared up in front of him, blinding him for a moment. The legionaries had done well – they had gathered, efficiently, in full uniform along the high parts of the fort, staring out into the unconquered territories, their bodies protected by their shields. He walked up the steps and,

looking out, he saw with satisfaction the torches of the three neighbouring forts, one out in front, in a forward position – they would be
the men at risk if there really was an assault. 'Should we give an alert
along the whole Wall? Should we light the beacons?' There was a
full alert about once a month; usually it was a drunk legionary or
some of the unconquered peoples coming too close out of bravado. In
his years on the Turf Wall only two of these alerts had been justified.

He would make sure and then send them back to bed: 'Tell me
why I have been woken up?' The junior officers looked down or in
any direction but at him. He asked them, word for word, the same
question again and one of the older, more trusted men ventured a
reply, though curiously he mentioned no names. 'The gate was ajar,
the one facing out into the wild lands.' Cocceius shook his head. Then
they had been right to wake him and he would be right to set off a
general alarm. But something, he felt, was not being said here. The
men knew something they could not tell, probably incompetence on
the part of a guard. Of course, there had been incidents in the past,
when one of the milecastle gates had been left open by legionaries
bribed to let Picts through into the southern territories: Picts who
wanted to trade or even Picts who wanted to go south and be
recruited. But a gate left open in one of the principal forts, that was
more serious. No Pict would try and get into a fort unless he wanted
to overrun it. And, if this Pict had wanted to get in, then he would
have needed an accomplice and a lot of warriors. Cocceius was still
sleepy. It had not yet occurred to him that maybe someone had wanted
to get out. 'Shall we set off the general alarm, Centurion?' 'The gate
has been secured?' All nodded. 'First, we will look carefully around
the fort. There is time.' They went off and began this task, taking a
number of legionaries with them and talking in hushed voices among
themselves. He stared for a second across the courtyard at the place
Trifosa was billeted and then walked up to where the rest of the
garrison were standing.

He did not address the men. But he strolled to a piece of wall, vacated by the guards who would undertake the search, and gazed out into the darkness, only illuminated by the torchlight and the distant constellations of the neighbouring forts. He was quite awake now, but there was nothing stopping him imagining. And so he did. He thought of the dispatch rider coming from Rome with the official notice that he was to be released from service. He saw the man landing at Rutupiae [Richborough] and standing below the enormous arch, built where the first legionary had come ashore at the time of the invasion of Claudius, then snaking his way up to Londinium and the marble palaces to give his messages ... Among these the discharge. Then he listened to the beat of the dispatch rider on the Great Northern Road, passing through the rich and fertile villa lands, where the Britons were now domesticated. Up, into the stormy hills, where many still went almost naked and on to the Stone Wall that he could picture in his mind. Then, on into the deltas where the wildest Britons lived: the ones he had been taught to fear when he first came, all those years before, arriving as he had from the Emperor's Horse Guard in Rome, sent north as a promotion, a favour of sorts.

And after the courier would ride on to the Turf Wall, where he stood now, and this man would leave his messages and be brought up to the observation tower by some garrulous legionary and shown the end of the world, the mountains and highlands of the north, where even full Roman legions only went for summer exercises, the dangerous glens. Out there in the wilderness, the natives crawled and passed through the undergrowth on all fours; in and out of the swamps and marshes, living like wild animals. They were not Celts. Rather they spoke an ugly and chthonic tongue that none could make any sense of and that sounded like sliding scree.

After the messenger had been shown these sights, Cocceius would gather his things and head for the gate. Many legionaries and centurions on being retired preferred to settle in Britain; they had sometimes lived there for the best part of thirty years when the moment came. Often they had forgotten their families and their homes. But

Cocceius had never forgotten his birthplace in the east and before every battle and every attack he had always sworn that, should he be spared, then he would return with the money the Emperor would give him on decommission, to the gardens and fields he had been promised there. He did not despise Britain as did many of the men; indeed, he had set up altars to the spirit of the island, Britannia – may her tattooed breasts be blessed! – knowing full well that it was the little indigenous gods, not the giants of the Roman pantheon, that could do the most to protect him. He had been punctilious in his respect to all the Britons he came across, unlike those others in the fort, forever making up names and insults for the natives. But he would sooner die in an ambush tomorrow than spend his final years among these moors and hills.

And then, there was the central part of his joy: he would not return alone. There was also the girl. It had happened a year ago. The old Jewish trader Salmanes, who sold to the Romans at the fort, and kept his mart just away from the buildings, on the safe side, had announced a slave auction. Of course, slaves were easily procured at the frontier – sometimes more cheaply than a horse – and he had not expected great things from it. He had gone more with a sense of curiosity, for there was something satisfying about seeing the enemy at close quarters, made safe and reduced to the value of a handful of coins or a ton of wheat. He also, even if he never would have admitted this to his fellow-officers, liked hearing Salmanes tell his strange stories: always about that Jewish priest who had done this or this faithful worshipper who had done that. He had, for once, a good excuse too. His duties meant that it would have been difficult for him to attend the auction. So he had gone, with this explanation, to the hut where Salmanes lived alone, and, outside, chained and shackled on the wooden boxes normally used for transporting fish, were the 'goods'.

Salmanes had outdone himself. There was not a single Pict. Instead, the Roman was presented with two Somalian brothers, a Greek, a young child saved from exposure by the Jew himself, and of course, the girl. While Cocceius walked into the compound, the Jew told a story about a hero of his religion, whom the Emperor of Rome had sent soldiers to kill. The story was the normal pleasing nonsense: band after band of these soldiers were converted by this zealot before they could carry out the Emperor's orders until, in the end, the Emperor himself gave up and converted as well to the worship of the God of Israel. But Marcus Cocceius Firmus was listening with only one of his two ears. He had noticed her as soon as he came in. He could tell she was British, not just by the lines of her face, but also because she was the only slave on offer who had not had her feet brushed with chalk, as the law required for slaves from outside the territory.

He could not approach her immediately, so he skirted around looking at the men. He asked Salmanes questions and was surprised how cheaply the slaves were being sold. The two Somalians were runaways, that would knock an easy third off their price. The old fox would have lied, but they had been branded on their thighs and upper arms. The child was weak – Cocceius wondered if he was not, in fact, a victim of the falling sickness [epilepsy]. The Greek had a back red from old beatings and lacerations; the centurion laughed off Salmanes' description of this man's learning, he was clearly a master's nightmare. Salmanes would even extend the guarantee. The normal six months he would make a year. And it was not true that the man was a suicide. But Cocceius walked away as quickly as he could. There was something that was not right there and a good rule was never to buy the long-serving slaves. They were the artful, cunning ones.

Then, taking the most tortuous route possible, he came at last to the girl, and the two men stood before her, Cocceius feigning indifference. He had seen Britons for sale before, of course. But she was unusual. She was not a barbarian from the hilltops; he could see from her reactions that she understood his Latin. Nor was there a tattoo on her. She had been caught in a spot of trouble and sold on,

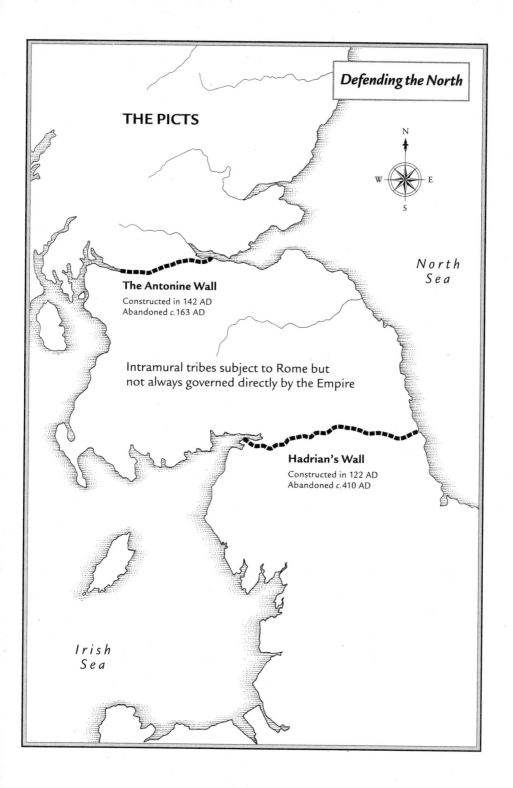

Defending the North

THE PICTS

N
W · E
S

North
Sea

The Antonine Wall
Constructed in 142 AD
Abandoned c.163 AD

Intramural tribes subject to Rome but
not always governed directly by the Empire

Hadrian's Wall
Constructed in 122 AD
Abandoned c.410 AD

Irish
Sea

explained the merchant. She was a blue-blood, from a noble southern family, the Atrebates: the great-granddaughter of the last king of the Britons, Togidubnus no less. Cocceius had never heard the names. He reached up to her neck, where the receipt of purchase was tied, and took it off her gently, but not so gently as to arouse the old man's suspicions. There was no description of the crime for which she had been responsible. But it had been done on the Governor's orders. It was her family that would have offended and been broken up. It happened. Taxes not paid, mutterings of revolt, supporting the wrong candidate for Imperial office, an intemperate speech ... The males were killed on a pretext, the women and children sent to market. Knowing the Governor, it was probably his idea of a sadistic joke that, instead of sending her over the waters to the Continent, he had sold her north so that she could spend her time not in a house, as a well-born slave should, but out in a field. He looked more carefully at the note: no, in fact she had been bought in Londinium, only to be turned into ready cash a few years afterwards. Having been got rid of so quickly she was unlikely to please as a servant. But then a servant was not what he wanted.

Cocceius was well aware that they had stood there for too long: 'And how much will you sell her for tomorrow?' The Jew grimaced and talked of absurd figures – she was a pretty girl, she was of good birth, she could bear children. Cocceius knew that Salmanes might have already slept with her. Any number of men might have slept with her. He thought of the money owing to him and the money that he had stored away. He would not go through the humiliation of bidding for her in an auction, with half the camp watching. If he bought her it would have to be now. She was freezing, her skin all goose-bumps, her lips white, and yet she stared past the centurion with a queenly contempt. That decided him. 'How much?' Salmanes looked at the Roman pleasantly. He had a nose for these things and had understood from the moment that the centurion had entered the enclosure. This poor fool had spoken too quickly, had moved too slowly towards her, and, in any case, love, like a cough, cannot be hidden from the wise.

Salmanes ummed and ahhed, talking about the vast expense of transporting, the possibility of a better deal at auction. Cocceius did not respond; while the girl seemed to be close to tears. But Salmanes had a secret: he liked the Roman. Three years ago when the last of his family – his son – had died at only fourteen, the centurion had been kind. He was a *goyzm,* a gentile. But he was a good man, a heaven-fearer. And Salmanes had seen many bad men in his time. He had spent his infant years in Alexandria in the huge Jewish community there. His mother had been dragged off when he was still a child and forced to eat pork in the coliseum in the city. His grandfather, a man of ninety, had been made to undress in a court, so they could see that he was circumcised. Salmanes' father had come to the north to escape these embarrassments and inopportunities, but here too the thugs that passed for Roman soldiers had mocked their God or troubled them on Sabbath. And nor had the Almighty been kind: his wife and only child stolen away before their time. But this Cocceius, he was a good man. Of course, the merchant could hardly justify a loss on those grounds; and so he reminded himself too that the Head Centurion was powerful in the fort. It would not hurt his business to strengthen their friendship.

Salmanes turned to Cocceius and looked at him carefully in the eyes. Then he named a price – a bartering price, of course: he did not want to insult the centurion by giving the girl away. But Cocceius simply nodded and folded up the guarantee. He would send the money over afterwards, he stated. Salmanes was taken aback. He would have to find another occasion to make it up to the Roman. What an unfortunate wretch. The old Jew tried, at least, to laugh, pinching the moody face of the girl and announced that her name was Trifosa, 'Delicious' in Greek. But Cocceius was not amused. He just nodded and walked her towards the fort then, after ten feet, he let go of the chains and told Magnius' daughter to follow. The centurion had chosen a room for her away from his and he had found a padlock, to protect her from the other men. The first of his brother officers who made insinuations he demoted and publicly dressed down. After that, all understood that the new girl was not to be borrowed or mentioned. And soon, he even stopped using the padlock when she went to sleep.

Well, Cocceius remembered it all now. That had been six months ago and, in a month, at the very latest, he and his Trifosa would be on the road away from this wall that separated the barbarian Picts from the merely barbaric British. In three hours it would be dawn and the dispatch releasing him from service could come that very morning. It was not likely. But nor was it impossible. He had already decided that he would not wait to be paid. He had enough money to let the wages of the last month go – even if he earned twelve times what the simple soldiers on either side of him could hope for. He would have it left behind for another altar or for the soldiers' guild so the cohort would remember him with a plaque. By the time it was hauled into position, they would be far away.

He had never touched her in all that time; but he had talked to her often about the Black Sea and the villa in which they would both live. He had led her to understand that she would not be a slave there. His home province was not an Athens or a Corinth, where a quarter of the population were enslaved. As in Britain, slaves were relatively few. She would speak her Latin and within ten years no one would know if she had been Celt or Roman, slave or free. She would bear him children and they would be buried together in the cemetery of his parents, from where it was possible to hear the water lap against the shores and the eagles crying overhead. He had still to win her trust, of course. She had been treated badly. She had seen her family destroyed, torn apart; though she would never talk to him about this. He understood that it was difficult for her. But he wished that, sometimes, she would be kinder to him, treat him with care. That very day, that very morning he had talked to her about the villa and how they would soon leave Britain behind them and start again. However, she became sullen whenever he spoke in this fashion; and today she had been especially ... he searched for the word ... unco-operative.

But Cocceius could wait, for whatever she did, no matter how she moved, grace entered her movements and attended her steps. And everything was worthwhile when she spoke to him in that surprisingly pure Latin. It was the strangest things that did it. Sometimes he would ask her questions about her parents, about her home and get nothing: she simply would not answer him. But, at other times, she would speak. Three days before, he and some of the others had gone on a boar hunt in the valley, on the Roman side of the wall. They had brought nets and several British hunting dogs with them, and they had come close to killing one of the largest boars on the chase, one that had defied every Roman who had gone after it since the fort had been built.

He had told her all this with excitement, not expecting any kind of response. Instead, she had spoken of the boars of the woods of her home. They too ran and escaped and killed and there were legends about their poisonous tusks and how, once, a mighty king had followed one particularly big boar across half the country and had had to ride it out into the sea to slay it. Then, as soon as Cocceius had begun to ask questions about this boar, about the name of the king, she had remembered herself and had become silent again. And when he had returned to the question of the villa – there were no boars there, but other animals to hunt – she had grown rude, not looking or talking to him. He knew masters who would have whipped a slave for far less, some who would have done worse: his mother had bitten her slaves when they behaved with a tenth of these bad manners. But it didn't matter any more, because soon they would be away from Britain. He would discard her certificate of purchase into the sea at the channel ports, when they were climbing onto the boat.

One of the more capable officers walked towards him. He was cold and serious: 'Centurion, we have checked the fort as you instructed. Rest assured, there is no one who came in from the outside. But we cannot find your slave.' Cocceius looked at the man, aware that, in the hushed tones with which he was speaking, ten others could still hear him. He would have to be very careful. 'Then someone has taken her?' The man looked across, but said nothing. He simply did not reply. 'Someone must have taken her! They must have come in the gate and taken her out there', Cocceius waved at the desolation on the other side. Now he had to think. In the forts on the Turf Wall, horses were almost useless for military operations and so there were few. But they would be able to round up a dozen. He gave instructions. Of course, no one had come in and taken her. However, if it was thought that she had run away and, worse, had left the gate of a legionary fort open – horrible images came into his mind of wild beasts mustered around her, snarling and preparing themselves – he did not think that he would be able to save her. They would say that all nineteen forts and milecastles, from the west to the eastern seas, had been put at risk.

The fool! What did she think she was doing? He had told her, that very morning, how they would be away from Britain in little more than a month. And if she had escaped, why did she have to go in that direction? She did not speak the Picts' language. What did she expect to do, fall on their bestial mercy? He shouted again for horses. And his men carried out their orders efficiently, not wishing to rile him. Cocceius was a disciplinarian. He was a cold man. But he was fair and those serving under him liked their commander, notwithstanding his exaggerated pieties and the absence of humour for which he was famous. However, even the most stupid of these, even slowly Cocceius himself, must have realised that it was useless; that nothing but death or the horrors of a Pictish raiding party could save the girl. And now all the confused faces earlier in the night, the men who had refused to look at him, came back to the centurion. There must have been a witness. From when they had woken him from the dreams of the villa he wanted to build with her, all those thousands of miles away, his junior officers had been terrified, not knowing how to say what they knew.

The patrol, the one that rode the perimeter in the morning, came on her; they found her in a ditch in the first rise of the glens. She was shivering from the cold and hardly, in truth, hiding. Cocceius was frantic as they brought her down to be handed over. But he knew that there was nothing that he could do. The prefect in charge of that part of the wall had sent for her and had given instructions that she was to be bound – though the patrol had not taken that step while bringing her to the fort. Once the message had been given, she was bundled up like a sheep and laid over the flank of a horse. Invisibly, Cocceius' men set out to protect their centurion. They gave the girl water. None hit her. And the men who took her away included – by the unspoken but conspiratorial consent of all there – those who had served longest with Cocceius, whose loyalty was unquestioned. But, even as she lay across the horse – and she must have known by then what awaited her, she had grown up in the Atrebates' house where there were slaves – she refused to look at him, to beg help with her eyes. And, when he passed by to tell her quietly that he would do everything he could, she did not answer him. And she was right. A runaway slave, who has committed a crime, no longer belongs to his or her master, but to the courts and to justice and, more often than not, to the coliseums and arenas of death. The best he could do was to send a verbal message with his second-in-command, pleading for clemency – anything in writing would put him at risk.

On the evening of the next day old Salmanes sat unhappily in his shop. The story of the escape had reached him in the early morning, and he imagined the poor, sad fool of a centurion waiting in his room for news that could only destroy him. The prefect was a heartless man, one who had never hesitated to use the power vested in him . . . There had been that nasty business with the Jew Tax, a couple of years ago, when Salmanes had only just managed to avoid being called into his offices. And by now the sympathy of Cocceius' fellow-men was failing. If the prefect was convinced that the girl had left the gate open deliberately, it would mean that she had willed a Pictish attack on the sleeping fort inside, that she had plotted murder. In that case, Roman law was horribly clear: how barbaric the gentiles were ... And the soldiers had now let excitement overtake their innate and proper loyalty to the centurion, gossiping and judging. In his shop, earlier that day, he had heard three of them speaking about the murder 'that British hussy' had tried to work on them. Salmanes had launched into one of his stories about the Jewish rabbi Rashi. But the three had been impolite with disinterest and walked away, speculating on how many nails the crucifixion would need. The old man fell back into his meditation and sometimes thought that he could hear the girl screaming. It was absurd, of course, she was three miles away. But in those hours he was constantly aware that no confession of a slave was deemed to be worthwhile if it was not reached through careful and professionally applied judicial torture.

Then the horse had arrived: the man who carried the prefect's orders to the fort. Salmanes walked along, outside the shop, towards his store rooms, and he heard the voice calling out to the man on the gate. The two soldiers saluted each other and the sentry asked immediately about the hearing. The horseman grunted: 'They didn't use the rack, just flogged her.' That was a good sign. It meant that they wanted her alive in the end. 'She has been sentenced to life in a salt-workings in the Fens.' The old merchant walked away. It could have been worse; those sent overseas to the copper mines rarely survived two weeks before being overcome. But life in a salt-working! He had seen the wretches in those places, runaway slaves, all scarred with floggings, ragged shirts, heads shaved, irons on their legs and sometimes arms too, yellowed from confinement: it was a principle that they were never allowed to go outside. If the sentence had been given that afternoon, they would already have started chaining her up for the journey. No idyll on the Black Sea; no new life for her and

Cocceius. Surely even Trifosa would prefer exile to what awaited her?

But then they were all cursed. He, for example, would never find his way to the Holy City now. The Romans had burnt it and destroyed it and they had, afterwards, built a new town in its place, while the Emperor said that no Jew was able to look on this terrible sacrilege – their very approach was outlawed. He shrugged. And yet when he had been young he had dreamed that the Temple would be rebuilt and that he would walk, on the Day of Tabernacles, through the cloisters ... And the Messiah would stand amidst them and would send out his armies to conquer the five empires of the world: the Persian, the Roman, the Ethiopian, the Indian and the Chinese; and righteousness would spread from the north to the south and from the west to the east. But those Romans had destroyed it all. Let Cocceius and Trifosa and all the rest of them perish with their salt-workings and their prefects and, yes, let perish too the fools like him who sold them supplies.

Cocceius walked uneasily into the shop. Two months had passed and he had studiously ignored anything to do with the girl, including the place that he had bought her. His orders to march had arrived, late of course, and he would have gone without saying goodbye to the Jew. But a message had come asking him to bid an old associate farewell; and this Salmanes had borne no fault in the matter, though it was through him that she had been conjured into his life. He would stay only for a few minutes, would talk to the merchant politely. And then, he had already decided, the morning after he would leave without saluting the garrison. He wanted no more of any of them. But to this Salmanes, who had asked, he would show his respect.

The merchant seemed to have aged horribly in those weeks. Death was working its way into the corners of his eyes and the skin hung loosely off his face. It was as if, finally, he had realised that he was alone in the world. At least, Cocceius had another twenty years of life, the gods being willing, before he went; this was what he tried to tell himself in the moments when he thought of her. And now he had the money in his hands for that house on the Black Sea and specially written letters introducing him to the council of veterans there, who would provide him with land. Then perhaps, just perhaps, he would still have children. It was not impossible. And he sat and listened, attempting not to show his boredom, as the old man told one of his endless stories – it would, in any case, be the last.

This time it was a particularly stupid and tedious one. A Jewish priest, one of the greatest, asserted the merchant, had been asked by his wife to save her sister, who had been condemned by the Romans to a life in a brothel. The rabbi agreed, but swore privately that if he saw this woman had given herself willingly to men, then he would do nothing. And so he went to the brothel and stood before her, dressed as a gentile, and asked for her body, for a short time. But she refused, saying that she was unclean, that there were other prettier girls, that she hated men ... And the rabbi had realised that this girl had resisted all who had come to debauch her. So the priest of the Jews bribed the brothel owner and came away with the girl.

After that the alcohol on the table before them diminished and the details became confused. The man who had been bribed by the priest of the Israelites was driven through hardship to the worship of the one true God. The true priest himself was saved by the one true God, through stratagems involving harlots and banquets. And Cocceius no longer understood, if he had ever understood, and shook his head until, at last laughing, the old man took him by the hand to the back room and told him to enter it with this candle, for he, Salmanes, had found a gift for his friend to take away with him. Cocceius asked how he would know it and Salmanes replied that the Lord of Israel would show it to him, as he had shown salvation to the woman trapped in the brothel, and the Roman passed into the other room with a small pottery lamp.

Salmanes felt suddenly an intruder in his own shop and walked out onto the large expanses of heather that the fort guarded. What a fool he was. It had cost him the best part of two years' money to salvage the girl. To persuade the chief of the salt-workings into handing her over and to set up the charade that some British tribesmen had stolen her out of the building and then, by chance, that he had seen her in one of his trips south and bought her up again. Of course, she was destroyed. It had been only six weeks. But she had been frightened, the spirit pushed deep down inside her; her skin was like that of a lizard and the beatings she had received showed not only on her shoulders but also across her lower back – the salt had healed the wounds quickly and made them into ugly scars. Worst of all were the tattoos. They had written that she was a runaway on her arms and on her thighs. But they had not tattooed her forehead: an oversight that the salt-works owner had used almost to double the price. If that fool of a Roman wanted her then, he could still take her to the shores of the Black Sea and make his home there. Though she would have always to wear long sleeves and, after what she had seen, her eyes would never meet those of others easily.

⚓ Historical Background: ⚓

In the 120s, the Romans built the Stone Wall (Hadrian's Wall) as a frontier against the still-unconquered northern Britons; then, twenty years later, they pushed the borders forwards again, absorbing what is today the Scottish Lowlands, and built, *c.* AD 142, the Turf Wall (the Antonine Wall) on the very edge of the Highlands. Both walls were constructed to hem in the peoples beyond and, if not prevent movement into Roman territory, at least control this movement and make return journeys with booty impractical. The defence of the Antonine Wall lasted only about twenty years – the exact date of the Roman withdrawal remains controversial.

In that time, at one of these forts, Auchendavy in Dunbartonshire, we know, from the dedications he made, that a centurion Marcus Cocceius Firmus was in residence. It seems that this Cocceius, who later retired to the Black Sea and who had served in the Imperial Horse Guard, also crops up in a legal digest for a case that was evidently worth remembering. He had had a slave woman who had been condemned for 'a crime', was sentenced to hard labour in the saltworks, from where she was later captured by brigands, and repurchased by Cocceius himself. The ruling is about compensation: the question of whether the state should be responsible for paying for the repurchase or not. But it also provides us with the outlines for this story. The slave girl's name is not recalled so we adopted 'Trifosa', the name of another British slave from this period. (Britons did sometimes end up in slavery at this time, as, for example, a certain Regina buried at South Shields, who was of a southern British tribe, the Catavellaunians.)

At Auchendavy, at the same time as Cocceius, lived Salmanes; we know of his existence from the tombstone he put up to his son. It has been suggested that he was a semitic, perhaps a Jewish merchant who came to Britain to cater for the tastes of Syrian archers in the region. Jerusalem had been destroyed in the period before our story and replaced, in 131 AD, with the Roman city Aelia Capitolina, to which Salmanes alludes; his views on the coming, conquering Messiah, meanwhile, reflect contemporary Jewish beliefs and it should also be noted that Jews at this time seem not to have been averse to the conversion of the gentile.

The Picts lurk in this chapter. In the next, in the period after the Antonine Wall had, for unknown reasons, been abandoned, and the Roman frontier fixed permanently on Hadrian's Wall, they strike: a nod to what was perhaps their most successful campaign against the Roman south dating to the early 180s.

CHAPTER EIGHT

Defending the North, **184** AD

Lucius Artorius Castus, grandson of Claudia and Togidubnus,
leader of battles against the savage Picts

The Turf Wall [the Antonine Wall] was abandoned not long
after Trifosa and Cocceius left Britain. But, as one defence falls
another is manned: the Stone Wall [Hadrian's Wall] was again
heavily garrisoned. And as one of our line departs, so another
returns; for Artorius, the grandson of Claudia and Togidubnus,
came to the island in these years to command a group of auxiliaries sent by the Roman government. His sword remains in
our possession to this day, leaning against the door of the shacks
that we are now reduced to inhabiting; and should the barbarians
arrive my little nephew says that he will lift its rusted blade
against our enemies, as Artorius did against the Picts in the year
of their invasion ...

The Picts came down from the moors and mountains in small bands of ten or twelve, one for each of the extended families, the septs. Then, as they reached the paths that ran down the large river valleys, these small groups began to coalesce. Young warriors had the most dangerous fighters of rival septs pointed out to them. Some of the old hands exchanged snarls and frowns. But it was understood – the new High King had let it be known, and all feared this one who had proved himself a master in war – that there was to be no fighting except against the Romans. As the hours passed, these streams of men ran together into other streams and became rivers, each carrying their own standards and wearing the tattoos peculiar to the different federations – the Dolphins, the Bulls, the Dogs – and these ran, in turn, in their thousands, into a lake at the preordained meeting place.

The Pictish army, in fact, gathered on the ground in front of the now abandoned Turf Wall – the proof, the High King had told them, that the Romans were not invincible and that they could be forced to retreat. There they worked their way over the ruins and looked curiously into the abandoned fortlets. The Romans were always thorough. Their retreat to the Stone Wall had been meticulously planned and they had taken away every nail and hinge and anything metal that the northerners would pick over and use for their own ends. But there were still curiosities. The Picts found abandoned altars with strange symbols carved onto them, they found graves that black crows had pecked open for flesh. And, as they waited for the signal to move, they climbed along the ragged remains of what had been the long wall, hurling clods of earth at each other like children.

While the army gathered, and for a good month before, embassies had passed into the territory of the Delta [Scottish Lowlands] tribes. These tribes were Celts, not at all like the Picts who spoke their own language. They were not governed by the Romans; indeed one of the main reasons the Turf Wall had been abandoned was the untrustworthiness of these half-tamed northerners. And they were certainly not citizens. But they had sworn loyalty to the Emperor and rendered taxes to distant Londinium. The Pictish embassies told those tribes that the new High King threatened – and all had heard whispers of this man who had united, in six short months, the disparate federations together – the direst consequences should any of the locals inform or tell Romans of the approaching army. These embassies had reminded the Celts that the garrison on the Stone Wall was the lowest it had ever been; that most of the legions had been withdrawn to answer needs on the Continent – the Germanic barbarians threatened to overrun the Rhine frontier. The High King had also sent word out that the *arcani* or hidden ones, the Roman spies who worked in the tributary tribes and dressed as merchants or travelling priests, bringing intelligence on any hostile movements south, must be sought out. Some were sent on wild-goose chases to peninsulas and islands, where in reality nothing was happening, and others were simply killed off and left dead on mountain slopes or thrown into ravines.

Then, on the night of the second day after the army had started to gather at the Turf Wall, the forward party came to the Stone Wall. They took their small Caledonian horses past the wide Lowland rivers and rode within a sensible distance. They pretended to be hunting hare. But they were hardly convincing, for they were stunned by what they saw and showed it. Standing ten feet high and bleached white by slaves – the local tribesmen called it the Great White – the Wall was everything that they had been led to believe and more. Their grandfathers had told them about it – their grandfathers, who had been the last to be foolish enough to attack it. They had told them that this was all that stood between them and the rich lands of Britannia, where fat villa owners lived in houses with gold cups, gold coins and gold statues. They saw, too, movement on the wall – soldiers were walking along in twos. But no patrols came out from the castle or the milecastles: there were too few of them, the garrisons had been cut in size. It was possible to pass through the wall for a fee. It was necessary to go to the Great White in the morning and queue; and for a coin or, perhaps, some pelts and corn, the Romans would let you across to trade on the other side. The Romans were fools. The new High King had made it his business, a month ago, to send men with wares at almost every one of the eighty crossings and they had confirmed what rumour had affirmed, namely that the Romans were few. The riders rode back. They did not have to ride so far as the Turf Wall. They met the army already traversing the plain.

There were maybe half a thousand on the Great White itself; the Pictish army numbered twenty or thirty times that number. Nevertheless, the High King had decided that they would wait until night for the attack. Late in the day the barbarians crossed the rivers, moving forwards with and like the dusk around them. Then, when it was black and the lights were lit on the distant Wall, one every twenty paces and many more at the milecastles, the army, in total and unaccustomed silence – soon they would make all the noise they wanted – moved forwards again. The warriors had listened well to their king before he had given the order. He had reminded them of the frequent summer patrols into their territory when the Romans hunted Picts as if they were deer and burnt their little houses and opened up the grainpits to the elements; of the women and children brought south to the slave markets; of the humiliation of the tribal gods. Well, this time it would be the Romans who suffered. But to do this they must be silent. And silent they remained. Then at an agreed signal – the call of a curlew on the moor – all came to a stop and only the harpoon men continued to crawl towards the barrier ahead of them.

They had previously been directed at a point where a mile-tower protruded rather more from the line of the fort than was usual. In normal circumstances there would be eight men sleeping there. They had reason to believe that this time there were no more than six. Six men against a Pictish army of thousands! Not even, for, at that moment, only one man stood where the lights shone. The Picts moved to the very perimeter and the man turned and, perhaps alerted by a sound, looked directly at them – but they lay just outside the circumference of light. They tensed now and, as he turned again, came up on tiptoes into the bright arc produced by the torch, bending with their harpoons ready, sliding on, rapidly and silently. They had six shots and if he turned now one would still, surely, reach him. But he did not turn. He played harmlessly with a stub of torch that had gone out before its time. The Picts moved closer and, when the Roman looked back and saw the six naked men gallivanting, in what must have appeared a strange dance, the closest was a mere ten feet away. This was the moment – if the Roman shouted then there could be problems. But, if he tried to light the signal or stood stock-still with dread, then they had him.

He reached for the torch to hurl into the beacon. But, as he did so, the first harpoon hit his back, hooking itself on his armour there. One other caught around his legs – if he were ever to wake out of this nightmare he would have a nasty scar to remember it by. But there was no danger of him awaking now. The two Picts who had got a hold pulled at the ropes. He tipped over the wall and, as he was falling through the air, they were running at him, hurling themselves into the depression below. There were shouts from within the milecastle. The Picts didn't understand Latin. But if they had they would have known that this was a warning to shut up. For the clatter of the harpoons that missed had been taken as an act of carelessness on the legionary's part: a dropped cup or helmet. Two of the Picts held his mouth closed, while the other sat on the limbs and began carving.

Another shout came from within the milecastle. But the Picts were so enjoying their first kill that they did not hear it. Indeed, one had already started to saw at the neck of the dying Roman and others were opening his chest and his stomach to the elements, when the door grated ajar. The new legionary, one of the five left, strode out onto the tower shouting a Roman name and almost tripped over a length of rope attached to a harpoon. Legionaries dreamt of these harpoons: they had found enough bodies of those who had been dragged down for them to enter for ever their marching-ground mythology, along with Dacian witches and Germanic high priests. The Pictish harpoon … and there was one before him. He knew full well what he would see below and was not making that mistake. He would need luck now; he would trade in a letter from Venus recommending him to Mars for luck in that moment! He grabbed at a torch, as another harpoon sounded on the wall next to him nicking his thigh, and threw it upward at the beacon. Then he screamed and screamed and screamed. Even if the beacon did not catch, his companions and the next milecastle would be … But the pitch in the beacon caught and, after a flicker, the light jumped into the sky. The milecastles on either side had been warned by the shout a moment before and the beacons there flickered too. In ten minutes, the wall would be lit up from sea to sea.

To the Picts waiting in the darkness, it seemed as if the Great White was engulfed in flame, its whiteness adding to this effect and, for some moments, they marvelled at the extraordinary sight, until the horns called and they stood shaking the numbness out and jogging at the monolith before them. The four remaining legionaries had now emerged from within, strapping armour on, and looking to where their colleague was pointing at the Picts in the grass, and the disembowelled, decapitated legionary below. Perhaps they were thinking of the revenge that they would work on this group of naked savages when the deadly music from the dark jerked their heads up. And then came the others. Not a war band, not anything as simple as an army, but a nation: thousands upon thousands of the undressed northerners passing into the light of the fort, almost as far as could be seen on either side.

The Picts took the best part of the night to overcome the defences on the piece of the wall they had chosen. The Romans were too thinly spread to offer assistance to each other and it was simply a question of knocking down doors or burning out or up the few pockets of resistance that remained. They had little use for slaves and so the legionaries were dispatched quickly. The High King knew that messengers would already be racing south on the roads to the capital of the north, Eboracum – their destination. It was unfortunate that the alarm had been given so early. But, sooner or later, they would have to fight. The army settled on the other side of the wall, full of spirit. The cold did not bother them yet and there was plenty of barley and dried meat to hand around. The Romans were always careful to provision their forts for a year. Indeed, the raiders had depended upon this, for they carried no more than two days' food. They lolled in the fields chewing and talking, and then slept until dawn when the war horns woke them.

The warriors gathered back into their clans, and set off south. Most had never been beyond the Stone Wall and novelty was all around them. They marvelled at the road covered with grit, at the large swathes that the Romans had cut from the northern forests; tree stumps were everywhere. They marvelled at the inscriptions, inscriptions that they could not read, put up to dead notables fifty or a hundred years before. But, if the army was happy, the High King was careful. The Romans prided themselves on acting quickly after a provocation or an attack. Ambush a party of ten men who had wandered out of their fort and by evening ten settlements would be burnt. The Romans never waited and, now the Wall was breached, it was only a matter of time before they arrived. Not for forty years had the Picts faced the Romans in the field – the last occasion, in the meadows on the edge of the Highlands, still being talked about among the oldest.

By nightfall of the second day, the army had moved almost sixty miles to the south. For a Roman legion that was good speed; for a barbarian army a miracle. And the High King, subsequently, became calmer. At Eboracum was the Sixth – the so-called Victorious Legion; well, even if they had wings on their feet, the Victors would not call the northerners to a reckoning that night. But he was not taking any chances for it was always possible that a local Roman commander, in charge of a few dozen auxiliaries, might get a silly idea into his head about a nocturnal adventure. His men, if set upon at night, would take real fright. So he placed guards as efficiently as he could around the hill. But he also knew that it would be, at least, two days before anything larger than a cohort reached them. A small fortlet was turned over for food and a few more Romans killed. There were no villas yet, and no towns of any importance, no towns, anyway, that were worth sacking.

Then dawn came again and the clan leaders walked towards the hollow where the king had been trying, vainly, to sleep; most of the men had dozed huddled together in the cold. The elders were a little less enthusiastic than the day before. Some looked dismally around them at the unfamiliar countryside. They distrusted any land where wheat could be grown in fields, used to the glens. Others looked north, where somewhere, hidden in the mountains, their hamlets and farms were to be found. Then they turned to the man who had brought them this far; and promised to bring them to the walls of mighty Eboracum. Were they to set off straight away? They had heard that villas appeared on the road to the south; and villas, rumour had it, were where the real treasure was. But the king shook his head. Then were they to head back to their homelands? No one dared suggest this. It was presented as a flitting, rather shocked question. But none would be disappointed if this was the monarch's decision. Again, the king shook his head. The Sixth would already be on its way, he explained; if his informants had been correct then the Governor of all Britain would be with them. He had chosen this place, he passed his arms around carefully, because it was here that they would meet the enemy. They would have at most two days. Perhaps only one. They must prepare the ground carefully and follow every instruction he gave with exactness. For the first time, the clan leaders looked at the landscape around them with strategic interest. They had spread their camp over several large fields, in a forest near the Roman road. To their back was a gorge.

A third of the Picts were sent out to forage, burn and generally to enjoy themselves. Anything built by human hands for ten miles around was to be set alight. And yes, of course, the inhabitants killed – no time for slaves. The rest were to prepare ditches to get ready for the Romans. They were to wait in the ditches along the gorge. Still others were set to work on the trees. Using long blades that had been brought from home and cutting, three or four at a time, they sawed their way into the trunk, until the tree was almost ready to fall; and then, gently, took the blades out, propping up the tree for the moment when Roman legionaries would pass underneath. The Pictish king moved through his men, reminding them of the importance of what they would have to do. Some seemed slighted at the thought of an ambush. Why couldn't they fight the Romans cleanly, out in the open? But those who had seen the legions in action knew what the first *pilum* shots would make of the Pictish infantry, however brave, and these spoke restraining words. Then, after assuring himself that the work was everywhere proceeding to his satisfaction, the king turned back up to the ridge. It was impossible, he kept telling himself, that the legion would be there before the next day. But, with the Romans, one never knew. The day wore on and no legion appeared on the horizon. The raiders returned from every direction. Not a man had been lost: it boded well. By evening, he was content. They would almost certainly arrive the next day and, by then, he and his army would be ready.

The next dawn, when the clan leaders hobbled in, he waved away their impatience and worries and told them simply to gather all the men on the slope below him. The Picts came out onto the green and stared up at the man who had led them further than any Pict had ever taken them before under arms. He warned them that later that day the Romans would arrive. Many of them had seen the Romans fight. The Romans were powerful. But they were not powerful enough, for a good deal of the soldiers had been transported away. Now, it was the turn of the Picts. They were, he shouted – he knew that less than one in five of his warriors would be able to hear his words, so vast was the army before him – the last of the people of the earth, the most northerly dwellers of the most northerly island. Until recently they had been shielded by their remoteness. But now their homelands lay open to the attacks of the Roman carrion-makers who patrolled far into the moors in the springtime. And these pillagers would never stop until they had wiped out or subdued the Picts as they had subdued the other British peoples. For the Romans to robbery, butchery and rapine gave the lying name of government. Indeed, they created deserts and called these deserts 'peace'. Now would his people follow him to victory in battle? Or would they submit to taxation, labour in the mines and slavery? A cheer rose and hung over the crowd, and finally he told them to take their positions. By nightfall, the Romans should be among them.

The Picts moved back to the ditches. The king realised full well that he was risking everything. Already there were grumbles about the lack of food. If the Romans did not oblige him by walking into the ambush by twilight, it might be too late. And, as he knew from experience, the Romans rarely obliged their enemies anything. Midday came and went and he continued to walk among the men, talking them up, stopping them from thinking of their bellies and home, reminding them of how the Romans would arrive. At the beginning of the afternoon he climbed the hill once again, but still nothing. Then, just as the first traces of a purple dusk swirled up from the sky edge, there was noise on the road ahead.

The Romans would come first with their *speculatores* [forward riders] – he had had no illusions about that. And so he had placed some men on stolen horses ahead on the road, and ordered them to bolt at the first sign of the enemy. Indeed, he had ordered them to shout and make a racket as they passed along the road. And now there came shouting. And the Picts pushed down into the undergrowth or into the ditches. Then, sure enough, the ten he had given mounts arrived, galloping. Scouts from the watching-places ran to him. There were several thousand men visible, coming along the road. They were marching fast and in order – the Sixth Legion, it had to be! They would be quiet only a little longer. This was the most delicate part of the operation. If the Roman scouts believed that there was a Pictish army in the area and that it was fleeing – the Romans would expect a Pictish army to flee – then they would rush in without taking the necessary precautions. If, instead, there came a scream from the undergrowth at the wrong time, they would realise that they were about to enter a trap and withdraw. The king sent one of the scouts back. He was to instruct a larger band of some three hundred Picts to start racing up the hill, as if escaping from the enemy. The order was given and again the Picts waited in an unnatural silence. Then, the scout who had carried the message returned; he whispered into the king's ear. The legion was approaching at full speed. Could it be any better? In fact, it could. The scout begged to inform him that close to the head of the legion was a man dressed in white, orating almost as their king had that very day. The Governor was with them.

Every minute now was agony. His army was excitable: they had been brought up to make noise in war, not to resort to stealth. If only one man were to shout out of turn or to become agitated then it might yet spell disaster. The ground moved beneath him with the weight of the approaching Romans. They were taking the trackway trustingly, spread carelessly along it. The Picts, they believed, were fleeing; were probably dispersed. They would just have fun killing stragglers and those who had recklessly forgotten the might of a determined legion. The High King, kneeling in one of the middle ditches, could hear a voice in Latin: a centurion ordering his men to keep quiet – that was unfortunate. By the monarch's side was the horn and the man who would blow it. The king knew that his hornman would blow on it as soon as the first Roman drew level. The voice of the centurion came again and then he could see the flashing of Roman sword hilts in the green shadows ahead. Their packs were full; that would weigh them down, if they did not have time to remove them. He closed his eyes and waited. Then, he opened them and could see the first cohort of the Sixth walking eight abreast. He could make out the hair, the eyes and their insignia and the blotches on their skin and the tired lines in their faces – they had marched at an absurd speed north. But there were also conceited and confident faces that deserved their fate. He nodded and the horn sounded.

The scream that came up from the Picts was lost in the screams of the Romans. At strategic points along the way the sawn trees were pushed onto the approaching army, breaking their line and killing or maiming those caught beneath their boughs. There were also screams as the tattooed Picts emerged from the undergrowth and launched themselves at the legionaries. There was no time for the Sixth to form shield walls or react together. Only the back third of the legion, which had not yet entered the woodland, managed to pull itself into order. But, by the time the lines had tightened and had set off pushing through the trees, the Governor's head was already being carried by one Pict in his teeth and the Romans left in the forest were so many dwindling units. The tail of the legion stood stock-still and awaited instruction; then, as if by general consent, realising the hopelessness of the situation, they stumbled backwards. At least, they could return and give some kind of defence to Eboracum. Walking slowly in reverse they picked their way up the hill, ready to defend it. And then marched rapidly back down towards the plains from which they had come. The Picts were brave warriors, but they were not disciplined and, despite repeated blows on the horns, they would not come to order to chase the maimed legion. Instead, they baited the survivors among the trees or picked at the flesh of dead Romans with a ghoulish fascination.

The next day and the next day and the next day the hungry but triumphant army continued down the road. They had left behind them groves full of the dead enemy and talked among themselves about similar triumphs and open gates at the place that all assured them was the most glorious city in the world – Eboracum. They attacked all the buildings that they came across, almost absent-mindedly, not now expecting any resistance, and they shared what food they could find. Animals were butchered on the way and cooked there and then, whole septs dropping out of the army to fill their stomachs. It was not Roman practice, but, with the exception of some auxiliaries, there were no Romans between the Picts and civilisation now – unless one counted, of course, the wrecked and demoralised remains of the Sixth, creeping back to ignominy. The Picts would deal with them in time. Another evening came and spirits continued high, though many had eaten little. Then the king was awoken, while it was still dark, by one of the clan chiefs. Something strange was happening down the road. The front of the army had been disturbed by Roman scouts, but not normal scouts. For a moment, the royal leader felt fear: was it possible that another legion was on its way from the south? But he dismissed this. It must be some foolhardy prefect after glory and an early death. He smiled and ordered the army to prepare and move forwards with the sun.

But, as the light came up, the Pictish monarch was faced by some-thing that bemused him. Straddling the Roman road ahead of them was a force of horsemen about a thousand strong. Without infantry he and his men would have nothing to fear, of course; horse on their own, even Roman horse, cannot do away with an army fifteen times their size. But there was something about its disposition that called for caution. The dawn was gleaming off their armour and the armour was not like that of normal Roman horse, restricted to the rider. It enveloped the horses too. The riders had small peaked helmets and carried what seemed to be enormously long javelins. They were Roman allies, no question about that. Then he saw their standard, a long tube of red silk with a dragon imprinted upon it; and he cursed. He had travelled and knew something of the world: these were Sarmatian horsemen from the steppes of Asia. His informants south of the Wall had told him that some had come to Britain only a few years ago. But he had presumed that they had been removed again to buttress the armies on the Continent. This could be more difficult than he had at first thought. Yet, if these were all that lay between his men and Eboracum . . . He ordered the clan leaders, who had gathered worriedly around him, to get back to their men. They would have to force their way.

Lucius Artorius Castus hesitated in front of the Sarmatian cavalry he commanded and watched the Picts messily form up across the plain. His men would catch them before they could make battle order. In fact, many seemed to be only waking now. He was dressed not in the uniform of a Roman equestrian as became his rank, but in the mailed coat and coloured clothes and peaked iron hat of an Asian steppe warrior. Artorius had long since settled on this form of dress as a courtesy to the Sarmatian tribesmen whom he led and had brought to Britain from the Danube frontier four years before, when they had surrendered to the Emperor there. Indeed, other than the fact that he was at the front of the column and that the rider to his side carried 'the silk dragon', he was virtually indistinguishable from the mass of men behind him. His only concession to Roman custom was that he hung on the side of his horse a Roman cavalry shield; the Sarmatians refused to carry shields, trusting in their mailed horses and their reinforced coats made of splintered hooves. And, instead of their long lances, he held a Roman sword, lengthened for use against dismounted enemies, that he had named, using their Iranic language. As they came onto the flat ground where the enemy had gathered, he broke into a canter and, with his free arm, signalled the units to spread out as they approached. As always happens when horses gallop, the well-knit lines separated and became ragged. But then, as the frightened faces of the Picts came within sight, in their Iranian tongue the howls of joy of the Sarmatians echoed ahead of them, for his men loved war.

The first hints of the invasion had come to Artorius five days before: a beacon on a hill had brought the news that an alarm had gone up on the Wall. In itself there was nothing strange about this. The alarm was raised once a month and only once a year was it a matter of any import. And so Artorius had thought little more of it. Then the next message had come ten hours later – this time a courier. He had been woken, it was deemed so urgent. The Wall had been breached in the east; all commands were to prepare to rally. There was no reliable information as to numbers; but it was an army of Picts. They would – despite the present dilapidated state of the Imperial army – not have dared to breach the wall unless they could, at least, match a legion in the field. Artorius returned to sleep, thinking for a moment of the men he knew on the eastern part of the wall; he pitied them. But what could an army of Picts, even two or three thousand Picts, do against a legion? In Eboracum, the flower of the north, there was the better part of the Sixth which, if it had been weakened for the Emperor's eastern adventures, was still able to muster an impressive number. Besides, the Picts would never make it anywhere near Eboracum. They would practise their savagery on the border. There was neither sowing nor reaping in this for him. He turned over and went back to sleep.

And, for the best part of another day, he had believed that. Messages from the north informed him that the garrisons on the western part of the Wall were intact; and, though the milecastles had been given up, the forts there were well defended. Likewise messages coming from Eboracum informed him that the legion had already rallied out to meet the enemy, under the guidance of the Governor who had, unbeknownst to Artorius, been visiting the city. Another two days passed, and the first clues that something was not right were now feeding back; by then Artorius had reluctantly taken to the road, crossing the Pennines. The equestrian remembered his experience of disasters on the Danube ten years before as a young centurion. It was always best to keep mobile, but, while moving, not to put too much store in rumours. He stepped up preparations for his men, and sent his own messages south; he could not believe that the Sixth had been bested by mere Picts. It was nonsense – simply impossible. However, he took one last precaution. He sent out scouts from among the Sarmatians. If he was going to act he wanted to be quite sure of his information.

On the morning of the fifth day, the message was brought by a witness. Not only had the Sixth been seriously bloodied, but the Governor had been killed in battle. They had surrounded him as the Romans were attempting an ordered withdrawal. Artorius listened. The Picts had worked an ambush on the legion, hiding in one of the northern woods. They had used tree traps. They had also fought with unusual cunning. Some had worn armour taken from the Romans to the north and they had not allowed the cavalry to work around their flanks. It was as if they had known exactly what to expect. There were survivors who talked of necromancy, others of spies. And what was left of the legion, rather than defending Eboracum, were threatening to mutiny. There was even talk of declaring their legate Emperor.

Artorius had had several years of contact with the Sixth and it had never convinced him as a proper fighting force, certainly not for the northern frontiers. And then there was the Governor. He was a fine soldier, of course; or rather had been. But it was always foolish to hand over a legion in a dangerous situation to a man of his kind, one who had made his reputation on the basis of daring. If the Sixth was out of operation then there was no question. His was the largest force in the north. It would fall to him to protect the road. Artorius had deliberately bypassed Eboracum on his way, not wanting to involve himself with the Sixth, especially if the legion was in the business of

fomenting revolt. Instead, he had taken his men rapidly up the Great
Northern Road, meeting escaping Romans and Britons. They talked
of tens of thousands of invaders; though, of course, civilian estimates
of such things could never be trusted. And then, the night before, his
forward riders had returned. They had made contact with the Picts.
And so to this morning and the attack and the terrified barbarians
reaching vainly for their weapons.

Most horse within the Empire attacked with javelins, ducking and
weaving. Some, brought from Armenia and Persia, were little more
than mounted bowmen. But the Sarmatians were unique because
they quite simply bent low, stretched out their long lances and charged
straight into the enemy. In his early career Artorius had had to face
the men now under his orders and had learnt, painfully, just how
effective this attack could be. Indeed, only after two unfortunate
encounters had he been able to better them, by forming his legionaries
into a square on the frozen Danube and dragging the attackers' horses
down as they came close. The Picts would have no chance of doing
that. They had only one point to their advantage, their bulk – they
outnumbered the Romans many times. But again, as Artorius knew
from experience, numbers could often work against an army, especially if they were forced to retreat. And, as the Sarmatians ripped into
the wide front of the Pictish multitudes, the northerners immediately
buckled and war screams turned into screams of terror. Their only
chance would have been to stand firm. But, instead, the wings fled up
the slope behind them. Artorius pulled his horse to the side. If they
held there, then there might still be a fight. But as it was ... The
retreating Picts poured into small valleys and between the trees. They
were doomed. Near home, in a territory that they knew, perhaps a
third would have escaped alive. But they were six days' march from
the Wall, which was already being re-manned. He would have the
luxury of hunting them all down. He doubted if more than four or
five dozen would ever return to the glens.

Two hours later the field had been cleared and, with his

second-in-command, Artorius walked over to look at the corpses lying there. One in particular interested him, because the body carried the heavy silver chain necklace that among the Picts indicated royalty, and the Sarmatians had dragged him into the centre of a grassy bank so that he could be inspected. The equestrian took the head and cleaned the bloodied face with his spit. Next, he called to his second-in-command, Tammonius Atrebates, a man distantly related to him from the south of Britain, and pointed at a comfortably fitting Roman breastplate and, then, at a scar-like mark under the chin – the inevitable result of twenty-odd years of wearing a Roman helmet with its tight, lashed string. 'He was a legionary?' Artorius nodded and his junior continued. 'Looks about fifty. He will have finished his service only four or five years ago. He will have come home with money and quickly made a reputation for himself as a native who knew the Romans and could defeat them. He will have been the natural leader for a Pictish sept, then a tribe and then he will have made alliances and become a warleader, one of their high kings; and, of course, he knew Roman tactics. It is an old story: if you teach a barbarian how to fight properly never let him go home.' Again Artorius nodded and then, after a moment's consideration, spoke. 'In fact, I knew him. He served under me in the Fifth Legion. He was recruited by an officer twenty-five years ago, by an old officer named Marcus Cocceius Firmus on the Turf Wall. This Pict was a fine soldier. I put him in command of the square when I met the Sarmatians on the frozen Danube.'

⁓ Historical Background ⁓

This chapter was written to give some idea of the threat that Roman Britain faced from the north. Specifically, it recalls a large incursion of 'Picts' from beyond Hadrian's Wall in the 180s: 'The most serious war was in Britain where the tribes in the island crossed the wall that kept them apart from the Roman army and did much damage, killing a general together with his troops.' We know very little about this attack except that an important Roman (a 'general') – perhaps the Governor – was killed and several Roman forts wrecked. That Lucius Artorius Castus was, as has sometimes been suggested, the saviour in this crisis is beyond proof. But he was the right person in the right place at the right time: an able, perhaps brilliant Roman officer in the north of the Roman province with a large number of Roman auxiliaries, Sarmatian cavalrymen, under his command. He is also among the most credible candidates for the 'historical King Arthur' – Artorius is the original Latin form of Arthur (see further the end notes).

Tammonius, meanwhile, is the hero of the next chapter, which takes us into one of the most stable periods in Romano-British history.

CHAPTER NINE

Scandal at the Villa, c.220 AD

Tammonius Atrebates, grandson of Magnius, a villa builder and villa owner

Artorius eventually returned to his homeland a limping, aged veteran; here in Britain they still sing of his deeds and implore the help of his ghost against the savage Saxon, who ravages our settlements and homes. His lieutenant Tammonius, my great-, great-, great-, great-grandfather is, on the other hand, not celebrated among the people. But our family remember him with just as much esteem, for it was he who restored the fortunes of the Atrebates after the disgrace of Magnius and it was Tammonius who founded the villa where, until the recent disasters, I and my kin lived. So vivid were the stories my grandfather told of this one that I can almost see him walking across the lawn, as the evening comes on, with a nervous slave tripping behind ...

At the villa a summer twilight had arrived. On the closely scythed lawns, where slave and master walked, the painting on the statues' faces had shaded away in the dark. Beyond them between twenty and thirty pillars of smoke rose into the clear sky from the fires of tenants on the estate and neighbouring landowners. Then, in the distance, shone the Woody City [Silchester], covered with the ant-like figures of those men who had been set to build on its walls and who would continue to do so until all traces of light had disappeared. Tammonius Atrebates, owner of the estate, pointed at them irritably and began to complain. The villa owner had several familiar rants and this was one of the better-known ones: Britain had now the safest borders in the Empire so why did taxpayers such as himself have to spend money on defences that would never be used?

Six months before the slave Calgacus would have saved up these words to repeat to his fellow-slaves in the dormitories after dark, imitating the high, booming voice. But that evening he was hardly paying attention to what the old man was saying. Rather he was looking down at the two bundles in his master's arms. Two bundles as if a farmer had wrapped turnips in rough cloth for market. But at the end of the bundles there were not shoots or sprouting green but small human faces. And even at only a few hours of age the two faces were recognisably twins. The newly born were not held with particular care. The cloth had been worked rapidly around them and did not so much protect as engulf their little bodies. And Tammonius' hands grasped the feet of both children so their heads hung down onto his rotund belly and sometimes banged against each other as he took steps.

They had left the outhouse from which the confusion of the mother's voice still echoed only to halt as the master enjoyed his favourite view; he was becoming increasingly nostalgic with age. He had built the villa himself only thirty years before. True, the Atrebates had had a shaky century – some had even been enslaved – but he had restored the family's fortunes, clawing it back with guile, lawyers and well-placed friends. In the courts he had won portions of the old tribal lands and after returning from his time in the service of the state – as he was happy to tell any man, he had fought in the Pictish Wars – he had called the mosaicists and builders and gardeners in and showered gold on the free and whips on the enslaved. Yes, his mansion with its muralled walls and neat red roof was further from the Woody City than an ambitious man might have wanted. But the view more than made up for that.

As the night came on he murmured now to Calgacus the old tales about the place – druidic stories of albino piglets and wolves who became men. And, as he was speaking, the screams of the woman echoed again around the compound; she was searching for her children. In the approaching darkness it was just possible to see that the screams discomforted Calgacus, though he tried not to show this. But his master seemed unable to hear them and only the mewing of one of the bundles beneath awoke him from his reverie. Then, sighing and talking of the unpleasant task that awaited, he started again to troop across the lawns.

Slaves were running everywhere now, lighting the torches that hung along the pathways and from some of the trees in the orchard. The orchard, Tammonius' pride and joy. He walked off the flagstones and looked up at the blossom and instructed Calgacus to tear some down for him. He did not use Calgacus' name but called him his 'first-class tool'; it was a joke shared only with the best of his men. One old Roman writer had said that there were three kinds of farm instrument: the kind that speaks – slaves; the kind that cannot speak – cattle; and the kind that cannot move – hoes and the like. On another evening, Calgacus would have laughed along with his master at this. He would have perhaps asked Tammonius from which author such wisdom had come. Would have even been brought into the library and watched as the librarian lifted rolls of parchment down from the shelf ('Well, it is not Cato') where they lay under the hanging sword, a gift of his master's old commander from his time fighting in the north.

But, instead, as Tammonius filled his mouth, nose and lungs with the incense of the blossom and began to quote a Greek lyric, Calgacus stared covertly down again at the children. Could he see himself in their bleary, unformed faces? It was possible; the pale, white, northern skin perhaps, the noses certainly were not unlike his own. It had been a terrible, terrible mistake; but that did not change the fact that they were his. She had been a new slave from Germany, sold across the border by the tribesmen, the enemies of Rome, and then juggled through the provinces from market to market, bartered for more and more as she travelled west. It was no secret that she had been bought for her blonde hair and striking, beautiful face. His master had always had an eye for lovely slave women: his contingent of serving maids were of an extraordinary calibre and much praised by visiting dignitaries.

Calgacus, who had been in the household from his youth, who had always been treated with respect and love by the family, had been foolish beyond words. The slaves' quarters were strictly segregated into male and female sections. Slave families were forbidden and what children there were came from the liaisons between the males of the family and their charges. But he . . . he . . . His master's dreamy voice came to Calgacus as if from a thousand miles off. And Calgacus, though he had not been schooled in Greek, understood that there were pearls and dolphins, storms and death in the words. And he seemed to be on the surface of the water and looking down at the bottom of the sea, where he could spy the two small faces staring up at him. But then the tone changed and he realised that his master was talking to him again and that Tammonius had reverted to his no-nonsense British Latin.

'Well, Calgacus?' 'Forgive me, master, I did not hear.' Tammonius stared into his slave's face as if to brush away this impudence and avoid what many of his worthy neighbours would have resolved with slaps. 'I said, Calgacus, that you should carry what you have spawned. The walk is a short one, but their weight has already tired me. Come, the time for games has finished. The night is approaching.' Calgacus held out his arms and received the twins. Tammonius then set off again, now carrying a bough of blossom in his hands and, as they came close to the house, he stole a sideways glance at the slave. 'I have noticed that you are very quiet tonight, Calgacus.' The slave made a barely perceptible nod and then looked down. He knew his master; and he had promised himself that whatever happened he would not beg or show emotion. But in that sentence he also recognised the voice: the gentle, malevolent one that Tammonius used on occasion. He would have to be careful. 'You know that many would be grateful that I have not had you scourged for what you did to my slave on my property? Certainly, I had to restrain my wife and son from taking a more traditional revenge. But I consider myself a forgiving man ... And yet I receive no thanks from you.'

Then, just as Calgacus was about to risk an answer, his master swerved away and pointed excitedly at the wall. The villa was painted on all sides, as was the custom among the richer of the landowners, and here the artisans had been called in only that week to put up something that all had been assured was the Bay of Naples. Willowy figures raced towards a boat and in the cove Ulysses or another hero of the long-dead shouted to his men, pointing at a stalking giant figure walking between volcanic and fuming peaks. Calgacus' eyes rose and on the mountainside he saw wooded dells and demonic faces reaching out like snake heads and staring at him.

He and she had always met in the dell below the villa. It was too risky in the house itself. But down by the river no one from the family came. And the valley was always empty. The drought of the year before had put an end to two of the tenant families, who had farmed the lower fields and who had now vanished into the workshops in the city. It was true that there were always perils, even on empty land. The dispossessed had recently formed into bandit parties calling themselves *bacaudae*, 'the warriors', and there was also the danger of escaped agricultural slaves with the manacles still around their necks. But, lying close to the top of the clearing, he had been able to see not only the girl beneath him, but also the fields around and, in urgent backward glances, the trees. There was no peace, of course, and they could never be together for more than a few minutes. However, as Calgacus was one of the chief slaves and was in charge of assigning her menial duties it was possible, it could be done. He would send her away from the house and himself go and inspect, not every day of course – but if Tammonius was on council business in the Woody City every two or three days, for the head of the Atrebates had been elected. And after the first excitement it became something with a frantic regularity about it. And it could well have continued. But one day she had refused him and, in her broken and embarrassed Latin, revealed that she was pregnant; she had been sick in the quarters and some of the other female slaves had nodded and reassured her, thinking that it was the master's. Calgacus' first hope had been that Tammonius or one of the sons had slept with her. They had not.

Then there had been the days of decision. It was well known that abortions were worked in the Woody City at the public baths. A wizened lady from the Temple of Venus borrowed a room and carried out her trade there. But they had not been able to arrange for the girl to visit the town, for it was a ten-mile walk and her absence over that time would certainly have been noticed – even if she had been able to pick herself up afterwards and limp back. In desperation, Calgacus went to the house of the tenants in the lower valleys where a midwife lived. Her family was starving, children swarmed past him at the door with swelled, empty bellies, as another year was finishing badly for those who lived on the land. Calgacus offered her oats smuggled from the barns if she would only come and see the girl and cause a miscarriage. But the midwife was stubborn and called him a dirty slave for an imagined slight in the period when he had collected rent for Tammonius, and drove him from the door with stones and insults. Then, in desperation, they had turned to herbs: to the plants that were said to induce movements in the womb. They – for by now five or six slaves knew – had attempted to procure the necessary white flowers and even found some in the fields, though mostly they returned with grass. But eating the bitter white flower did nothing to her.

And, at last, just as they were discussing whether it would not, in fact, be possible to disguise her pregnancy and fake an extraordinary illness to cover labour and its aftermath, something terrible happened. Somehow word came to Tammonius of his new serving girl's condition. Calgacus had never discovered how. It would have been a slave escaping a beating, or perhaps the hag who had hurled stones at him. He remembered only the unhappy day when he had been summoned to the dining hall and the girl stood wretched with tears dripping from her and the family sat around: old Tammonius, his wife and the boy Victor, who was to take over the estate on his father's death. Poor Calgacus had had many happy memories of that room for it was there that he had first been introduced to the household and had served Tammonius' relations when they came together for one of their orgies of boar meat and bear claws. And, as a young man, he had listened to these elders who one minute spoke in a dainty Latin of a new wine or of a new poem that had come in from Londinium and the next began to discuss vendettas and council votes in their own earthy Celtic. But today he was not here to serve but to be served, for with two slaves standing guard at the door behind him he felt as if he was the beast on the platter, basted and ready to be eaten by the furious assembly.

Tammonius veered carelessly away from the painting and moved further along the path. Now he was no longer carrying the children he passed more quickly. And he talked about important business that the council would discuss in the next days at the great chamber in the Woody City, modelled on the Roman Senate, where the elected spoke in the presence of the Eagle of Jove; and where Calgacus had often been seated as a factotum for his master, running hither and thither with letters, fetching drinks and food. There was talk too this year of sending Tammonius to the Council of Britain in Londinium or the Colony, he said. But as he spoke his pace remained the same: fast and regular as he moved away from the house towards the outer gardens. There were no torches, for no one cared to walk in this place towards night. Guards were sometimes sent down or dogs let loose to make sure that the starving tenants did not sneak up over the fields to the cabbage beds, where some of the new and exotic Roman varieties had been planted: the carrots and the onions that had set the entire district speaking when they had arrived. But, at this time, there was nothing but the last of the dusk to show them the way.

As they reached its threshold it was as if Tammonius suddenly realised where they were and what they were doing, or perhaps it was just that he had run out of words concerning his inconsequential activities. He turned and looked at Calgacus. The slave had not been favoured in the past months after the disgrace of the pregnancy, but Tammonius had always had an affection for Calgacus since that day he had pulled the screaming Pictish boy from the dead bodies on one of the battlefields; the child had had no tattoos and so Tammonius had decided not to kill him and later that year he had refused to trade his Calgacus to a neighbour for thirteen heads of cattle and a water-meadow. And perhaps now, glancing over Calgacus, he saw something like agony in the face of a man, a man whom he had, after all, had at his side for thirty-five years and whom he had watched grow.

Tammonius halted and stared carefully into the slave's eyes and then down at the two bundles in his arms and lifted the bough of blossom across and gently flicked it against Calgacus' cheeks. 'You must see that there is no other way. We can afford no other mouths in this house. The whole countryside is starving. The clouds do not bring rain. Did you not see that family that came to me today?'

Calgacus had seen them. They had been driven from their ancestral lands by the expansion of a villa on the wooded plain below. They had come to beg for a hovel. They had waited for two hours in the reception area and then, with guards around them, they had been escorted through into the main hall where Tammonius was eating. They were from a proud family and remembered, though now the tribes were long since gone, that Tammonius Atrebates was of the royal line of the old Atrebates – perhaps he would recognise the obligations of blood. Their clothes had once been good. But the years had shredded the neat weaving and expert cutting so their coverings hung ragged. And even though the men could speak a tolerable Latin – fatally, they admitted they could neither read nor write – Tammonius had let it be known that he could do nothing with them.

Instead, he had been kind suggesting that they sell some of the younger ones for their own good; they might be taken up as house slaves and they would be treated well. He had pointed Calgacus out as an example of the happiness that awaited them. Why, he would buy the pretty young one himself: he motioned to a boy with a snub nose and a kind of snarl hiding in his lips. It would give the family some sustenance. And then he had thought aloud that the men should consider a military career. The Britons were being taken up into cohorts all over the Empire; they might end up in Africa – Tammonius' eyes glistened as he described places he had never been but often read about – or on the marches of Persia. He would write them a letter, for it was not too late for them; he called out for a butler to bring more chicken and the eyes of the youngest seemed to levitate out of their heads as the platter was carried in. Then they had been sent back to the gates, escorted even more heavily on their way out, through the rooms with, their expert mosaics, their twisting silver and hanging paintings radiating wealth and well-being. And, as they had reached the gate, Tammonius' heir, young Victor, had thrown a ball through them; he was playing the game 'triangle' with a brother and a slave who had been pulled off his duties for the purpose.

Calgacus rarely came to the vegetable garden and though he had heard of their destination it was by reputation not by visits. But Tammonius, with his horticultural interests, knew the land better than any slave. He passed easily down the main path and then took a side route to the left where a long finger of earth extended out past the rest of the beds and rose bushes. When the villa had first been built it had been one of Tammonius' experimental vineyards; but the grapes had never, even in the brightest years, quite satisfied the Atrebates. And so afterwards it had been converted into a simple vegetable plot with grassy margins. Then, as new statues arrived and space in the barns had been taken up by cattle, Tammonius had decided that here he would keep the statues that no longer interested him, but that he could not quite bring himself to part with.

Calgacus had sometimes seen this graveyard of stone from a distance. But he had never troubled to go and inspect it himself and he doubted he would ever come again. There was Pan dancing with his hair pulled up, not in the Roman fashion, but with the cut of a Celtic warrior in days of old. There was a lovely Venus with her eyes and face painted – but her side had been chipped: probably by the fall of a neighbouring statue. Then there were the Three Graces made by a local artist who had cared not one jot for classical norms. The lithe, nymph-like servants of beauty had been converted into wide-hipped, wild-haired, almond-eyed harpies. Tammonius, however, did care for classical norms and the frieze had been upended and made to lean against an unimportant Roman emperor.

Calgacus looked at these relics and then his eyes glanced like a trapped animal around him. But once again Tammonius led the way.

Through the statues, through a ream of brambles, through the long grass to the place where the garden tipped away into the valley below and there, at the utmost extremity of the Atrebates' land, stood a mound of rotting vegetation. Withered herbs, old parsnips, excrement, tangle weed, streaks of ivy and a half-eaten rat had all been thrown there by a gardener and allowed to fester. Then, in a couple of years, the pile would be dug over and fed back into the earth, smooth black soil carted out around the fruit trees. As they approached the pile Tammonius stepped aside and signalled for Calgacus to pass. He did not look directly at his servant, but sent his eyes over the heap before him. 'You know, it is a quick death. There are no clouds tonight. It will be cold. Then there are the wolves, of course. Look at that …'. He pointed at the teeth marks on the rat that were large and lupine. 'It is part of their round. These young ones will know nothing of it. Why, they are already sleeping! Come on now put them down and let's get back.'

Calgacus stared down at the pile of decay as his master listed what still remained to be done that evening. And the babies felt heavier in his arms. He had thought about this, of course, in the days before. They had said nothing to the mother. It was felt that she had burdens enough and would, in any case, be punished afterwards when she was quite herself once more. But to Calgacus the family's decision had been repeated again and again: twins or no twins. The slave had thought of every possible solution. He would drown his master in his bath and blame it on an old heart; but the rest of the family would take the same revenge, perhaps with added venom. He would threaten his master with some of the secret knowledge that he had amassed about him and say he could sell it to his rivals in the forthcoming election campaign; the walls of the Woody City were always plastered with graffiti in the run-up to the elections, graffiti describing the peccadilloes of those standing. But he would be dead by morning if he so much as insinuated such a thing. He had thought that he could pay one of the tenant farmers the little money he had managed to amass to collect the children after dark. But who would then keep the twins safe? He had thought …

He had thought many things. Some were so absurd that they would not have appeared in one of the Greek or Latin novels that arrived in the house every month from the copyists in Lugdunum [Lyon]. And now at the end he had failed. His children, the first, probably the only of his blood to be born, were about to be put on the compost heap of the Atrebates for the wolves. He bent down and laid the children out – he had not learnt to tell them apart – and then lifted his eyes to escape their inevitable, bawling dissatisfaction. He noticed though that Tammonius, instead, was watching them with interest; almost as a scientifically inclined gardener examines the stigma on a flower. Or, no, the expression was changing: was he about to berate Calgacus for not taking away the crude wool that had been wrapped around them? Calgacus could stand it no more.

There is no need to record the words that he spoke. The apologies beyond anything he had ever made, his eloquent regret, his self-hate, his oath of perpetual loyalty – somewhere in that long lamentation he swore that if his master wished he would throw himself on the same funeral pyre and their ashes would be blown together over the fields. He would never touch a woman again, let alone one of his master's slaves. Indeed, he would inform on those that did – and Tammonius was to believe him that some did. But, though the burly villa owner smiled and dried his slave's tears with his tunic sleeves, he could hardly allow the children to survive, children that were a mark of one of his dearest servants' betrayal. What would the neighbours say?

And then it was as if Calgacus was filled with the breast milk of the muses. So be it. It was not for either to decide. Let them leave it to the gods. If the children were there by daybreak then it meant that they were fated to live. Would Tammonius not, at least, grant that? The master glanced over at his servant and smiled wanly; he knew the borders of his garden better than any other. Had he not lain in his bed the last thirty years? And had the wolves not always come to the fields at the edge of the buildings and yelped and screamed their way into his sleep? And would it not keep his favourite slave sweet to see that, yes, the gods had willed it. Pulling Calgacus off his knees, he affirmed the pact: the gods would decide the fate of the twins and the twins, he knew, would lose.

Calgacus paced in the wing at the opposite end of the mansion of the Atrebates. He had been allowed to go to bed early; but he did not even attempt to sleep. Instead, he walked up and down the corridors trying not to wake the other slaves and then crouched in a heap on the floor listening to the owls outside. The first wolves sounded at a little before midnight: and he heard barks from the hounds that ran loose in the garden and that until then had remained near the house asleep or sniffing at the bones thrown out for them. The wolves had come earlier than expected. And he prayed that the mother did not know of the terrible game that was being played that night as she slept. He also imagined and wished ill on his master lying peacefully in his bed, perhaps waking and straining his ears. And he listened to the beasts' silence as well as the noise. Had they stopped baying to eat? He waited and listened again. Then more noise. Then more silence. And then the silence stretched over hours towards dawn.

A guard was posted at the door and had personally been given instructions that Calgacus was to be allowed out only with the first light. The guard was a stubborn old Briton who had long ago taken a dislike to Calgacus and had rejoiced in his downfall, so there was no possibility of an early exit. The two then stood side by side on the threshold and watched as the black slipped into red on the hills; and when the first beam shattered the sky the Briton stepped aside and Calgacus, despite himself, aware that even at that early hour the workers chained together in the field would see him as they trooped out, ran. He sprinted past the orchard, past the picture of the Bay of Naples, past the vegetables, past the hedges, onto the last piece of the garden, weaving around the statues. And there before him was the dump and on it was nothing, just a tangle of reddened wool where the night before he had left his children.

He didn't shout out. He didn't curse. He just walked forwards and picked up the bundle, then, pushing on, he walked up to the top of the heap and saw the first limb, a fat baby's arm with its fist closed, and he stared down into the sloping meadow and saw what might have been other pieces, all pink and red. And, just as he was about to turn, he heard the cry. It was like a tune blown through a reed. If he had moved back even a moment before he would have missed it. He walked into the taller grass. The baby – it was the boy – had been savaged. His leg, he ascertained picking the child up, was chewed down almost to the bone, though miraculously he was otherwise uninjured. Only his head had been cut slightly in a fall – in ripping open the fabric the wolves had perhaps been more interested in the wool than in what it contained and his son had been thrown clear some fifteen feet. 'Augulus, Augulus,' muttered Calgacus, 'I will call you Augulus.'

ᎭᎭ Historical Background ᎭᎭ

This chapter is set in an era when the island, shielded from the raids and wars that made life in, say, Gaul so dangerous in that period, prospered with wealthy villas and well-managed estates. Infanticide as described here was common in the Roman Empire and there are some hints that it was practised in Britain, including evidence of 'late abortions' from the baths at Silchester and the skeletons of over ninety very young children from Hambleden Villa in Buckinghamshire. Tammonius is a good Celtic name that seems to have been popular in the environs of Silchester – two of the very few inscriptions from the city include it; while Calgacus is one of the few 'Pictish' names we have, and is found in Tacitus.

One of the features of this period of stability was, as set out in the next chapter, the slow rise of Christianity.

CHAPTER TEN

A Persecution of Christians, **c.280 AD**

Iamcilla, daughter of Victor, a Holy Saint of the Holy Church

Tammonius' son Victor had only one daughter, the saintly Iam-cilla. She was a Christian – though in those times the faith of the Nazarene was despised in all the world – the first of the Atrebates to turn to that religion. And when this young girl heard that the secret church she attended had been raided and that persecution was spreading throughout the province, she and the others she could find took to the roads. They hoped, vainly, to find sanc-tuary in the house of the Christian Augulus, once her father's slave, now a freedman settled on the Great Northern Road ...

Of course, travellers often came to Bridge Fort [Water Newton] on the Great Northern Road: seasonal workers heading for the wheat fields of the south, retired soldiers returning to an almost forgotten farmhouse after half a lifetime, equestrians and senators on their way to new postings. However, this party of seven had aroused suspicions from the start. There were more women than men, though this was not a family – different races were represented in the group. And they were also travelling light, with only a sack between them; had they, perhaps, left wherever they were coming from in a hurry? Then, the moment they had arrived in the settlement, they had asked – this had been their fatal mistake – for the house of a goldsmith named Augulus. A man who, while not a Jew, ate the bled-out meat of the Jews: a quirk usually sufficient to snare a Christian. And so a discreet watch was kept on this building until, in the late afternoon, one of the newcomers left his lodgings with that same bag that they had before carried between them. There had been no one to follow him. But he returned an hour later with nothing, though he was sweating and had evidently walked a good way. He had gone out – there could be no doubt – to pass on something incriminating to others of his faith, for those inside had realised that they were being observed. At that point, an application was made to the town magistrate and the guards were summoned.

It did not take long for the shopkeepers and street sellers to understand what was happening; this was a party of Christians fleeing from the latest round-ups. The officials who policed the small settlement had come and were knocking on the door and these officials had been joined by legionaries sent from the nearby fort and a member of the town council. The residents, gathering rapidly now, cheered on the representatives of the state, enjoying the noise and the confusion, babbling among themselves. Some complained of the wicked atheism of this cult that denied the gods of the Empire – it was for this reason that the legions had lost in their recent battles. And had the Christians not tried to burn Rome itself down? Others talked of their cannibalism, as in their holy day ceremonies those of that faith ate human flesh and blood. While the more recondite scandalmongers described the 'love feasts' practised in Christian houses. A dog was tied to the only lamp in the room, the congregation sitting in eager expectation, and then meat was thrown, the light being expunged as the dog jumped forward, and the most terrible sins of lust and incest enacted in the darkness. But now these criminals would be brought to justice and . . . The door was, at last, opening.

Some wanted to throw stones: but the presence of the legionaries encouraged, instead, moderation and the crowd limited itself to taunting the party as it emerged. One, a pale girl of little more than twenty, announced that she was a citizen and demanded to be treated with respect. She was visiting the house of one of her father's freed slaves. And the guards did, in fact, hold off until Augulus was dragged from his lair screaming in Latin. The head of the mission was then handed rolls of parchment that had been hidden in the roof space. He took them in his hands and examined them. They were in Greek, a good sign that Christianity was at the bottom of it somewhere, for the Christians disliked the language of Rome. He opened one and had his secretary hold the end as he stretched it out: 'Christ' – he pointed at the prohibited word. He had no need to read on. He told the culprits, simply, that they would be taken back to their place of origin and charged as Christians there; the gold merchant Augulus who had sheltered them would, instead, be tried in the town itself. The crowd erupted. The shame of it: a Christian in their own community! But now they might also have some fun. One managed to tear at the pale girl's hair, another spat and many lunged as the guards loaded the incriminated onto the cart that had been brought for them.

The little band ignored the screams around them and the pale British girl, Iamcilla Atrebates, closed her eyes in prayer; at least the silver ornaments from their altar had been passed on to a sympathiser and would not be melted down by the pagans. And, in any case, they had known what awaited them as soon as the news of the persecution had arrived. It was a danger that all Christians had to live with at all times; usually it was a flood or an earthquake or even a miscarriage that set off the lynch mobs. But they could be avoided, especially if one was of good birth as she was. However, when the Governor ordered there were no exceptions . . . Iamcilla herself had been warned by a breathless messenger, sent from a neighbouring villa, and had escaped alone just before the inspectors had arrived, for she was the only Christian in her family; and being a Christian in Britain was a solitary affair. In Egypt, where half the population was of the faith, persecutions meant civil war and armies. But the only Christians she had ever met were the handful there with her, the congregation of her church. No one would and no one could protect her. Still, there was a consolation, for if, with her blood, He meant to light the lamps of holy martyrs, then, in this northern island too, the Cross would rise above the temples and send its roots into the soil. She closed her eyes and prayed.

The party were transported in the cart away from the Bridge Fort, as soon as their home, the Woody City, had been established. The legionaries, who rode by their side, did not speak. And the Christians spoke only among themselves. For normal criminals the period after arrest and before condemnation was a simple one. There was nothing to do except await sentence. But Christians were cursed with choice, as the magistrate would not immediately have them punished. Rather, they would be given an opportunity to repent. They would be shown a statue of one of the gods or more probably the Emperor and asked to swear to its divinity; if they did so they would be free to go. And, for this reason, there was much to talk about as they prepared themselves.

There were still some who claimed that to swear loyalty to the demons of Rome meant nothing; for it was forced and afterwards the Christian could carry on as before. This was nonsense, of course. They all knew that. But was it a soul-killing sin to turn apostate and then turn again? The youngest with them, an adolescent boy who had escaped from the villa next to that of Iamcilla, said that he had heard cases of Christians being received back into the Church. But he was shushed by their deacon and by the others, who quoted the practice of the North African Christians. There the lapsed were treated as the already damned. Apostates could *never* be forgiven. The little group must stand firm together or Hell awaited, as it awaited the ones who rode with them. The escorting legionaries grinned at each other; and the front horseman trotted over, unsheathed his sword and hit the deacon on the head with the flat of the blade. After that, there was little talking. And Iamcilla was relieved – while fearing her relief was a sin – that when they came to the Woody City, it was dark and there was no one to see her humiliation.

The magistrate had been forewarned about the captives – there had been rumours for days of a group on the run – and had taken steps quickly; it was in his interest to avoid deaths and encourage repentance, above all of the noble girl, one of the Atrebates family. And so it was that, the very next morning, the door of the cell where Iamcilla had been left the night before was thrown open and she was brought face to face with her aged father, Victor. There were no recriminations, only words of persuasion. He implored her, begged her by everything that was good and fine in the world, to shift from her absurd resolution. All she had to do was give up these pointless beliefs and sacrifice to a statue of the Emperor with some incense. If she did so then he could take her home with him and all would be forgotten; he was sure that he would be able to arrange this now. If she refused, she must understand that he could not protect her. It was true that he had once been a councillor, but now that counted for little – and they were taking the whole thing very seriously this time. There had been cases of executions in Verulamium [St Albans] two days before. A Christian soldier had been publicly decapitated. He continued to speak. But something strange had happened to Iamcilla on hearing of this fellow-citizen, who had shed his blood so near to where they stood, and she shook her family and its words off her. 'Father, do you see this vase here?' He nodded. 'Well, could it be called by another name?' 'No', he admitted, not yet understanding. 'I too, in just this way, can be called nothing save a Christian.' Her father was so angered that he strode towards her as if he would scratch at her eyes. But, though enraged, he thought better of it and walked away, taking temptation with him.

Later that day, a servant came with her three-month-old child. The family had sent it; they believed that if given her baby, starved without its mother's milk, she would relent. But it was not so and, holding her daughter in her arms, Iamcilla called to the Christians dispersed among the cells on the corridor between murderers and escaped slaves. And these called to her and to each other in the dark, wanting only the company of others of their faith. The governor of the prison soon tired of this, for the noise reached his room, and even, he decided, criminals awaiting death had the right not to listen to impieties at all hours. And so it was that the Christians were removed from the corridors above to a dank hole in the cellar, where they could hardly breathe in the confined space. In fact, a room fit for four had been given over to six and the baby girl of Iamcilla. It was only because the deacon, the same who had got away their precious altarware in the hours before they were caught, had some money and bribed the guard to let them out and wash that she was able to bear nursing her baby in that dark cell, its mouth chapping her nipples. But she was faint with hunger and was happy when she could give the child to her mother, who also came in an attempt to persuade her from the path of righteousness. And soon the news returned that the child, who had been accustomed to feed only from her, fed from the breasts of a country woman and suffered nothing for it. The little congregation in the dark took this as a sign of their God's favour and muttered prayers.

Alone of her family her brother Publianus was sympathetic to Iamcilla's cause: he had even been to the hidden church with her and his name had been inscribed there. But he could not understand her loyalty to the course of death. If she were a Christian, he asked in his visit, would God not send her a vision to show that the Highest really wished for her to perish – for he, who was untutored, believed that impossible. And, in among the black walls, she prayed for this fervently and that very night she dreamt a dream that was to become famous for its clarity and spread from the mouths of the faithful to doubters and to the ones who had not yet known the name of Christ.

Iamcilla, once asleep, saw a bronze ladder that stretched as far as Heaven, a ladder that only one believer could climb at a time. On the side of the ladder were stuck many evil things: she saw swords, spears, hooks, daggers and spikes. These tore at those who did not climb the ladder with sufficient care, while at the base of the ladder was a dragon that frightened all those who would climb there. First went the deacon of Iamcilla's church and he climbed and, looking down, he told her: 'Do not let the dragon bite you!' 'He will never harm me', she replied, 'in the name of Jesus Christ.' After this, she stepped on the dragon's roaring head and, taking it as her first step, began to ascend. When she reached the top – the climb was long and hard – she came to a beautiful garden, where an ancient shepherd milked his sheep. He turned when she climbed there and spoke: 'I am glad you have come, my child.' She took the milk of the sheep in cupped hands and drank of its sweetness. After she awoke she told all those Christians present that they would most certainly die. But she also, the prophetess discovered in their midst, described the wonders that awaited them and the sweet taste of the beverage.

A few days after, her father Victor came again. He was sick with worry, for he had heard that there was to be a hearing. 'Daughter, have some pity on my white hairs. I have favoured you more than all my other children. Think of me, your mother, your aunt and of your daughter who pines without you, your husband who despairs of his position and his heir. Do not be proud for you will destroy all of us! None of us will be able to live freely again in this province if you are condemned; we who are of a noble family of this place, a family that lived here since before the Romans came. Think of your warrior ancestors, think of me, the noble Victor.' But she shook her head. She was a warrior of Christ. Only that would satisfy God. Nothing else. The interview saddened her though. Her father truly loved her, and she thought that he alone of her kin would be unhappy that she suffered. And old Victor spoke to her, not to a child but to a woman, with words that would shake the foundations of the world and with tears in his eyes – he seemed to have heard rumours of what was being prepared for them. But she could give him no consolation other than to say that it was in God's hands. And he left, wretched with sorrow, refusing to kiss her.

Her father did not come again to the prison. But the flow of visitors to their doors, with the days, grew. Full permission had been given for friends and relatives to call, for if only one of the Christians could be persuaded then the magistrate was sure that the rest would peel away and an important victory be won. Yet, in among the begging guests came others who had long been curious of this new religion and wanted to know more, some who had attended masses in the hidden church in the slaves' quarters on the estate, where Iamcilla had first heard of the one true God. They did not implore the Christians to change, but sat in the presence of men and women they considered martyrs and touched them with extreme reverence, as living relics. One man brought news from Cambria [Wales] where two others had been put to death for Christ and described the triumph in the days that had followed. All Venta Silurum [Caerwent], where the killings had taken place, had talked of it and many were intoxicated by the bravery of those who had died. The churches that had emptied were now filling again and Jews had abandoned synagogues, Mytharites their underground Cellars of Mysteries to come to the truth. But the man had spoken too long of the sufferings of the martyrs and, after he had gone, the little group sank into a numbing silence.

Two days later, the Christians were eating a sparse breakfast when the guards arrived and bustled them off. The magistrate had decided that the hearing was to be held immediately. Some of the prisoners, Iamcilla perhaps most of all, felt pangs of shame. But they were strengthened by the idea of the godless observing them, for a mob of townspeople had gathered. They must not bend now or it would be an insult on the head of the Incarnated One. Her father was there and came forward with her baby daughter, who pulled at Iamcilla's simple white covering: 'Think of your child! Perform the sacrifice,' he sniffled. Then, when the magistrate asked them whether they were Christian, all answered yes and her father surged forwards again. But the magistrate, with no respect for his age or the station old Victor had once held in that city, instructed soldiers to throw him to the ground and beat him with staves. And Iamcilla felt the blows as if they were beating her – this was even worse than the torture of seeing her daughter for the last time.

The magistrate stood up. Wild animals had been brought, he said. These Christians must be made an example of. Sighs from the crowd, excitement, pleas from family members. The martyrs had prepared themselves for metal and nooses, but not claws or teeth and some found it difficult to breathe. Now, the magistrate would ask a last time: were they or were they not Christian? He waited a moment and started with the youngest. He had marked out the adolescent as being especially vulnerable, and, certainly, he was pale and close to tears. Would the boy sacrifice? The beardless one waited a moment and then spoke slowly and deliberately: 'I am a Christian.' After that, one by one, the magistrate questioned them and none hesitated. Indeed, it seemed to those watching that they could not get the words out quickly enough in their enthusiasm. And, in the forum, sympathisers muttered the words under their breath. Afterwards, the guards were summoned; and the Christians returned towards the prison actually laughing with the joy of the sentence, for soon they were to be in paradise.

One of the girls was a slave named Innocentia, who had given herself to God and his Holy Son only some weeks before Iamcilla. She lived on the estate where the church had been hidden and was heavily pregnant, almost eight months with child. They would not send her into the amphitheatre until she had given birth. And this woman was terrified that she would not be able to die with the others, above all with Iamcilla, whom she considered her sister in Christ, perhaps having to suffer at a later date, with criminals and bandits. So, together, they prayed that she might be delivered of the baby quickly – they begged, especially Iamcilla, whose dreams had set her apart as a person of power. And none were surprised when almost immediately the birth pangs began. In this and in many other things, they believed that God favoured them greatly in their last days and their confidence grew.

The governor of the prison had kept them dirty in the hole where they were imprisoned, for he believed that Christians outside would use their magic to free the martyrs-to-be if they were placed in better, more open cells. But with this new-found confidence they demanded to see him. Iamcilla went herself and stood before the man, who had once served under her father, and now with nothing save death before her, she told him that as they were to die, and die willingly mind, then it was only right that they should all be given proper quarters so that they could turn out well for the crowds. He blushed at her eloquence and they were brought to cleaner rooms and almost coddled by the guards, one of whom promised to visit the forbidden church where their road to salvation had begun. There was little time now. They would never know if he was good to his word or not.

On the night before the games, Iamcilla had another dream. The deacon of her church came to the prison doors and knocked violently. She opened the gates for him as if there were no locks. And he said to her in a kindly voice: 'Come, Iamcilla, we are waiting for you!' Then, he took her hand and walked with her through a horrid, broken country and holding her, said: 'Do not worry for I will be with you.' Afterwards they were on a long road towards the amphitheatre that glowed ahead in a wonderful light and she was left to walk this long road alone. Then, when she arrived, she turned around and saw the peoples behind her uncertain and lost in the world. The crowd within, instead, roared, and she waited for the animals, but none came. Rather, there was an Egyptian with a mangled face who walked towards her to fight. Her clothes were taken away and she became a man. Assistants appeared from nowhere and rubbed her down with oils.

Then, as she and the Egyptian were preparing for the encounter, an enormous official appeared in a purple tunic. He had sandals made of gold and silver and his head was so high that it lifted above the clouds. In his hands, he carried a branch and on this branch were golden apples. He spoke to her earnestly: 'If this Egyptian defeats you, you will be dead. But if you defeat him then you will win my branch.' He withdrew. And, she and the Egyptian fought, smashing with their fists until she, with a power she did not know that she possessed, floated into the air and hit the Egyptian from above. She grabbed his neck and threw him to the floor. Then she trod on his head. The crowd shouted exaltations and those who had rubbed oil on her sang psalms. The tall man gave her the branch and, kissing her, said: 'Peace be with you, my daughter.' Then she awoke and realised that that day she would fight not with beasts, but with the Devil.

The crowd was already angry when the little congregation started on its longest journey. From the other British cities had come the rumour that the persecution was grinding to a halt – and with so many Christians still arrogantly holding to their dangerous beliefs! Then, had come too the news that the Cornish wolves promised for the games had not arrived. Nor would the magistrate, who had condemned the Christians, grace the spectacle. He was needed in Londinium on urgent business. The Christians were, in any case, marched through the streets towards the amphitheatre that stood on the edge of the city with rabid lines of fellow-citizens abusing them. As they walked passers-by, family members, complete strangers assaulted them with their favourite insults for Christians: 'donkey worshippers', 'tinder-men', 'atheists'. And then, as they came closer and stared at the curved building, constructed like a giant receptacle for blood, there rose a more general cry: 'to the beasts', 'to the beasts', 'to the beasts!'

The four thousand seats had already been taken: seats had been sold for a fortune, so many clamoured to see the spectacle. And as those lucky ones inside heard the approaching six by the jeers of those outside, the very walls vibrated with shouted enthusiasm. It was said that sitting in an amphitheatre, even using hands to close ears and eyes, it was impossible to escape from the spectacle, which thumped its way into your very bloodstream. And some became so excited at a normal event that they threw their togas into the ring and were forced to walk home naked. This excitement, however, was nothing next to that felt by the spectators as the first Christians to be put to death in the town stumbled through the gates.

The Christians had not been able to speak to each other on the walk. They had been kicked not only by the crowd, but also by those guards who had previously treated them well, now caught up in the blood lust. Not one sympathiser of the Cross did they see in the streets, not one smile and by the time that they arrived at the stadium, they were sore and had been pelted. However, the moment they were brought into the side hall, where gladiators normally waited, all this changed. A man of Italian birth was preparing for them, on a long oaken table, certain costumes. He waved in a friendly fashion and smiled: 'Now, now, friends, it will all soon be over! But we do need you to dress up!' He pointed at the suits laid out before him: one dangling with grapes and a loose guitar. 'We have decided that the first of you will go out as Orpheus. We have a Caledonian bear ... Well, we'll let you discover that as you go along, shall we?' Anger surged in Iamcilla. Criminals were sometimes clothed as mythological characters to enter the stadium. In previous years in the Woody City they had seen a bandit, made into Icarus, propelled by theatre ropes into a cage of starved beasts. A woman poisoner was forced to mate with an ass or a bull, as lions were sneaked through the animal tunnel to kill both. And prisoners doused with drink or the fear of a still-worse end were normally happy to submit. But they were Christians!

She, who had been those long weeks before the meekest of the group, was now the most outspoken. She took up, with anger, this insult: 'We are here on the Lord's business. We will die if you wish it – we wish it too. But not disguised in these baubles, not to be mocked by your demons.' The others, though shaken from their walk, supported her. And the thin man became excited. He begged. He offered them only worse pain if they did not do as he said. He agreed to skip Orpheus or at least the bear. They could go out without a guitar and he would use dogs. It would be quicker that way. He would give them vials of drugs so they would be insensible to the pain. He even talked of his wife and family – he would never leave this awful job, if he did not prove a success at it. But none weakened. And, as the spectators became frustrated – the dancing had finished, the first gladiator fight had proved a disappointment – it was agreed to send the would-be saints out without the suits.

And so they were shuffled and pushed towards the entrance, where a second gladiator fight had been improvised to distract from the confusion within. Lucius, one of the most famous of the British gladiators, had starred in the first outing and was now sent against a young slave, who had been given some vague promises of freedom. But this inexperienced opponent was knocked around and, finally, left begging mercy to the stand where those in charge of the spectacle sat. The crowd usually would have let the lad go. But their mood was filthy – and they raged for his death. Lucius twisted the trembling boy up to sitting position and looked off to the side where the assistant, dressed in the garb of Neptune, the god of death, emerged, bringing with him the sharp killing blade, the youth all the while howling for a mercy that neither the crowd nor the organisers would consider. Only Lucius felt some pity as he opened the jugular. The Christians had been given a vivid lesson in how not to die. They must not scream, must not plead, must not waver; *for Lord I have set my heart on you and will not be destroyed for ever.* The guards were behind them and the Italian, who though he had used honeyed words, now showed himself all gall and vinegar, pointing his fingers, giving contemptuous instructions.

The first of them to be killed by the beasts (they were sent out one by one) was their deacon, his going hence proving surprisingly difficult. A boar that had been provoked to fury came out in a cloud of dust, but gored its trainer instead of the Christian. A bear that followed – one of those fearsome Scottish bears that were so fêted at Rome in years gone by – refused to leave its cage and dozed oblivious to the riot of sounds outside. It was given, in the end, to a hunting dog to rip out the priest's throat, and even then the wretched soul needed to be given the *coup de grâce* with a knife. He had held up his arms begging for an end …

Iamcilla managed also to cause scandal before her death. She was, after her refusal to don the mythological fancy dress, brought out into the arena naked in a net and left at the mercy of a bull. But the crowd, with commendable modesty, booed at seeing this young girl without clothes and she had to be brought back and covered before being offered up to the beast. However, once returned, the animal would not slay her and, after tossing her several times, ran off. So she was dragged into the centre of the arena, as the crowd exulted – finally, enjoying itself – and put out of her misery by one of the circle's guards. In fact, she guided his sword to her throat, helping cruelty to run its tired course.

⁓⁓⁓ Historical Background ⁓⁓⁓

The persecution of believers was a fact of life for Christians from the first to the very early fourth century. Our evidence for martyrdom, even for Christianity in Britain, is limited: Christianity seems to have taken longer to get going in the island than in the rest of the western Empire – not surprisingly given its distance from the Mediterranean urban heartlands where that religion struck its first roots. However, we do know of a few cases where believers were killed for their faith, though their dates are insecure: Alban at Verulamium, who later gave his name to this town, St Albans; there were also martyrs in Caerwent in Wales, including one with the Jewish or, at least, semitic name Aaron; and perhaps, elsewhere in the province, a Christian named Augulus. All of these died in the same general period as Iamcilla Atrebates – the dating of the British martyrs is notoriously difficult – who is killed in a fictional British persecution of the late third century.

I took as the starting point for this chapter what is known as the Water Newton treasure, the precious objects of churchware that are smuggled away at the beginning of the chapter; for the dating of this silver, as opposed to the date of burial, see the end notes. Iamcilla and Publianus and Innocentia are names found on silver pieces in this hoard. The story, from the arrest onwards, closely follows the experience of Perpetua, a Christian martyr from Carthage, who wrote an account of her last days, dreams and all: arguably the most moving, fascinating, readable text to survive from early Christianity other than the New Testament itself. Lucius is the only British gladiator of whom we know anything. His name is inscribed on a piece of pottery where he is associated with Verecunda the actress. The Romano-British equivalent of a scandal mag?

Persecution reaches a particularly high pitch in the later third century. But in 313 Christianity is legalised in the Empire and quickly after that the Empire itself becomes Christian, a situation portrayed in the next chapter.

PART III

*Decline
and
Disasters*

CHAPTER ELEVEN

Reunion, c.327 AD

Publianus, brother of Iamcilla, on a northern journey

Iamcilla's brother Publianus did not follow his sister to death in the coliseums; but he rejoiced when thirty years after her martyrdom the pagan Empire became Christian. He also proved dutiful to the obligations of blood. He remembered Iamcilla in his prayers, praying too that she would remember him. And, when another Christian, his distant cousin Helena, returned to the island, after most of a lifetime away, he went to meet her in the northern marches of Britannia with his son Silvius. Silvius was my grandfather and himself told me of the staging post in the shadow of the Pennines where they finally met . . .

They had told old Publianus that he would recognise his cousin Helena as soon as she walked into the room. Yes, more than fifty years had passed. But she would still be the same under the wrinkles and the rich clothes; the same girl who had left Britain half a century before, unmarried on the arm of a Roman notable, causing a scandal that had greatly excited all Britannia. Yet, in the Pennine staging post where he had been instructed to meet her, there had occurred an embarrassing incident: the head of the Atrebates line had mistakenly embraced a rich Spanish dowager down from the wall, while her furious daughter looked on. And he had not even noticed the severely dressed widow who waited in the corner; for his cousin had shrunk in height and in weight and the sun of the Mediterranean had singed her face for too many summers. Indeed, only the ring kept, in the British way, on her middle finger betrayed her island origins. It was that ring that she held up to him as he came near, allowing him to kiss it, holding it out too to his son Silvius. And then she said that she was ready to begin the journey south and asked some pertinent questions about the conditions of the road and the time they would ride. Then, almost as an afterthought, and disappearing from sight into the carriage that had been prepared for her comfort, she said that, no, she did not remember him though she recalled his mother.

This behaviour had surprised Publianus, for he remembered his cousin only too well from his younger days; she had been a flighty, unpredictable thing given to jokes and games. And, in truth, he did not believe that she could not recall 'baby Publianus'. But the head of the family was not easily riled and he did not allow Silvius to provoke him to anger on this occasion, reminding his heir that their guest was beyond the age of reason: what was she now, eighty? He did not say – it hardly needed to be said – that she also had the power in one decayed little fist, in a letter that she might write to her son or other magnates of the Empire, to have the Atrebates scorched from the face of the earth. In any case, after two hours of riding he had convinced himself that her early rudeness – her reluctance to talk and the ring waved in his face – had been unintended and, recalling fond times spent together many decades before, he rode alongside the vehicle sheltering her and asked about his dear Helena's health. But she was praying, rather too loudly he thought, and impatiently rebuffed his attempts at conversation, growling about the Lord in Hebrew and Greek.

And so Publianus rode to the front of the party of horses and watched the mist and twilight rolling down the hillsides; while beyond them the panoply of trees stretched, almost as far as his eyes could see, in every direction. In Londinium, in the Woody City, at the Waters of Sulis and a hundred other of the towns of the south Rome ruled. And walls, baths, sewers, theatres, schools and coliseums had been built to ensure that rule. But here in the north nothing had really changed for a thousand years. True, detachments from cohorts rode through the stifling vegetation, running backwards and forwards up the great roads – the only truly Roman territory in the north. Off these paved or gritted tracks, though, the tribesmen still lived in their dirty little villages – in the same way they had in the time of his forebear Commius; many still covered themselves in tattoos, and the clans that had been forgotten in the south persisted in their feuds and cattle raids here. Well, by evening they would be in a safe place and it would no longer matter. But for now Publianus felt that tremble of anxiety the wild places produced in him and remembered stories from his grandfather about the wars in the north.

He would not care to spend the night or any large part of the day in a wilderness like this. These wastelands were for passing through, not for living in and yet there, off to the side, hidden between oaks, were the circular huts of the natives and there, on a knoll, a bonfire had been lit. He heard the strumming of a *chrotta,* the barbarian harp, and immoderate laughing and drunkenness. If he had been riding alone or with only his son he would have been worried, even if the tavern where they were to stay was only a mile down the road. But as it was . . . He looked complacently around at the large slaves who rode with him only to see, to his horror, that one was remonstrating with his aged cousin, who had woken from her prayers. In fact, this energetic woman was pushing the slave out of the way – the carriage had come to a complete stop. And she was reaching her feet down to the muddied road, and leaving its protection behind. Publianus gritted his teeth. It would be a call of nature: could she not have waited? And in this of all places? But, instead of descending towards the river, where a beaver's dam had created a pool, this Helena was walking now towards the crowd of tribesmen and their fire. And then, just in case there could have been any doubt, she turned her head and, with the assured arrogance of one who has lived for decades in the luxury of Adriatic palaces, announced that she had set her mind on seeing this most interesting gathering for herself.

There had been rumours that his cousin had strange tastes; had gone digging up half of Palestine looking for Christian relics, for example. But at dusk in the Pennines, a circle of clansmen! Well, nothing had prepared them for this. Publianus and Silvius immediately set off to drag her back, if need be physically, from such madness. They had been told, after all, in no uncertain terms, in letters covered in Imperial seals, that they were responsible for her safety. But they took time to find their way off the slippery stones and she, in any case, was surprisingly sprightly, bouncing through the long grass towards where the tribesmen sat. And, as the two Atrebates reached her, the locals were already inviting the old woman to sit; an animal bladder was being offered her with the promise of last year's beer. And she stared at her distant kinsmen, almost daring them with her eyes to take her away now.

In truth, the crowd congregated there was not quite as bad as Publianus had feared. There were no weapons in sight, no woad, and an amphora of wine – probably stolen off the back of a jerking supply wagon – had been broken open in the corner. One managed a few words in incorrect Latin, begging him too to sit; even inviting the slaves over. And the old man sighed, telling himself that it would create less offence to wait for some minutes here than to cause a scene by tugging her away, a scene that could spark off anger in the mob. So, pulling gently at his son's arm, he brought himself down onto a damp horse blanket and straw that had been laid out there and into the sheltering heat of the fire.

The locals recognised, of course, that the travellers were well-to-do; their clothes, their huge horses and their carefully cut hair could leave them in no doubt as to that. And they began to ask questions as tribesmen always do: where were the noble gentlemen coming from, where were they going, what were they doing there, did they have things to sell, had they news from afar? Publianus and his son answered discreetly. They talked not of places but of distances with vague gestures to the points of the compass and they certainly did not mention the civil war that the well-connected claimed was brewing in Gaul, the result in no small part of the activities of Helena's son. But the ancient woman had no such reserves and talked frankly in a heavily accented voice. No, she was not a foreigner even if she had not spoken Celtic for many years. She was – though you would hardly believe it to look at her pasty kinsmen – related to the two Romans before them; the northern Britons laughed. She had come from a poor collateral line, and they also nodded at this for with their clans and large, extended families they understood the curse of the younger brother and the poor relation all too well. In fact, the old man they saw now – Publianus was his name – had, when a young man, barely acknowledged her for her father had been nothing more than an innkeeper, one not welcome in the family villa. But she had married well and, as if this point needed no further explaining, she rattled a gold chain that hung from her wrist.

The crowd smiled again, warming to this strange lady from afar. They had come here that night to hear a story from the storyteller – an emaciated man bowed his head at her from across the flames. But perhaps it was better that she tell them a story. Yet at this she shook her head. She had no stories to tell, she stated, but she would gladly listen to one of theirs; what stories did they know? Well – voices sounded enthusiastically – there was the one about the goddess Britannia, for every hill in Britain was her breast and the kings of old suckled sovereignty from out of her peaks. There was the tale of the fairies that dwelt in mounds such as those they sat on now. And, of course, there were the dragons. And the history of Artorius the Pure – they slurred his name, calling him 'Arthur' – the Roman cavalry leader who killed the enemies of Britain. And the storyteller, excited by this catalogue of adventure and marvel, rose to his feet and began to shake his hands in the way that was required of him and turned to the ancient lady. Very well, she would not tell the story. But she would choose the story that he told that night. Now, what story would she choose?

It was a great honour. However, Publianus' cousin seemed unconscious of it. Instead, a glint of something like mischief came into the old woman's eyes and she said that she wished to hear the story of Constantius and his love the Briton, Helena. Could he tell her the story of that famous pair? Silvius and his father stared at each other: this was *most* dangerous, it could lead to misunderstandings and scandal. But around the fire there was, instead, excited talking. Wasn't Constantius the one whose head they still sometimes found on coins – one of the old masters of Rome? And Helena had been his British love, whom he had taken away from the island and whom all had talked about in years past; for though little in the way of Roman baths or Roman villas reached the north, the Pennine folk were always fascinated by Roman gossip. Then, yes, they too wished to listen to the story of Helena and Constantius; for none had ever heard it told around the fireplace of the tribe. And, though the storyteller did not normally talk of the recently living or the recently dead he assented, and with practised swirls of his hand invoked the muses of the fire and the breath of the heavens and began with the traditional words: once, long, long ago ...

Once, long, long ago there was a man named Constantius, who was the son of one of the mightiest men in Rome and he was the best-looking and wisest of all men and he had everything except a beautiful wife such as kings require. And, one day, he held an assembly and he said: 'Today I will hunt.' And so it was that he set out from his palace in that city and went along the valley of a long river that is found in those parts. He ranged up and down this valley until it was noon, hunting all the while. And with him were seventeen princes. And, after they ate together on the banks of this river near Rome, Constantius fell asleep and the seventeen princes gathered around him with their shields to shade their sleeping lord from the harsh sun and they stabbed their spears into the ground to guard their master and one, gently, so as not to wake the best lord in the world, lay beneath him a long, golden sheet, letting him sleep the better.

And, as Constantius slept, he had a dream: a dream such as he had never had before. In this dream, he was making his way along the valley in which he rested, until he came to a mountain that was, he knew, the highest mountain in the world. And, as he began to climb this mountain, quite alone, he could see that it had the finest meadows of any mountain anywhere and, on the top of the mountain, these pastures continued gloriously so he could follow them. And, on the other side of these pastures, he came to a spring and saw that in the distance it became a stream and he followed this stream, which became a river, and slowly the river took him down towards the sea. And he travelled and travelled and the river tipped into the ocean. And, at the mouth of this river, he saw an enormous fort and there were towers in this fort made of different materials and, next to the fort, was a grand fleet, the grandest fleet that mortal has known. And, in that fleet, there was one ship that was ten times bigger than all the others and a hundred times as beautiful. And, on the boat, all the planks were made of gold and from land to this ship stretched a bridge of pure ivory and, in his dream, he went along onto the bridge with no fear.

Then, this boat with its fleet passed across the wide ocean and they came to an island. And this island was the most beautiful of all the islands of the wide world. And, once disembarked from that boat, he saw valleys and mountains and hills and woods and clearings and fields and farms; and there was a beauty and a wildness in the place that he had never seen. And so it was that the brave Constantius passed through the island, coming to a plain of trees, a plain of trees as small as the island that he was on was large and he passed into that plain and found a fort there, the most beautiful he had ever seen, and he entered this fort until he came to a marvellous circular hall, painted over in many different colours.

The roof was made of gold, the side of glittering gems, all worth twenty slaves. And, on the couches, in the centre of the hall, there were two red-haired men playing at a board game and laughing all the while. They were dressed in silk from the lands of the east and ribbons of purple held their hair, and their feet had on golden shoes of kings. And, at the base of the pillar that held the circular hall up, he saw an ancient man seated in a chair of white bone, a chair stamped with red eagles. A gold torque was on his neck and a gold amulet on his arm and many golden rings on his fingers. And this man was a king in his looks and his gestures, and in his hand was a piece of rock and from the rock he carved figures for his sons to play with.

And before the king, on a chair of red gold, sat Helena, a girl such as Constantius had never seen while waking. It would be easier to look at the sun at midday or wrestle with the waves than to stand unmoved in her presence. Her gown was of the purest with not a speck of dirt or wear and around her head was a tiara of royalty with diamonds. Never had a Roman seen any as beautiful as she. And she rose from her chair the moment that

Constantius arrived and he threw his arms around her neck. But, when he was about to brush his lips against her lips, a terrible noise erupted. Dogs in the hall woke and strained at their leashes. Guards, who had appeared statues, started to knock their spears. Shields were banged together. And, in the stables outside, the horses neighed into life and thumped their hooves. And Constantius, desolate, awoke in the wood near Rome with his seventeen princes. And, though his hands reached out to touch her, there was no one there. Not a bone, not a hair. He was alone with his friends in the forest. But he was demented with love for her. 'Lord,' said one beside him, 'it is the time that you normally feast. We should return to your father's mansion', he said.

The storyteller stopped and called for wine; he had spoken without a break and was desperate to drink, as well he might be. Publianus, instead, covered his face so none of them would see his expression. He had heard these Celtic fairy tales before, of course, and should have known what to expect – the confusion, the muddle, the twisting of the generations! There were many points he could have picked out: the description of the Tiber, for example, or 'seventeen Roman princes' – Rome had no princes, or kings for that matter. In fact, about the only thing that they had got right was that this Helena was a Briton. Oh yes she was a Briton all right, he could vouch for that; he stared bitterly at his cousin sitting next to him and for the first time he saw that sly look that had once permanently graced her face. And Constantius, the man who had done more perhaps than any other to drag the Empire into the chaos in which it had found itself in the last decades, had met her in Britain on one of his endless military tours. She had been sixteen – as Publianus knew only too well for, to his shame, he had been there when the mighty Constantius had stared across the hall in the forum of the Woody City. And that little fool of a cousin had stared back at him as the Empress of Persia might have looked at a cowherd. That had been what had done for Constantius and for her as well; the scandal of their association had been much talked about. But the storyteller had taken his fill of wine and was returning to his theme. What further nonsense would this British Homer introduce into his narrative now?

Friends, with great sadness Constantius returned to his horse and his home, the saddest man that had ever lived. And whenever his men wished to drink beer, he refused to go with them. And, in fact, the only thing that he did was sleep. For when he slept, he could see traces, though only traces mind, of that wonderful girl. And one day it happened that a trusted counsellor spoke to Constantius: 'All speak badly of you because you are no longer a lord to them but dream and dawdle.' 'Then bring me all the wise men of Rome and I will tell them why I am sad.' And the wise men of Rome came to him and he addressed them: 'Wise men of Rome', said he. 'In a dream I saw a girl. And since then, nothing exists for me, but the glow of her cheek.' They nodded wisely and said: 'You are sick with love and there is only one cure. Send all your retinue out into the world in every direction for a year to seek for the woman of your dream. And, in that year, if you live without her, at least the hope of her face will keep you from death.' And so the retinue of Constantius went out in every direction and they travelled to the edges of the world, asking for his dream, and, at the end of the year, they returned to Constantius, who now slept almost always and they confessed that they knew no more about that love he had met in a dream than on the first day they had set out.

And Constantius despaired then, for he had lived only to see his dream again. But his faithful seventeen princes knew better: 'Our Lord Constantius', they said, 'let us go out and hunt as you did that day when you dreamt and follow the lands you saw in your dreams. And so they went out and, in time, they came to the bank of the river where he had lain down and he said, 'I slept here and in my dream ...' and he pointed upwards to the valley. And so Constantius sent out seventeen messengers to go northwards to find his dream. And they galloped up the tall mountain that Constantius had seen and they wore on their body tokens of messengers, great feathers, so that no one seeing them would think to attack them. And they travelled across the meadows of the mountain to the larger river and down this river they rushed and then they travelled towards the sea, all the time saying: 'This is the route our Lord Constantius told us to follow.' And, at the head of the estuary, they saw the fleet and the golden ship within it that was ten times as large and a hundred times as fair. This was, certainly, the way. And, once on the boat, they asked where it was heading. And the captain of this boat told them that they were bound for Britain, the best of islands.

And they sat in the boat until they came to Britain and in Britain they crossed the swamps and ravines and empty places until they came to a wood and, in this wood, they came to a castle with a circular hall and the guards there told them that this was the Woody City. And they passed into the hall and there, inside, there were the two boys playing, there was the king working on his figurines for their game and before him, on the couch, was the girl Helena, brighter than fire. And when they saw her, they fell to their knees. 'Greetings, wife of Constantius.' And she, while showing them signs of respect, could not understand their words and thought they were mocking her. But the servant of Constantius explained: 'We have come from Constantius, one of the lords of Rome. He has seen you in a dream and since he saw you he has nothing save sleep and torment to see you again. Either you must come with us and become his wife or Constantius will come to this island and make you his wife.' She laughed at this: 'It may be true, what you say, but, in that case, tell your mighty Constantius to come and get me himself.'

Publianus smiled into a cup that had been handed him. Now that was worthy of the Helena he remembered, that haughty 'tell your mighty Constantius to come and get me himself'. And he had come and got her for himself: Publianus' father Victor had told him that the Roman had vaulted into her bedroom from a stable. But there had been no marriage; the young Helena was not of noble enough blood and she had become, instead, the man's concubine, dragged behind from province to province and eventually discarded when

Constantius married. If it had not been that she had produced a son, then he doubted that she would have ever been heard of again, would probably have finished in a Greek brothel. Perhaps it would have been better! And he started to laugh to himself, when the storyteller halted: 'There is one who does not listen to me here! He despises the tale I tell!' This could mean trouble. The head of the Atrebates would have to speak quickly. 'Forgive me, father, I am not of your blood and I do not know your ways. It is the finest story I have ever heard and I was laughing when I thought of the foolishness of the stories they tell in other lands compared to the stories of Britain.' Old Helena, grinning slightly, and the crowd, with more serious faces, looked up at the storyteller. He was a dangerous figure. He could send men away from the fire. He could blight and kill with his curses, leaving red scars on faces or pocks and rashes. But he seemed pacified.

Well, so it was that day and night, morning and evening they rode madly down the roads to Rome. Every day their horses died with exhaustion and every day they bought others and rode them and rode them until these died. And, when they came to Constantius, they told him that they had found his dream. And he discovered her name and her kindred and her lineage, for she was Helena of the line of the Atrebates. And Constantius summoned not only his men, but also his armies and he rode to Britain that was always disobedient to the Romans, and he conquered the island from the Picts and all others who resisted him. And he came to the fort with its wonderful hall. And saw the king, an ancient man, and the young men and the girl he had dreamt of was also there and she stood and he threw his arms around her neck and brushed his cheek against hers and that night they lay together.

On the next day, the girl Helena asked Constantius for a gift for her wedding. And he asked her to name her maiden fee. And she said that she would be Empress of Rome and that he would be Emperor. And so it was that Constantius agreed and in Britain he made many forts and walls and his wife Helena ordered that the straight roads be built. And, for seventeen years, Constantius remained in the island with his wife. And then he wrote a letter to Rome and in it he wrote: 'I am now the Emperor.' And, in Rome, the Emperor wrote back and said: 'No, you are not.' And so it was that Constantius prepared for war to deliver his bridal gift to Helena. And the prince set out for Rome with his army and the armies of all the Britons and he conquered the country of Gaul, and Germany and, after a year, he came to Rome and put the city under siege and destroyed it and so the Empire became his. Friends, my story ends.

Publianus turned to Helena and whispered her name softly, though none there would imagine, none could imagine that she was the same woman as the dainty princess of the fairy tale. She had been despised, left, forgotten, only receiving the respect due to her with the ascent of her son in the last years. But she had at least had the final satisfaction of becoming a song in the mouths of her people. And yet she was asleep. She had fallen asleep before the storyteller had announced that she was responsible for building the Roman roads of Britain: how she would have enjoyed that! And, for the first time feeling the affection that many years ago he had felt for the lost girl with the long black hair and the daring eyes, he instructed the slaves to lift her and carry her gently back towards the carriage.

⁓ Historical Background ⁓

This chapter is based overwhelmingly on one source: 'The Dream of Macsen Wledig', a medieval Welsh tale. But what has a twelfth-century Welsh tale to do with the Romans? Well, the tale recalls – in a distorted and mythic form – the love story of a Briton named Helena and an important Roman almost a millennium before and has, in fact, been used by classicists, dubiously, as a historical source. The muddle of the legend – and the point of the chapter is that legend hopelessly bends historical facts out of shape – seems to borrow from two different historical episodes, that of Helena, low-born, third-century wife or concubine of Constantius the Roman magnate (a 'Caesar' and then later a co-emperor) and that of the campaigns of Magnus Maximus, a tyrant based in Britain in the later fourth century who may also have married a Helena.

I have chosen Constantius as the lover over Maximus and, in our story, when Helena visited her distant cousin Publianus c.327 AD (towards the end of her life), her son with Constantius, Constantine, would have been Roman Emperor. It was in his reign that Christianity became legal and even fashionable in the Empire. The reference to Helena looking for relics in the Holy Land is a nod to the legend that it was she who discovered the Holy Cross.

CHAPTER TWELVE

The Police State, 354 AD

Silvius, son of Publianus, a poet

My grandfather, the poet Silvius, is remembered by his family today not only for his verses – we have, in fact, no more than a dozen scribbled rhymes – but for his suffering in the purges of 'Paul the Chain' two generations ago. And in these days, when we thirst for order, when the law and the land have been given up to the strongest, it is only right to remember that there can also be too much authority. For it was the tyranny of the unjust as well as the barbarian spear that destroyed our Britannia and, eighty years ago, led the spy Fullofaudes towards the venerable Silvius' house ...

Following his instructions the agent and courier Fullofaudes rode north to the Thames. He arrived a little before evening, and let his horse go on the outskirts of the straggling settlement that clung to the south bank: those disordered and anarchic taverns and houses where the administration of Londinium had no authority. The Imperial officer, disguised in the clothes of a simple traveller, then walked through the lanes between swindlers and beggars, watching the tenements of the capital to the north, picked out in the half-light of dusk, and the hints of marble in the streets beyond. And after, as the dark came on, he followed the loudest voices to the drinking places and stared vacantly into the faces of men who believed he was a fool. But all the time he listened. And he heard talk there of the latest arrests, for in the last months the provincial government had been rounding up rebels. The aristocracy of the island had backed the wrong side in one of the Empire's increasingly frequent civil wars; and the Emperor's most notorious enforcer, Paulus, aptly nicknamed 'the Chain', had been sent in to root out the traitors.

After downing four foaming beers, he left and found a bed in a cheap fleapit and tried to ignore the noise of the street performers outside. He did not trouble himself with sleep, for on the night before a job sleep always brought him nightmares. Instead, he read again the instructions, written out in minuscule on a ragged piece of parchment: the description of his victim's house and the name, Silvius Atrebates. They could not, it had been explained, simply arrest this Silvius as he had some vague connection to one of Rome's greatest families through a distant cousin, Helena. They wanted, instead, evidence that could be used against him. Fullofaudes anticipated no problems.

He left the small room before dawn and found himself standing at the bridge across the Thames as it opened with three or four men who had spent the night carousing or sheltering with courtesans in the entrances to tombs along the road. Fullofaudes had thought about passing over the river in the night and trying to enter by one of the five gates in the walls. But he knew from previous experience that the checks there were especially rigorous and that they might even try and make something of the long knife strapped to his inner thigh. Instead, he played drunk so as to be confused with the others and paid coin to the guard, lifting his shirt to show that he had no baggage to be inspected or taxed. Afterwards, walking over the bridge and into the city, he put on his hooded cloak. And all around him Londinium was coming alive. Hammer blows were sounding from his right where the distant cathedral was being built, encased in fragile-looking scaffolding. And past him scholars, traders and matrons hurried to their first appointments of the day or from the last of the night, shielding their eyes from the glaring sun.

The light did not alarm him as it would have in Rome for Londinium was a perfect city for his line of work. True, there were two long, paved streets that legionaries patrolled constantly. But, otherwise, it was a gloriously chaotic place, and most of the alleys and ways were winding, narrow and unroman. Fullofaudes waited until he came up against the old Temple of Mithras, now daubed with Christian graffiti, and then plunged into these small spaces, underneath six- and seven-storey blocks of flats. Then, after twenty minutes of meandering past street sellers, bakeries and men boiling up fish sauce, he came into the eastern part of the city where the most exclusive of the capital's citizens lived. Britain was famous throughout the Empire for its urban gardens: towns with long stretches of lawn and orchard. This had been true even in the very centre of

Londinium where the poorer folk lived. But now, as he came to the mansions of the richer Britons, the gardens were often larger than the houses.

It took him five minutes to find his bearings: bearings that he had memorised the night before from the piece of parchment. He had been instructed to look for a large, pinkish house built with Egyptian granite and, seeing such a mansion, he doubled back until he came to a gate where an ancient slave sat half-asleep. And, sure enough, there at the entrance was a statue of a Romano-Celtic god: a tall man with a dog by his side. There was no question; it matched the description he had been given. He had found the place. For another hour he walked in the neighbourhood aimlessly, keen only to avoid being noticed, disposing of the cloak that he had worn just in case the gatesman had been attentive. Certainly, he knew that the next part would be the most difficult. He waited until a bell sounded within the house, signalling that the master was coming to breakfast, and, satisfied, set off at a slow pace towards the entrance. As he walked he looked before him and behind him and then slipped his knife out, thrusting it into his thigh, away from the artery. He waited a second for the blood to start to flow. And then he screamed. He did so in Latin, but with a heavy Italic accent. It served his purpose that they thought him Italian.

Almost immediately slaves came running out, calling to the gatesman, to get help from the house; the ancient one set hobbling off into the grounds. But even as all were shaken by the blood on the roadway, they constantly turned behind them to make sure the entrance was guarded and the injured man could hear mastiffs growling in the garden beyond. He was carried swearing into the gatehouse where he made some feeble attempts to remove the knife, while describing all the time his assailant. But his hand was slapped away by the butler who had come out of the house to tend him. His master, he said, was clever with these things and it was best if he removed it. Next the city guard arrived. They had been told of shouts and an attack. The young man in charge blanched when he saw the wound; then stared into the victim's eyes.

It may have been the imagination of the butler, but it seemed that a significant glance passed from the officer, as if a traveller with a knife in his thigh had been something that he had been warned to look out for. But that was absurd. The butler hurried the guard away and continued to talk to the man to keep him lucid in the minutes before his master's coming. Why was he in Britain? The Italian talked of a pilgrimage to Cambria, he had needed a cure. All the men in the gatehouse laughed at that: he would need another cure now, they said. And where was his horse, asked the butler, who was the senior slave present. He had no horse, said the Italian, for piety's sake he had decided to travel on foot. The butler nodded, came to his feet, bid the man farewell and then walked out of the building. He alone of all those there had noticed that the man had a small horse whip tied to his ankle. He would talk to his master. These were, after all, dangerous times.

By now the excitement had given way to pain and the wounded man groaned as he waited for his Silvius to arrive. He had even become worried at the delay, wondered if perhaps they had somehow found him out, when a small, well-dressed crowd started across the lawn towards where he lay. There were three men: a large Briton in the tunic of an equestrian; the butler speaking urgently to him, but being ignored; and a thin, willowy man who was already staring at the knife that remained firmly in Fullofaudes' thigh. Then, behind them all came a young boy slave of six or seven with a bronze bowl of water, slopping carelessly as he walked. The one dressed as an equestrian introduced himself as Silvius Atrebates; and the debilitated stranger, despite his pain, started.

Silvius Atrebates? Surely not Silvius Atrebates the poet? The butler narrowed his eyes. But the master of the household smiled and admitted that he was, indeed, the poet. Had this Italian – Marcus he learnt was his name – had Marcus heard of his work? Marcus admitted that he had and surprised all by quoting some of the poet's hexameters. Even the willowy doctor, who was bending and examining the wound, grinned at the coincidence of it. They knew that Silvius' fame had reached the Continent; why only the year before that impertinent snob, the Gaulish poet Ausonius, had written some satirical verses directed at their master. But for Silvius to be known now in Italy ... All spoke as the slave doctor washed his hands in the bowl held out by the slave boy and, while this Marcus explained that he was a magistrate's secretary, the slave withdrew the knife and clamped clean rags down onto it with a yellow powder. Then, as the newcomer told how he had piously decided to walk to Cambria, to a place named the Shrine of Dreams, dressed in his poorest clothes, the slave who had performed the operation washed the blood off his hands and dried them vigorously on the small boy's hair.

But here was another coincidence. Silvius knew of this place, his eldest son now in his thirties regularly went there – they would have a good deal to talk about; the Briton's vanity had already been preened on hearing his poetry recited by an Italian. As they chatted the butler who had been bobbing along beside them, asked if he might not speak to his master alone. But Silvius brushed him aside and told him and the doctor to go to the kitchens. Then, as they walked away, he intimated that his butler was always full of theories and wild schemes; he had, the Briton started to rock with laughter, convinced himself that their guest was a member of the secret police! Now, if his new friend Marcus would care to walk a little in the garden he would be most pleased. Though, if the wound was too much, they could also rest for a minute on one of those benches. He pointed to a small arbour where seats had been fashioned out of stone. The Italian was ready to stroll around despite his injury, but he sensed that Silvius Atrebates would prefer to sit, for he was a sedentary sort, tipping into middle-aged obesity.

And so they sat. His host regretted again the attack and explained how lawlessness was growing in the province. Then he boasted of the various features in the garden and the stones of the house that his ancestor Togidubnus had had brought from the quarries of Lower Egypt three centuries before. He pointed out too the White Hill [Tower Hill] that loomed behind them and that marked the eastern border of the city and the end of Silvius' garden. It was Londinium's most famous landmark and Silvius talked of the legends that his own father had told him about the place when he was a small child and how he and his child friends had raced up and down it for amusement. It was said, he explained, that an ancient king of the British named Raven, a cousin of that god whose statue stood at the front of their house, had had his head buried in the hill. And, so the people insisted, while Raven's head remained there, Britain would never be invaded. The two men smiled at each other and at the pleasantry of the story: a further point of contact between them.

For almost two hours more, they spoke in the sun. It was an informal conversation, but the newcomer noted that this Silvius was not quite as foolish as he had at first seemed. Indeed, very gently he tested his guest's defences; where was he from, did he know that magistrate, how had he come to Britain ... But the tenor was one, above all, of friendship; for Silvius had found that rarest of things, a cultured man of the south with whom he could speak of the latest trends in the most fashionable Roman families. In fact, the only real distraction was that, from time to time, the butler appeared walking around the garden, intent on unimportant jobs, but evidently watching.

However, almost as abruptly as their conversation had begun it ended. At a flurry of movement in front of the house Silvius stood up and pursed his lips. Then, taking his guest by the hand, they walked as quickly as the pilgrim's wound would allow him over towards the gate where a row of six children had formed. The six were slaves and ranged in age from about three years to their late teens. They had been made to stand in order and chains and cuffs had been attached. Silvius shook his head sadly. As all the noble British families after the recent crackdowns, his income had been reduced, though perhaps he should be thankful his life had not been taken *yet*. He said the last word bitterly. Well, it was his daughter's dowry. He had to raise the money somehow, even if all the family would be furious when they discovered how he had done it. There would also be open revolt among the slaves. At the front of the children was the tall, willowy servant, the doctor who had removed the knife from the Italian's leg and who had been placed in charge of their short walk to the slave market. Silvius excused himself and then spoke to the children in turn, patting some and imploring others not to cry. The guest did not know what promises he used to calm them; but he was sure that they were the lies masters normally told their slaves on these occasions.

A welcome distraction came from the palatial buildings at this point, the bell again. It was time for the midday meal and, without asking the Italian, Silvius hauled him towards the house. As they entered the dining room the head of the Atrebates apologised for the reduced state of his household. His two eldest were away in the army and his second wife had died in childbirth only three years before; he gestured at a toddler rolling in the corner being brought to order by a nurse. His other children were spaced around on couches and looked down demurely as the Italian passed – one youngster even seemed familiar to Fullofaudes, though he could not think where he might have seen him before. Silvius, in any case, was speaking. He explained that he had brought them up to be modest in the presence of other adults; it was how he had been brought up by his father, they would not interrupt and it would be better not to ask them questions.

The Italian started to outline his own views on child-rearing when the butler – his face tense with suspicion – passed into the room. Silvius though was having no more of this. Winking at the guest, he took the old retainer aside and patted him on the shoulders, speaking until relief suffused and spread over the man's face. The Briton then turned back to his guest: 'I have told him we share a friend in Italy: I know, I know, a necessary lie. It is absurd but these are dangerous times and strangers worry the servants. You', he tapped the man's chest with his forefinger, 'are responsible.' The other laughed and now, completely at ease, accepted the invitation to take his place for the meal.

For several minutes they ate in silence and then, as if gaining his courage, the pilgrim described some recent gossip from the east; for he had cousins in Antioch and told of the massacres perpetrated by the government there. Silvius did not show any emotion as his guest spoke. But nevertheless he listened attentively. If another wished to be indiscreet, his face seemed to say, then he would not complain; how else was he supposed to get his news? The Italian, though, was careful not in what he said but in how he said it. The guest, for example, did not criticise directly, but called those who opposed the Emperor 'rebels' as was only sensible. And yet there was something in his tone that suggested he was a kindred spirit: that he would have wished, as Silvius, to have lived in a different, happier time. And, as the minutes wore on, they followed each other in the etiquette of criticism, gaining confidence from the enthusiasm of the other.

Silvius described the recent barbarian attacks in Britain, stating that the commanders of the province had not been able to defend the people. The Emperor should be told so that he could change his representatives. The Italian countered. In his journeys he had seen villas abandoned, villas where whole households had been emptied into prison carts and taken in for questioning, to the lair of the one they called Paul the Chain, the Emperor's special representative. Of course, if they were all traitors then it was only just. But, he left the doubt unspoken, were they all rebels or was it, as many said, an excuse by a cash-strapped government to confiscate? Then, as the food ran out, both talked excitedly of the old Republic and the powers of the Senate in the golden age before there had been emperors and inform- ers and secret police. The second amphora of wine arrived and from then small indiscretions were piled on small indiscretions until between them the two men had built a confidence in which they could speak without concern.

Indeed, sated and reassured, their hands, trembling from drink, touched. The Italian poured his host another glass, while asking him why this man Paulus, whom the Britons feared so much, was called 'the Chain'. Silvius shook his head. He had composed a poem on this very theme, he said; though he had not, to be safe, written it out. So the Italian asked him to recite it. But Silvius modestly refused the request. He would tell the Italian, instead, of the two explanations that he had heard in simple prose. Some said it was because this desperate ruffian loved using chains to restrict and to beat those who came into his prisons. Others claimed that it was because he trapped his victims in chain-like plots, going to great trouble to snare them in their own weaknesses and vanities. A noise outside in the corridor called the attention of the butler, who left the room. And his sudden absence – a tray had dropped and valuable glass smashed on the floor – seemed to remove the last semblance of restraint from Silvius Atrebates, who bent his head towards the Italian then spat: 'But whatever the reason, he is, this Paulus, a bad and evil man sent *by a bad and evil emperor.*'

The children, at least those who were old enough to understand what a foolish and dangerous phrase their father had uttered, looked up. The butler, who had returned from the domestic disaster in the corridor, began to collect plates, vainly trying to make enough noise to cancel out the unhappy words. While Silvius himself, suddenly conscious of the peril he might have put himself in, looked morosely into the wine, watching his own reflection there. Yet the Italian seemed not to have heard the incriminating sentence, but continued to talk of this Paulus and what he did to those who had supported the other side in the civil war. He had heard of men crushed and stretched on machines until they were like pulped fruit. He had heard that then they were carried out into the streets and, with their hands tied behind their backs, beheaded like common thieves: women, children, men, nobles, slaves . . . It was all the same to that beast in his jail. But, though Silvius tried to be polite with his smiles, he no longer contributed to the discussion and, within half an hour, the Italian was walking towards the doorway, full now of dandelion seeds, for an autumn breeze was coming up from the river.

He had tipsily refused a bed for that evening despite Silvius' protestations. He had refused too an armed guard to take him on the next leg of his journey; for he was, he said, like the poor man who whistled carefree through bandits, carrying no wealth of his own. And, after he had embraced the poet many times, he set out walking down the lane that he had been carried into, five hours before, moving towards the gate, where the gatesman sat in solitary silence. And he moved swaying slightly under the spell of alcohol, hobbling too from the damage the knife had done until he had assured himself that all was in place, and then a change came over him. His drunken gait disappeared. He straightened his body, as if he was on the marching ground. He tilted his head up and let out a piercing whistle, for by now he could make an unambiguous report about the traitorous family of the Atrebates. And from a house across the way came men. At the end of the street a stall was overturned and more men appeared. Horses that had been grazing in a field, while a road was repaired, were mounted and a group rode at the gatehouse. There was a scream as the gatesman realised what was happening and then a second scream – the last he was ever to make – as the old man was kicked down.

Fullofaudes walked slowly back towards the mansion. The guard captain who had seen him injured had been warned a week before to look out for a knife victim in the Atrebates' house named Marcus and to prepare accordingly. It had really been too easy. These foolish Britons . . . What match were they for him? Only the butler had had his suspicions. Fullofaudes was still curious about what had given him away; perhaps he would ask his own questions. He tightened his fist lustily. And there on the steps the house slaves were being kicked into place: most would be sold for the benefit of the Imperial treasury, once they had confessed their master's crimes. Then there was the family; he looked with interest now at the weeping children, and Silvius with a stony face, refusing his stare. And there was that boy again. He was one of the Atrebates' whelps. Yet Fullofaudes was convinced that he had seen him elsewhere. For a moment a half-memory came, but he was distracted by a voice behind him. 'Captain Fullofaudes, I knew that we could rely upon you. My master Paulus will want personally to reward you; though you will also have to testify.' It was his British contact: an angry under-secretary at the ministry of justice, who had blood on his sleeves from a morning's work in the prisons.

The under-secretary then asked where the criminal and his family were, Fullofaudes holding out his hands modestly at the line before him. But the British official did no more than run his eyes over the captured prey. These were not the Atrebates, he stated coldly. He knew that old fool Silvius all too well; and this was not Silvius, nor were these his children. Fullofaudes did not understand, tried again, still did not understand and then stood shaking his head. But the under-secretary, instead, acted. He walked up the steps and grabbed hold of the man whom the spy had spoken to all morning, who had spoken such outrageous words against the Emperor. 'I know you. You're the one with the perfect Latin and the perfect manners. The one your master is always boasting of. Where is he, you dog?' The man's voice was no longer that of a villa owner: 'I am only a slave. Please do not harm me, sir. I did what I did on my master's orders. He has left the house.' Now it was Fullofaudes' turn: 'It is impossible. No one has left this house except a body of slaves this afternoon.' Then almost as he said this his voice fell away, realising the truth. For at that very moment Fullofaudes remembered where he had seen the boy before. He had been the young slave carrying the water who had come through the garden when he was first stretchered into the gatehouse – he was the slave on whose hair the tall, willowy doctor had wiped his hands. All the demure children in the dining room had been slaves. And the 'doctor' who had escaped into the city with the slave children, actually the young Atrebates, had been Silvius. For the first and last time in his career Fullofaudes had been outwitted.

ᜰᜰᜰ Historical Background ᜰᜰᜰ

The Roman Empire was, arguably, never **a** particularly nice place to live. But by the fourth century it had become positively Soviet in its rigidity and lack of respect for ancient liberties. The price of surviving civil war and the barbarian tribes on its borders had been that of placing more and more control in the hands of central authority. And the agents of central authority included men such as Paulus 'the Chain', sent by Constantius II to suppress rebellious elements in Britain, arresting, in the process, a good portion of the British aristocracy. Here I have described some of Paulus' methods. His victim in this story is a contemporary of Paulus, Silvius Bonus or Silvius 'the Good', a poet. We have no evidence that they ever met and we only know that Silvius existed because his contemporary, the Gaulish poet Ausonius of Bordeaux, mentioned in the chapter, refers to Silvius 'the Good', a Briton, lampooning him and his poetry in a series of epigrams. Fullofaudes is an official associated with Britain in the next generation; he was killed at the time of the Barbarian Conspiracy, for which see Chapter Fourteen. By making him an *agens in rebus* (postal agents who sometimes doubled as spies) we are creating a not-impossible early career in the service of the Emperor.

Part of Roman Britain's and, indeed, the Empire's failure in the fourth century was caused by such sclerotic and unpleasant government. But there seem also to have been religious tensions; for Christianity, from being legalised, had now become legally dominant.

CHAPTER THIRTEEN

To the Temple of Dreams, **c.360** AD

Silvanus, son of Silvius

Silvius, through his wit, escaped death and saved his family. I turn now, instead, to my father the noble Silvanus; his corpse was burnt on a pyre only five months ago, as was normal with those who have refused the Christian faith. Actually, he was one of the last, if not the last, of the pagans; for in the wrecked Britannia of the last years the bishops alone squabble over our souls. And already, sixty years ago, on Silvanus' final pilgrimage to the Temple of Dreams [Lydney Park, Glos], the home of the god Nodens, leader of the Wild Hunt, he was one of a dying breed.

Silvanus Atrebates heard the dogs of the god at least an hour before he arrived at the Temple of Dreams; he was still walking over the rough ground in the valley below when the barking began, somewhere in the dark to the west. Doubtless they were being fed, hence their excited state. But to this particular traveller it seemed an instruction from the divinity himself to continue and not to rest by the side of the road, as he had, for the last hour, been sorely tempted to do. Others came with horses to pay their respects to Nodens, or Apollo as he was called by the Gauls and Italians, worshippers who could never accept the British gods for what they were. But Silvanus, who had revered Nodens, since his childhood, would have considered a journey on horseback an impiety. And so he had set off from the Waters of Sulis [Bath] three days before on foot. And, yes, he had been tested and punished by the walk into the uplands of Britain: the endless peaks and troughs, the rains, the blisters, even a crowd of jeering Christians who had seen his pilgrim staff. But this was his fifth visit to the temple and every time he had passed over these plains and climbed up to that magical bluff of rock his devotion had been amply rewarded.

Twelve years ago it had been prayers for a marriage: he had married two months after his return and had cradled an heir in his arms at the end of three seasons. Eight years ago it had been for their third child, a baby paralysed by an illness none had been able to explain. The child had died the very day that Silvanus slept on the heights; and Nodens in a dream – an eagle had soared against the sun – had told him that his darling's soul would be free to roam among the stars. Seven years ago it had been to ask help for Britannia that laboured under the change of Emperors and the civil wars and the chaffing of barbarians on her borders: he had had no dream that night but had left the temple bounds serene. Five years ago it had not been to require but to thank, for his father and younger siblings had only just escaped arrest for some invented crime. And now, after half a decade, he had returned. It was no longer his elderly parent who worried him. The groundless accusations of treason had been forgotten; the villa and other properties restored to the family. Rather it was something closer, something of his own. And he felt for the ring that his wife had given him when they had married. He could just pick out with his fingertips the face of Venus on its upwards side and fancied that the goddess, who had recently caused him so much pain, was smiling at her servant.

And there, as he brushed the ring, high on his left the temple came into view; burning candles, at least a thousand of them, spread over the holy place's fronting. It was the sign he had been waiting for. He needed only to turn from the road up towards those lights and he would be taken in and given comfort by the priests. He found the pathway. Then for ten more minutes he climbed, sweating, until he came to the steps that led to the godhead and he fell to his knees on the blessed paving stones as cloaked men slipped silently from out of the shadows and stood over him; and he saw among them Victorinus, the famous Interpreter of Dreams, who smiled at Silvanus and helped him into the inner sanctum. There were fewer lights there, and he had to imagine for himself the mosaics and the carvings of Nodens with his hound. As he walked, the temple dogs ran up to him and nibbled, for he dispensed from his pockets bits of bread and teasing half-morsels of meat that he had saved specially for them. There was a villa owner he knew who swore by these dogs. He had, in his youth, been injured in an action against pirates in the Irish Sea, half his stomach ripped open; and, on the advice of a shore official, he had been carried to have Nodens' dogs lick at his wounds, so curing them. Silvanus hoped never to require their holy tongues, but he scratched one behind the ears as he followed Victorinus into the corridor beyond.

As was customary after dark, Victorinus spoke only in whispers and only when it was absolutely necessary. For the most part there were simple sentences: questions or instructions, the worshipper being expected to put himself entirely in the hands of his guide. Did the pilgrim wish the god to speak to him in a dream? Silvanus nodded and so he was shown the cell in which he would sleep and was told to undress. The far-travelled one immediately did so and was next led by the priest towards the bath buildings where he would be purified. For an hour, Victorinus left him there, keeping watch outside, until Silvanus could almost not breathe from the steam; it pulled into his lungs and his eyes became sore. Then, just as it was about to overwhelm him, the elderly priest opened the door and signalled for him to leave. A temple slave offered him drinking water, scraped and dried his back and a gown was thrown around him for it was cold and autumn was turning slowly into winter.

He had thought that perhaps he was the only pilgrim to come that night. But, as he moved back towards his room, Silvanus, still gasping from the vapours, was to be surprised. For there, in the corridor, he brushed past a naked man who was being led to the baths and whom, despite the dim lighting, he recognised as his cousin Senicianus. Silvanus was made uneasy by this accidental encounter. Senicianus belonged to a collateral branch of the Atrebates who were characterised by their adherence to Christianity. Indeed, Senicianus' grandmother was a certain Iamcilla who had been put to death for her faith when that religion had still been illegal; while, with the exception of his grandfather Publianus, most of Silvanus' immediate relatives were staunch pagans. And he was glad that his cousin had not noticed him as he had walked past. For that bore – Senicianus was certainly not among his favourite relations – would be in a desperate state if he had come here, betraying the Christ child.

Inside the cell he was made to kneel and whisper the five or six sentences that explained his visit, the word 'wife' being repeated again and again. And Victorinus, without meeting his eyes, nodded and when the words were finished stroked the pilgrim's cheek. The interpreter then lit incense and walked out of the room while Silvanus made himself as comfortable as possible on the wooden planks that formed the bed. And the long day and the soothing bath had tired him so his eyelids were already drooping when the interpreter returned with a box. Victorinus gently slapped his charge and brought him back to a sitting position where he was given a small cup of bitter nard to drink – within it there were also the herbs that helped dreaming. Then the ancient one opened the box where a living bat had been pinioned to two sticks; and, as Silvanus watched, the priest removed the animal's eyes with a nail and placed these one by one into the face of a wax dog that stood next to the bed. Silvanus was also told of a spell that he could work at home: his wife must drink goat's urine, it could be mixed gradually into wine and she would not notice. The priest had, too, a tick that had fed on the blood of a black bull; that blood rubbed on his wife's stomach would certainly help; though it was a strong remedy, for she would find all repulsive, would not wish to lie down even with him afterwards.

But Silvanus was no longer listening. His eyes were closing: there had also been a sleeping draught in the bitter drink. And he only heard the words in waves: drenching, pleasant waves that came towards him. He saw the interpreter's face smiling and felt Victorinus lift his hand and admire the golden ring of Venus, then gently remove it and place it under the wax dog. And now his eyes had closed completely, and, as if from a great height, an ox hide had been laid out on top of him to help him with the dreaming – an old druidic trick. And then he was sliding into the waters of sleep ... And he knew that, apart from his dreams, the next thing would be Victorinus waking him in the sunlight to interpret the omens sent by Nodens and advise him on how to resolve the unbearable situation in which he had found himself in the last months.

And so it should have been . . . At midnight, the heavy gates were shut with a great bang; and this bang did not wake Silvanus. And the putting-out of the lights in the corridor as the priests retired also had no effect on the sleeper. But as one and then two more hours passed the oil lamp that had been left by his bed illuminated a face surprised and then pained: whatever the dream was that Nodens had sent, it was a terrible one. And afterwards, not more than two hours before dawn, long before he should have done so, he sat bolt upright in bed, the sweat pouring from his face and his eyes jammed open. By some great good fortune he did not scream, but, as if he was aware of the possibility, he reached his hand up and covered his mouth.

It was his fifth visit and he knew that this was not supposed to happen. He was supposed to wake in the morning and sit to find kind Victorinus before him, kind Victorinus who would ask him of the images of his dream. And they would discourse on how mating dogs meant war, how crucifixion was a sign of good fortune . . . But already, moments after waking, the nightmares he had seen were fading away to nothing. He knew only that in the dream he had woken from he had been walking in the dark and then above him he had heard the wild hunt passing through the sky. There had been the hounds and guards of Nodens screaming above and he had run and run until he had fallen on the heath. And then Nodens himself had come, standing over him. He had not seen the god – for who would gaze on divinity? – but he had heard his thunderous voice: there was danger, it said, the pollution of the holy places had begun.

He was not sure if such a dream could be said to be from Nodens, for he had awoken early and they said that the truest dreams came only in the morning when the lamps were flickering. Yet he knew from the small window cut in stone above that it was night and the oil lamp by his bed, which had half melted the wax dog with the bats' eyes, was burning strongly. He sighed. Indeed, he was about to lie down and attempt to call up the god again; when through the doorway he saw a light float silently by in the corridor. The appearance was ghostly, but he had also seen flashes of flesh; it was not a priest but another dreamer in the temple who had also awoken, for only the dreamers were nude. His cousin Senicianus perhaps? Silvanus did not shout out: something told him that that would be foolish. Instead, he reached for his wife's ring and slipped it protectively onto his fingers. Then he stood and, wrapping a cloak around him, passed into the corridor with the warm lamp, shielded in his hands.

He walked down this corridor until he heard the gentle growling of the temple dogs and saw, about twenty yards further on, the light of the other pilgrim. He was not able to see the one he followed now. But from the unsteadiness of the flame, moving up and down, he understood that the man was carrying out an operation of some kind. Then the slapping jaws of the dogs and their gulping explained it to him: they were being fed. Not a second too late Silvanus blew out his lamp. And he saw the figure in front, traced in the dark by the unsteady flame, walk some steps back towards him and ask quietly: 'Someone there?' There was no mistaking the voice: it was certainly Senicianus. But though there was no reason to remain silent, his mouth did not want to work. Perhaps it was that he hated embarrassing his cousin. But, as he stood, his heartbeat thudding in his ears, he realised that it was not that. He felt, instead, in danger, he felt in terrible danger. And when the light ahead of him passed into the inner sanctum he did not immediately follow.

For almost a minute, he waited in the dark considering what he should do. He should wake the priests, should return to his cell, go and confront his cousin ... But it was only when he realised what his cousin was doing that he moved. Of course, the righteous fool had lost his nerve, had woken and had decided that he should depart. And then it all made sense. That had been Silvanus' dream. The voice from the Wild Hunt had told him that the temple was being polluted and so it had been, for Nodens clearly objected to a Christian sleeping within his walls. Very probably it had been the god himself who had shaken Senicianus awake and had told him to leave. In a moment he would hear the great door open and his cousin escape down the hill. He walked forwards now with a smile on his face. And yet, as he took the steps, thoughts returned to assail him. Wasn't it strange that his cousin had gone nude to the door? Why hadn't he dressed? Then as he came to the main temple the silence perturbed the now fearful man, for before there had been dogs, the dogs that growled and ... Prompted by something under his feet he knelt down and with his hands came quickly to a canine body. The one he touched had died quickly, the poison had been fast-working.

As he was about to stand a long creak sounded from the heavy gate he had entered earlier that night, the gate surrounded by a thousand candles. It would take two men to open or close it: Senicianus was not alone. And sure enough now there came harsh whispers from ten yards further on, where the wooden portal stood. Some, but only some of these whispers belonged to Senicianus. And through the space there came not the timid flames of candles but the angry lights of torches. Silvanus might scream, of course, but then he would be their first victim. Instead, he rolled towards one of the niches – the interior was now half lit by the intruders – and curled up behind a statue. And he, like a fool, had thought that Senicianus had abandoned the faith. Why, Senicianus had been the spy sent within. And his friends? They were all Christians, of course: all of them. There had been many cases in the last months. Purifying the island they called it; for the Christians, once lambs, had turned to lions. Temples attacked at night or even in the day in isolated enough locations. Worshippers and priests beaten, statues smashed. Statues smashed ... He groaned for he, like an imbecile, had secreted himself behind the largest and most tempting. He would certainly be found.

He was about to scrabble for the cells, hoping to hide himself when the mob burst through the door, banishing the shadows with their torches. There were about ten of them; and they were not frightened, had not taken the trouble to mask themselves. And as they looked on the interior of the temple so did Silvanus, for earlier that night the dark had hidden it from him. The lights lit up the great mosaic of the sea god – Nodens in one of his aspects – dolphins and mermen dancing around him. Gold was hanging from every stone hand and from every lamp-holder. And for a second, the solitary pagan and, despite themselves, the Christians shared in the wonder of the sanctuary: one of the most famous in the west, made all the more impressive by the violence of the torches. But then the terrified Silvanus heard his cousin giving orders to his companions to spread out and bring to the front the priests and pilgrims so that these would see justice done; and he pointed at a statue by the door that they would start with. Axes appeared, another had rope and they began to pray aloud as they turned to the stone monolith, promising, in God's name, to bring the demon trapped within to destruction.

Silvanus considered the long walk he would have to take to the door and knew that he would never make it: even distracted, the Christians were too many. Was it best to throw himself on his cousin's mercy? But that was lunacy. His cousin hated him and his pagan ways. He remembered a time only a month ago when he had been walking in their home town with his two sons and he had pointed out the little church where the Christians went. He had meant nothing by it, but those outside, knowing him, had roared insults; there had been Senicianus among them. Another time they had happened to be invited to the same meal and had argued. It had all started with the ring of Venus he had on his finger, Senicianus saying that it represented an inexcusable evil. And, of course, Silvanus was the only one who knew who his cousin was, the only one who might incriminate him. He would not be allowed to leave the temple alive if he fell into their hands.

'Bring down the fire from the skies, Lord! Bring down the fire from the skies!' There was no lightning, but the statue in the corner toppled over with a sickening crunch, the mosaic below it splintering under the half-ton of stone. And, as the statue rocked on the floor, half-naked and naked men were driven from back where the sleeping quarters were. A guard had been knocked down, said one of the Christian avengers; and the others shouted their triumphs for they had kicked a devil-worshipper, or set alight a tapestry of water demons in the corridor; while the unclean dogs – they pointed to the corpses of the hounds – were slain. Then, finally, the old priest Victorinus, the Interpreter of Dreams, was dragged into the confusion. He had not known to read the signs his god had sent him and was thrown over the upturned statue that one man had begun to attack with a blade; the stone head rolled off its stone neck and was lifted and thrown against an altar. Then Senicianus picked up the diminutive interpreter and carried him towards the shadows, where he would be made to answer properly for his sins.

But as these attacks worsened and the rage of the attackers increased, interspersed with whoops of joy and cries of 'the Anointed One', Silvanus saw his first and what might be his only chance to escape. A Christian who had dragged out the only other pilgrim in residence that night had become over-enthusiastic in his attacks, knocking the glassy-eyed man – still drugged from the drink he had taken to sleep – against the wall, punching him and kicking him repeatedly. But better to carry out this act of vengeance he had had to drop his torch, which rolled only a foot from where Silvanus was crouched. Hardly breathing, Silvanus stretched out his fingers and took the torch and, standing, he started to move towards the over-turned statue still being assaulted on the floor. He could feel his hands sticky with nervous sweat on the torch as he moved; but he took care to walk normally, he must show that he had no fear, that he was one of them as he stepped over the bodies of the dead dogs lying around.

For a moment it seemed that he would do it. He stared one of the other Christians in the face as he passed and only a flicker of confusion came over that marauder. He yelled at the entrance as if there was a sacrilegious object there and kicked stupidly at a stone pedestal. Then, coming towards the gate, he bellowed insults about the heathen and felt the night air beyond. But between him and freedom, in the half-open gateway, a man was bending over a heap of cloth. Silvanus watched with horror as this figure span around and he recognised Senicianus with a bloodied knife in his hand and below him the body of the interpreter Victorinus. His cousin was evidently sickened by what he had done, yet perhaps also exhilarated, was certainly distracted and took a moment to realise who was before him. The two stared: Silvanus considering his chances of escape and life, Senicianus trying to come to terms with the presence of one known from his home.

Silvanus acted first, while the dagger was still bent down, and charged at his cousin hoping to barge his way past him. But he was pushed sideways and fell into a corner. Almost as soon as he was on the floor he begged for mercy, but Senicianus either did not hear him or did not care and dived onto Silvanus' back. For a second they wrestled uselessly and then the knife came towards his throat, still dripping with Victorinus' blood, while their hands tore at each other. Silvanus felt a light wound close to the top of his chest and then a smash on the side of his head. One of the other Christians had arrived and was pounding something stone against him; it was the same man who had dropped the torch that had allowed Silvanus to attempt an escape. Then he heard that Senicianus was screaming about the ring, the ring of Venus on his hands: it was a defiled object and should be destroyed or cleansed. He was going to chop the man's fingers off to ...

But at that moment there was a crash like thunder, a crash that made the floor beneath them shudder and a terrible scream, a scream of death. The Christians began to shout among themselves. Silvanus could not understand their fear – but a wind blew through the open temple as if Nodens himself was re-entering and reclaiming it. And, as he tried to lift himself up and push his cousin from him, a blow from the side made contact with his skull and Silvanus slumped unconscious to the floor. He remembered only his fist tightening to protect the token of his wife's love: if he had lost her, he would not lose it.

The locals arrived only at dawn. It would have been foolish to come in the night, for no one had known how many Christians there were ... In the early morning light though they ran up towards the temple where smoke was billowing, rejoicing when they learnt that the damage was not as bad as they had feared. The burning came from heaped temple robes and only two statues had been brought down, one on top of a Christian, now dead beneath it, a sign that Nodens was protecting his temple and a sign that had caused the defilers to flee. The old priest Victorinus – much loved in the area – had been stabbed once, but it had been a leg wound and he was already being nursed in bed by acolytes. A pilgrim moaned in the outer room, his naked body covered with black and blue bruises. And, in the entrance, a man was almost hysterical about a ring and a wife he had lost; they could make nothing of his words and so passed on. The reinforcements from the village persuaded the temple staff not to make a complaint to the Governor, nothing in any case would be done; and then assisted in cleansing the inner rooms of the outrages of the Christians.

<hr>

⚬⚬⚬ Historical Background ⚬⚬⚬

Historians have long argued about the relevance of Christianity in fourth-century Britain. One proof of its likely popularity is the fact that by the early sixth century it was the sole religion of the British Celts. Another proof is that in the later fourth century there were violent, probably Christian-inspired attacks against pagan temples, especially in the Severn region where Lydney Park is to be found. What I call the 'Temple of Dreams' did, in fact, have dreaming cells and an Interpreter of Dreams named Victorinus, recalled on a mosaic inscription: while its god was Nodens, equated with the classical deity Apollo. It used to be believed that the temple was built in the mid–late 360s. In fact, there had probably been a temple of some sort at the site for as much as a century before.

One of the names associated with Lydney Park was a certain Silvanus who, on a tablet, cursed an associate named Senicianus who had stolen a golden ring of his. Just such a ring – the Vyne Ring that sometimes has been said to be the inspiration for Tolkien's fictional ring (see end notes) – was found at Silchester with a Christian-style inscription recording one Senicianus. It has often been suggested that, given the date and the relative rarity of the name Senicianus, the ring mentioned and the ring found were one and the same. That, in any case, was the starting point for the story recounted above.

Instability within Britain may have been one of the factors in bringing the province to ruin. But, as we will see in the next chapter, there were also external threats, perhaps in Britannia more than any other of the western provinces.

CHAPTER FOURTEEN

The Barbarian Conspiracy, 367 AD

Gratian, grandson of Silvius, ambassador for the Empire

Silvanus' eldest child, my brother Gratian, was not so fortunate as his father in escaping unwelcome death. He was born in a period when the carrion birds had started to circle in the sky above his home – they remain there to this day – and was sent, while still young, beyond even the Severn, to pacify the worst of these, the Scotti barbarians in the west …

Gratian Atrebates rode along the western road with a certain wariness. It was not the towns with their locked gates and fearful guards that had unnerved him. It was not the empty labourers' huts and the occasional glimpse of terrified citizens, running through trees away from his ten-strong armed escort. It was not even the towers of smoke rising from the broad valley of the Sabrina [Severn]: barbarian raiders were, after all, only barbarians, never mind what colour they painted themselves or how long they grew their hair. No, it was rather the words of Commander Fullofaudes, the words he had used when their long interview had concluded and Gratian's mission had been fully set out. 'You are a fine patriot aren't you. You revere Rome, I know. But you love your Woody City and this island of yours?' Gratian had nodded passionately and had begun to talk of a great-great-grandfather. Yet the commander, who masterminded intelligence in Britain, was having none of it and held up his hand: he was used to this kind of nonsense from the Britons. 'If you achieve your mission there will be great things for you here.' He signalled at the palace around him, one of the last in Londinium to retain its marble lustre from the golden days. 'But if you come back from that pirate scum without a deal or, worse still, lose the booty on your travels', he pointed now to a heavy sack lying between them, 'then there is an interesting post on the Red Sea that I'll be putting you in for.' The young and ambitious Gratian trembled at the thought. He would do anything to avoid Arabia and thirty years among the fish-eaters and troglodytes of the Indian Ocean, with occasional hunting trips out into a sandstorm for diversion.

Of course, so far it had all been quite simple. There had been the normal array of angry refugees, asking what Rome did with its taxes if they let the enemy enter in this fashion: where were the guards, where were the legionaries? Gratian could have answered that they had urgent business on the Continent, that the Danube frontier was ready to snap again and that the Empire was tottering on the edge of yet another civil war. But it was no good lecturing commoners on Imperial affairs – the high-stepping gods do not attend to the dogs that bark at their feet. And so he pushed through the rabble, hustling his concerned escort forwards with terse instructions, ignoring the shouts about the Scotti, the name that the simple Romans gave to the raiders from Ireland. On the western coast of Britain – and they were less than ten miles from the sea there – the very word was enough to send matrons into a death swoon, for they were the worst kind of savages. Their only clothes were the wild beards that covered their chins and cheeks while, on their foreheads stood the devil's mark, tattoos of horrible whirling lines indicating their prowess and the number of murders that they had committed. And, somewhere in the cloak of smoke and ruin before them, there was a small army of these Scotti. True, they were split into their packs for what they called 'wolving', but dangerous nevertheless, even to a man riding with armed troops. It was them Gratian had been instructed to reach.

As the small party came towards where the road entered the wide, shallow valley of the Sabrina, they had their first sight of the casualties of war. It was a medium-sized villa; or rather it had been a medium-sized villa. The Scotti had set it on fire. Straw had been dragged inside and lit on the mosaic-laid floors, calcined and blackened now. And most of the walls had already caved in under the heat that had been created there. From the top of the well in the courtyard protruded the body of a cow, while an old man wearing the colours of an equestrian had been run through on the grass lawn that stretched down to an orchard. A more efficient band of robbers – a group of British ruffians, for example – would have just got the valuables and perhaps some likely-looking captives for slaves and then run. But the Irish were different: their attacks always started and ended with the furious annihilation of persons and property.

The party trotted down into what had once been a garden with its nymphaeum, their horses flinching from the heat wafting out of the still-blazing house. Gratian was about to scream at them to continue their ride towards the river, where the Scotti would certainly be heading, when a small, echoing shout reached them. It was a cry for help in Latin, a child's cry. The men rode confused around the garden until these shouts led them to the well. As Gratian protested, their mission required speed, they hauled out the cow that had been jammed into the well's neck and the calls became louder and more distinct. It was a young girl, a little girl trapped somewhere below. It was a typical Scotti tactic. They would have thrown the bodies of the old and the young down; for they would have been little good as slaves in the markets across the ocean, though usually they, at least, had the courtesy to slit the throats of those they discarded in this fashion. One of the men suggested lowering a torch. But Gratian could imagine the jumble of limbs; for it was there that most of the owner's family would have ended. His orders were clear, they came from his seniors: 'No, we must ride on! There will be slaves hiding out there', he gestured at the wooded slope. 'They will save her. If not the parties from the town.' None of the men answered and he had not really convinced himself. But much depended on their mission. The very fact that the child was still alive meant that the raiders were near. His men could hardly have failed to understand that.

For three hours they followed the muddy prints and the signs of fire back to where the boats had been left. There, before them, were the large uncovered footprints of the raiders, hardened by decades of running through the heaths of Ireland, and there were also the sandal marks and hobnailed bootprints of those the Scotti warriors had captured. The disposition of the prints showed that these Britons were being herded like animals towards the place where the Gaels had come ashore. After four miles of following the river path, more footprints joined this pack. The Scotti divided once inland and the raiding parties, having picked over the landscape on their own, were now evidently coming back together. The escort looked at each other nervously and most of all at Gratian. They could hope to take on eight or nine of the Gaels, but not a full contingent. However, the Roman slapped his horse and cantered on and his fellow-riders continued in silence until they could see, in the hazy distance, the disembarkation point.

Even from afar it was possible to distinguish between twenty and thirty of the Irish curraghs – the leather-sewn skin boats that they used for their raiding and that could hold as many as a dozen men. They had sailed into the estuary and these rafts had been left there with a substantial party of guards. There was a large crowd of slaves. And there were the marauders back from their raids, sat around fires where meat was being cooked – the boat guards had indulged in some sheep-rustling while waiting. The escort groaned. They were outnumbered fifteen to one. It was hopeless. If they had caught the party before it had got back to the boats then just possibly . . . But now there was nothing to do, except go home and leave those who had been taken to their fate.

The riders pulled hard at their reins, but Gratian turned on them angrily. 'I didn't tell you to stop!' He carried on moving towards the mass of figures. Among the enemy, the warriors had by now noticed the Roman presence and some started to their feet, throwing off furs and reaching for spears. Gratian continued at a trot, silently damning the men by his side for holding back. The Irish could smell fear. He knew that much. The raiders were now forming up, some keeping by the boats to guard their catch. And Gratian tensed. What if it were all a mistake? Could he trust to the horses and the men, never mind Commander Fullofaudes' information: Fullofaudes had never cared for his family? He knew only that the worst thing he could do was to slow down.

A sharp intake of breath from a rider on his left signalled a spear sailing through the air towards them. It fell far short in the turf. And walking out from the pack, as if to retrieve it, came a large Irish man, covered in dirt from his day's adventuring with copious, embarrassing quantities of body hair. Gratian whispered a sharp 'halt' and then waited. The man continued to walk, staring at the Romans and clapped his hands once. It was the sign. Now, Gratian thought, they were at the mercy of the gods. He turned to his second-in-command: 'You are to ride back and tell them that contact has been made.' The man looked confused. 'Repeat the message!' The man did so and Gratian dismounted saying, almost as an afterthought, that the horse were to go with them and walked forwards with the sack that had been entrusted to him. He did not bid the party farewell and no sound came from their mouths. Instead, he repeated to himself, as he moved closer, the lucky words: 'You will go, you will come back, you will not die', over and over, as if his life depended upon it.

The tall man had his hand on the spear, but had still not wrenched it from the earth. And he waited till the Roman came side by side, then spoke in a perfect Latin that totally belied his appearance: 'I was worried that you would not get here on time.' Gratian, at first, was lost for words and shuffled uneasily. 'Will they not suspect that you are one of the *arcani* [spies] if we speak here?' The man laughed. 'They know I have dealings with the Romans. And, like all the barbarians, they admire it. You'll see. I told them that I served in the army in years gone by.' Beneath the blooded, dirt-blackened, tattooed face the man showed about fifty years. 'And how is it that you speak Irish?' The rejoinder was sharp, the spy angrily upbraiding the newcomer: 'And who are you, my commander?' Then he relented: 'I grew up in Dumnonia [Devon and Cornwall]. My father was a Gael who settled there – he followed my mother across the border, as they say. Now, come on we have no time to waste. They will be pushing the boats into the water soon.'

The two men strode across the middle ground; and, as they came into hailing distance of the raiders, all leers and taunting faces, Gratian had to resist a strong temptation to look behind, where he thought that the horse might still be waiting. But, before they had covered many more feet, the Scotti warriors took up all his attention, hissing and growling. Then, as he reached the centre of their circle – and he was carrying several lifetimes of silver in his bag, with nothing to stop them from taking it – an elder walked towards him speaking the Irish tongue with rapid, aggressive jabs. He looked at Gratian, staring into the equestrian's eyes, then threw a fur wrap aside exposing, in this way, his left nipple.

The spy spoke: 'Get down and suck it!' 'What?' 'You heard me. Suck the nipple, otherwise you are quite dead and perhaps so am I. It is their sign of friendship, in this way the chief becomes your Mother and no one will harm you.' Gratian had heard much of the Gaels' barbarity over the years, but this he had never come across. Yet, obedient to the instructions from his guide, he bent down and touched the man's nipple with his lips. 'Don't come up too quickly!', came a warning snarl in Latin. 'They think it is offensive, but don't overdo it either. Very well that's enough.' Gratian's face, drained white, emerged from off the chieftain's dirty chest. The ancient Gael pulled him in with his lurid, white arms, hugged him and spoke some words. 'He says that now he has a Roman son.' 'Very nice, I am sure', replied Gratian, looking at his new extended family. But the Gaels, who had greeted Gratian with such hostility, and had watched the ceremony with only passing interest, were now bored and turned back to their work, which included hauling booty onto their boats and kicking at the captives.

Gratian was pushed by the *arcanus* to one of the curraghs. The two men clambered inside, over a bronze sculpture of Mercury and a beautiful gilded cross. 'How will they fit all those', Gratian gestured at the captives, 'into these things?' The *arcanus* stole a look at the Roman: 'They won't.' Already from the crowd of prisoners were screams. The Scotti were wading in, pulling some from the group. And by instinct the unfortunates had guessed what was happening. 'They'll leave those who would earn less in the markets: Roman slaves are so common now that they barely fetch a cow on the other side.' Gratian tried to acknowledge this comment nonchalantly, but did not manage it. 'There are worse ends, you know. If these were Saxons, the sort that raid in the Cornerland [Kent] and in the Fenlands, then you can imagine what would happen . . .'. Gratian knew: before being loaded onto the boats, captives were forced to draw lots and the unlucky ones were sacrificed to the blood-hungry Teuton gods, crucified on the beach, their innards tipping out of their stomachs. 'These poor souls will be dispatched like chickens. Perhaps they're the lucky ones. Look at him.' The *arcanus* pointed at a delicate adolescent who was being walked over. 'Fifteen, sixteen, villa owner's son. You can see it from a good mile away. Never lifted a spade. Never sweated work. Can read and write Latin. Can speak it like a Roman lawyer. And what's his destiny? He'll spend the next fifty years on one of the hills of the Holy Island [Ireland] watching sheep. Remember him when you hear the screams.' The more valuable Britons were now reaching the boats and that very boy was lifted into the seat next to Gratian. Then, from further up the hill, came a dreadful pitched begging. The boy closed his eyes.

Gratian had been told that it would be a difficult crossing and that he should, on no account, let go of the gift that Commander Fullofaudes had given him, especially not when he were to fall asleep. But the Roman looked at the boats around him and smelt the foul stench of the raiders and the fear of the prisoners. Many things might happen in the next days, but it was highly unlikely that he would sleep during the crossing. Not that he didn't wish to be away from it all. The boy, who called himself Patricius, was asking him why the mounted soldiers had not saved them and why Gratian, from his dress a Briton of good birth, was speaking with the enemy: questions that Gratian found uncomfortable – he had a boy of his own at home. He tried to answer, but his words seemed forced even to his own ears. And he was relieved when one of the raiders gave this brat a clattering face-slap to shut him up.

Gratian did not, as he had guessed, sleep that afternoon or that night. But by dawn, as Ireland loomed towards them across the waves, he nodded off and was oblivious to the other leather coracles, peeling away from the vessel in which he snored, heading to their own coast-lines and beaches. The boy Patricius was moved, whimpering, onto one of these other curraghs by the raiders, pulling at the cloak of the sleeping Gratian. But the Roman continued to doze until almost midday, when the sun started to break through the Hibernian clouds, teasing his closed eyes. And, when he finally awoke, he was confused to see that the boat was alone, rushing through the water – Ireland off to their left. Only five men remained in the vessel and, in their midst, the Roman was, at least, pleased to see the *arcanus* sitting opposite him and his 'Mother', the guarantor of his safety, by his side. 'Where are we going?', he managed sleepily. 'To the Home of the Sun. It is in the north.' Gratian nodded and said nothing, as the chieftain whose nipple he had attached himself to the night before caressed his new son's cheek.

The young Briton had been told by Commander Fullofaudes that the missions to the south of Ireland were the best. The south had a veneer of civilisation. But to go to the north, where the meeting had been arranged, was more dangerous. It was there that the Attacotti lived – the worst of the Irish. The ones who ate human flesh and who . . . He blinked and tried not to think of it. It was bad enough that his Mother's arm sagged around his neck, half-closing his windpipe.

For three more hours, they travelled up the green coast. And then, suddenly, quite unexpectedly, they veered inland, not towards the pebbly shore, but into the headwaters of a small estuary, riding angry waves. Even the chieftain took one of the paddles and the sail was dragged down as they moved towards landfall and a collection of fifty or so rocks by the side of the sea-bound river. Then, at a shout from the front of the boat, and to the surprise of Gratian, these 'rocks' started to move out of the fog. The spy noted, in an offhand manner, that this was their escort – the faces of warriors were now becoming visible through the mist – and that, at all costs, Gratian was to remember his instructions.

Whatever happened he was not to stray from the group: as he had no Irish blood in him, he would be killed or enslaved if he ever left the sight of his Mother. Gratian said he understood. The spy continued. He would also have to pay for his passage through the various kingdoms to the rulers of the territory: Gratian nodded again. And, added the spy, he was to honour their gods whenever possible. He would also be wise to make no reference to Christians, a veritable plague among the captives from Britain, and a religion that the Irish chieftains despised. Gratian assured him that he was not of that religion – or that he was only for purposes of promotion. Well, said the spy, showing his nerves for the first time, it would be wise for Gratian not to mention any of the Roman gods either. Once more, Gratian nodded. Then, as they were coming to shore, a question: did he understand the Gaelic tongue? Gratian confessed that he understood a few words, as it was a cousin of the British-Celtic spoken in his home town. The spy nodded and then spoke for the last time – by now men were wading out to pull the boat in. If Gratian were to understand references to killing he was not to worry, the Gaels talked a lot; while he stayed within reach of his Mother, he would be safe.

They walked for two days through that ragged, terrible island, a trip that Gratian would never forget. The Irish countryside was not unlike that which he had seen in parts of Cambria: forested hills and endless, soggy river valleys. But in Britain, even in the wildest parts, the clan chiefs and respected members of the old tribes lived in villas or on the best farms. And, while there were rumours that, in the west, some still indulged in old customs – a sacrifice of a man here, an illegal cattle raid there – this was nothing more than rumour. And, yet, here it was all horribly real. There were no settlements other than the large circular forts that the Gaels called 'raths': with body parts hanging from entrances; with cows, stolen in a recent attack against neighbours, masticating on mean clumps of grass. And, as they passed through one valley or plain or across some wooded hillside, they would stop first and justify their presence, showing that they had permission from one of the more important kings in the region or, simply, that they were on the big king's business. At this point Gratian would be expected to reach into the large purse, which Commander Fullofaudes had provided for this purpose, and shake a few silver coins out. And then off they would go, till the next village swarmed out from one of the fortified strongholds to meet them.

By dusk, when they settled down for the night in one of these hellish and unsanitary places, they had travelled little more than ten miles. In Britain a man in a hurry could cover, with the right documentation, on a pristine Roman road, the same in a third or a quarter of that time. Here, though, there was no documentation, except a strange, slashed code that was cut onto sticks and, as to roads, Gratian glanced bitterly at the muddied track that they had travelled along. Then, before he plunged into the depths of the fortified hamlet, he looked around to make sure that he was still within easy distance of his Mother. And, there, in the twilight, he saw something that made him uneasy. Two men were walking, not towards the settlement, but away from it. He blinked in the dusk. They caught his attention because they did not wear rags and furs like the other Irishmen he had seen. They had, instead, leather cuirasses and their blond hair was caught up in pigtails. He smiled to himself. They could almost be Saxons, for occasionally he had seen members of that race in the coliseum or the slave markets. A frightening, terrible people. But that was absurd. In Ireland, on the loose, Saxons ... And then one of the figures, hurrying into the night, turned back towards the place where the Roman stood and, for just one moment, just one moment before

Gratian was pulled away by the village chief, he saw what it was impossible to mistake. The hair had been shaved back from the forehead and the sides of the head to give the impression that the face was much larger than it really was and the pasty-white skin was clean of tattoos. There was no doubt. He had just seen a Saxon. But what was a Saxon doing in Ireland?

On the second morning, the vision of the night before was obscured by the tedium and fear of their journey: the pattern of village and tax toll bitterly repeating itself. Now they were farther from the shore the natives found the clothes of the Roman all the more curious and mockable and the tariff to allow the man and his bodyguard to pass through rose. Then, towards midday, the *arcanus* dropped back from the front of the column to where Gratian walked with his Mother, the elder chieftain. 'We are approaching. Remember that this is a holy place.' Almost as soon as the words were out of the spy's mouth Gratian made the slight rise and was confronted by a field, well within view, full of fires and warriors – he estimated between fifteen hundred and two thousand men. And there, most extraordinary in the centre of the field, a massive, circular construction twenty or thirty feet high round the perimeter. It was man-made: he had no doubt about that, one of the temples of the Irish. 'The Home of the Sun' [Newgrange], whispered the spy who was walking alongside. 'Remember Dagda. That is the god you must thank.'

The escort, who had made the journey inland, started to disperse into the crowd, greeting old friends and shouting insults at rivals. And Gratian, who had longed to be away from these men for most of the previous hours, found himself suddenly alone and vulnerable in the midst of the enemy. His Mother, at least, took his hand, stroking his short Roman hair, as if to indicate to those around that the new-comer belonged, while the spy had other things to do and, after warning him again to thank Dagda, pushed his way into the mob. However, if the villagers had made a fuss of Gratian as he had travelled across country, the warriors were strangely indifferent to him. Some glanced over his clean-shaven face and, trained for treasure hunting, looked with professional interest at the sack he was carrying. But it was clear that they had seen Romans before. Most of them had, certainly, raided Imperial territory and thrown their share of citizens down wells or hassled terrified villa owners towards the boats.

As they had been striding across the field, the huge, circular temple had been coming closer and closer, rising before them, threatening to dwarf them – the walls of rocks and turf were four times the Briton's size. He had been struck before by its grandeur. But now something else impressed Gratian: its power. And the Gaels who had gathered around understood this and even appreciated it, pushing him slowly to his knees. The words of Commander Fullofaudes came back to him, words given only ten days before in that meeting that had promised to change or perhaps end his life: 'Others who have been to the Home of the Sun tell me that you must bury treasure at its confines.' Gratian scratched at the ground, as these words returned, earnestly scraping the hard soil away. Again, the Gaels seemed to understand what he was doing and some helped him, using their feet to remove the clay. Then, as carefully as he could, he took out the remaining coins from his now almost empty purse and placed them gently into the earth. After, he tried to pray for a moment – perhaps it was also a cry for help to the spirits of the place. But the Irish did not understand his meditation and, upset by an interruption in the ceremony, called out and used hands and feet to push the soil back over the coins, so, in only a matter of moments, the hole was no more and the fragments of precious metal were covered.

Gratian stood up, relieved that the first of his tasks was done. But he was taken aback to see that, off to his side, another man was going through the same motions he had completed moments before. At first, he mistook the digger for a Gael; he was certainly a barbarian. But, after a second's examination, Gratian who had been in the north of Britain earlier in his career, recognised, with shock, a Pict – a Pict who, at least according to the bull tattoos across his shoulder, was a member of royalty, while, from his neck, swung the twisting wave of silver that only the most senior of the Caledonian families carried. What on earth was a Pict doing among the Irish? It was well known that the two peoples loathed each other. And, yet, here there was a man on a diplomatic mission, just like himself. First, the Saxons and now the Picts in Ireland: Gratian gawped.

The Gaels, who had been preoccupied with making sure that Gratian dug a proper pit to honour the sun god Dagda, had left the Roman for a moment. But, seeing his expression of surprise, hands reached out for Gratian's shoulders and warriors intervened like a carefully pulled curtain between him and the Pict. Immediately the man whom Gratian had not been supposed to see vanished from view and the Roman found himself, instead, being propelled through the crowd towards the king: the word was muttered by several of those around. Gratian continued to struggle to look behind. But after only ten yards something else distracted him. He had been jerked forwards to a child-sized mound not of earth, but of Roman coins and treasures. And there, inspecting it, stood the man whom Gratian was to greet as monarch: a surprisingly small Gael with bushed, savage eyebrows, covered in a purple cloak, an insane parody of those the Roman emperors wore, with a golden torque around his neck. The royal one had seen Gratian. But he took a little longer to pick at the piles of valuables before him, brought to him by his warriors from all over the coasts of Britain, for the raiders had been busy in recent weeks.

And then, satisfied that he had seen enough, he lifted up his face and stared in a way evidently meant to chill the Roman's very heart, Gratian finding it a simple matter to oblige him. 'I am Niall. My ancestors fought at the Alps themselves, Roman!' Gratian had heard of the boastfulness of the Gaels and meekly nodded as the *arcanus*, who had reappeared, translated. 'Now, what message from the king of the Romans?' Well, it was only Commander Fullofaudes, Chief of Intelligence, but it seemed to Gratian that a little majesty might not go amiss. 'Oh Great and Fearful Master of the West, the Emperor, I mean the king of the Romans asks you that you call off the raids again for this year. For this reason, I have been sent here to the Home of the Sun', he gestured at the house of Dagda behind him, 'and also to offer you certain wonderful treasures so that your men may stay in their own land.'

He took the sack and silver cascaded out, carefully hacked from plates and altarpieces and measured exactly into pounds. The Gael king looked at the silver in a bored fashion. It would be a substantial, but hardly a defining contribution to the heap before him, and he spoke back to Gratian, waving at the translating spy. 'His Majesty the Gael king says that he will earn something like that in one lucky raid on Britain. Why should he give up fifty raids when the Roman king offers him only these baubles?' Gratian was not to talk of the British navy, which had been something of a failure in recent campaigns; nor were there any shore forts on the western coast to protect the lands; nor, indeed, was he to hint at an invasion of Ireland – that had long since been given up by the powers that be. However, there was something else he could give, and this, Fullofaudes and the Governor had hoped, would be decisive.

'But the king of the Romans offers another treasure, Great One. He has decided, in His munificence, to allow the Irish tribes to continue to settle in the parts of Cambria nearest the sea. And he has agreed that settlement be no longer restricted to the Peninsula of the Men of Leinster [Lleyn Peninsula], but also opened up to certain territories in the south.' The Gael king listened with polite interest as these promises were made. But he did not trouble to disguise his thoughts: the king of the Romans was certainly in desperate straits if he was giving up his lands in Britain – all that they had heard about the wars on the Continent must be true. This expression worried Gratian, who decided that now was the time gently, imperceptibly to threaten: 'If the Gaels promise no more raids this year then our Leader will not drive the settlers out, as is certainly in His power to do.' The king hesitated for a moment, removed some of his dinner from his moustache, and then, as if having made a decision, snapped his fingers at a boy, who gathered together the silver that had been poured out on the grass: 'The king of the Irish will consider this kind offer of his brother the Roman king. And, while he is considering it, he will instruct all attacks to cease.' Gratian bowed low. It had worked. He would be rewarded for this far beyond what was normal for his years. He saw himself a magistrate or even seated at the Council of Britain in a decade's time. Nothing would, nothing could stop his ascent. 'And now we will prepare your escort to take you back to Britain so you can give your news.'

It was all over. Gratian had been spared the unwelcome responsibility of feasting with the Irish monarch, this terrifying five minutes of interview had been enough. And, the best of it was that the Gaels must now guarantee his safety to be sure that the message would return to Britain. He could, of course, have warned the Irish monarch that the Roman Emperor would be most displeased to learn that the Gael was in contact with other enemies of Rome. Gratian had, after all, seen the Pict and the two Saxons. But an instinct for self-preservation told him that this was not in his best interests; though, of course, he would be sure to include it in the report written back in the comfort of his villa. And so it was that, smiling, already dreaming of his office in the palace in Londinium, he was led by the *arcanus* away from the field and its haunted walls to where his Mother and a much reduced escort were waiting. They climbed onto the slopes and, as they were coming to the hilltop, he stared one more time at that strange temple. And, maybe it was a trick of the dying sun, but next to the glinting pile of treasure he glimpsed the Irish king, who stood speaking to a couple of men, one with yellow hair such as the Saxons have and the other with a silver necklace like those that the Pictish nobles wear. Gratian shielded his eyes to get a better look, but felt the *arcanus* pulling at his arm, pulling him away from Dagda's House.

The next days bewildered Gratian, who only ever had an imprecise, though not unhappy memory of them. Whereas they had taken two days to reach the Irish king, they took ten to return to the sea. Of course, excuses were given: a religious festival, the danger of heavy rain when it did no more than drizzle, the chance to meet a fellow countryman – Gratian was dragged fifteen miles out of his way to be introduced to an itinerant Roman eye doctor and a party of merchants, who had bravely come inland to sell their wares. At other times they did walk, but always in the wrong direction, no closer to the sea. Sometimes going south, sometimes north. And, at the end of one day, when the rest of his party were asleep, Gratian climbed a slope and was shocked to see the Home of the Sun, the Temple of Dagda below him, now bereft of its treasure pile and warriors.

At first, he was made uneasy by this obvious deception. But then, he concluded, quite naturally, that his Mother did not want to lose his company, wanted even to show him something further of Ireland before giving him up to Britain. Certainly, it was the chief who now paid for the right of passage between the different kingdoms. And there were, in truth, wonderful moments in those days, moments he would never forget. They spent a night in a rath with one of the famous Irish jugglers. At another settlement, a druid was brought in to see him and talked of the times when the high priests of the Celts had led armies into distant Italy. Gratian felt a sting of melancholy for what was certainly among the last of those ancient philosophers. He visited slave auctions and was tempted to buy back Roman citizens or snap up some muscular Irish brave, who had been caught on the wrong side of the hill when a raid had come to an end. He was even taken to see one of the famous Irish hostels, where travellers could stay for free and where he learnt the joys of roast Irish swine. Then, finally, on the tenth day, he was led to a harbour, where a Roman ship was moored. The captain was informed by the *arcanus* that he would have an extra passenger and there, on the gangway, the Mother fondly took leave of his son, while the *arcanus* clutched the young man's shoulders, telling him to salute the old country. Gratian climbed the

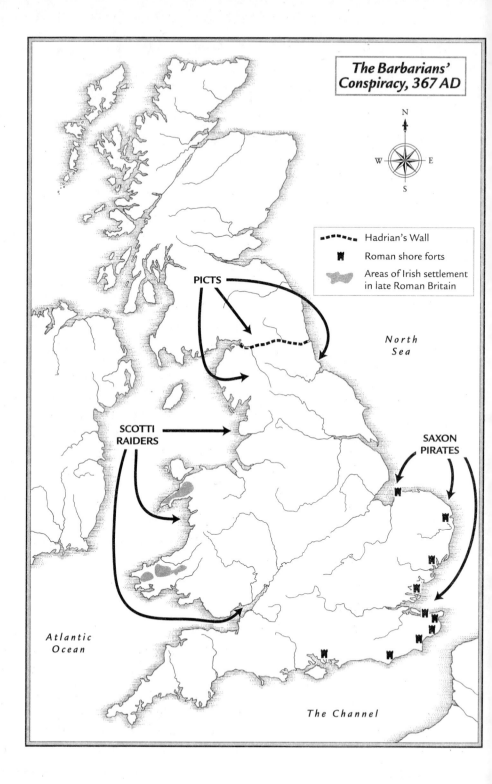

The Barbarians'
Conspiracy, 367 AD

N
W E
S

Hadrian's Wall
Roman shore forts
Areas of Irish settlement
in late Roman Britain

PICTS

North
Sea

SCOTTI
RAIDERS

SAXON
PIRATES

Atlantic
Ocean

The Channel

ship, almost sad to leave the Holy Island behind, and waved at men he considered his friends, and stood there waving until the boat had clipped the twelfth wave.

The *arcanus* watched the boat put out with relief and satisfaction. He, like many of the *arcani*, had sold out to the enemy long ago, for it paid better and the risks were considerably less. And, in many ways, this useless mission had served him well. He had managed to stay away from the fighting and had won a substantial prize of silver from the Irish king, not to mention the promise of his own kingdom on the Boyne. The Roman would soon discover the deception, of course. It had been planned for a year, the joint attack by Picts, Saxons and Gaels on Britannia. And already news was creeping back of remarkable successes. The head of the British coastal defences killed, the Governor trapped under siege in Londinium, the leader of one of the legions mortally wounded and bleeding to death in Eboracum [York]. This fool Gratian would have been killed as well, should have been killed as far as he was concerned. But the Roman had taken the nipple and the Irish respected these archaic practices. Well, that conceited diplomat would soon get what he deserved. If his commander survived Gratian would be put on the first boat to distant Arabia to manage the locals there. The spy looked for one last time at the trader, now urging its way into the sea, and imagined the larger island beyond full of flames and the warrior representatives of the three allied peoples, hurling themselves at dwindling Roman defences.

⁓ Historical Background ⁓

We know from the Roman historian Ammianus Marcellinus that in the year 367 '[the Emperor] Valentinian was appalled to hear that a conspiracy of the barbarians had reduced the provinces of Britain to disastrous straits. Nectaridus, the commander of the coastal parts, had been killed, and

General Fullofaudes surprised and cut down … at that time the Picts …
together with the warlike Attacotti and the Gaels, were wandering around
and causing great devastation.' What scholars normally refer to as 'the
Barbarian Conspiracy' in fact involved the simultaneous attack on Britain
of several different barbarian peoples including the Picts (for which see
Chapter Eight and the notes to that chapter), the Saxons and the Irish or
'Scotti' as they were called. We do not know to what extent these attacks
were co-ordinated, perhaps by roving barbarian ambassadors (as we suggest
here) or, rather, if they were a fortuitous coming together of all the province's
enemies: for an ultra-sceptical view see Philip Bartholomew, 'Fourth-
Century Saxons', *Britannia* 15 (1984), pp. 173–7. The result for Britain was,
in any case, appalling and the invasions worsened, because of the betrayal
of the spies beyond the borders, the *arcani* who assisted the enemies of
Rome. The province seems to have been overrun, while unhappy elements
in the native population were also driven to revolt and it took Rome a
number of months or even years to restore order.

Gratian was a Romano-Briton who came to prominence forty years later
(see the next chapter). Here, he is sent to Ireland at what would have been
the beginning of his career on a mission to the Irish High King from the
government of Britain. It has sometimes been suggested that hoards of
hacksilber (chopped-up silver), such as are known from northern Britain
and Ireland, and that were often weighed out precisely, may have been
'dane-geld' paid by the Roman authorities to keep barbarians away; and
similarly that the late Roman coins buried ritually around the edge of
Newgrange were to appease not only Irish gods, but also Irish warriors.
Patricius, the boy victim of the raids, was the only Briton to be taken into
slavery whose name we know: he was actually the young St Patrick – for
further details see the end notes.

The Barbarian Conspiracy is often described by historians as a fitting
prelude to the final collapse of Roman life in Britain forty years later, and
to other wider disasters in the Empire …

CHAPTER FIFTEEN

The End of Roman Britain, 410 AD

Ambrosius, son of Gratian, a young man of much promise

Gratian, my brother, avoided, by happy fate, a trip to the Red Sea, for Fullofaudes his commander was killed in the invasions of that year, invasions that scarred Britain for a generation. We will recount Gratian's later successes and final failure here. But only briefly, and in connection with the early adventures of my nephew Ambrosius, as little as twenty years ago: at the time of the collapse of the Rhine frontier and the revolt of the British garrisons. The winter of his journey to Italy was the coldest in living memory and blizzards blew down upon him from the mountains around ...

Ambrosius strode, as quickly as his blistered feet would allow him, through the whirling snow, towards where they said the Emperor was waiting. The sight of guards on horseback, just in view, told the exhausted man that he had, finally, arrived. It had taken the Briton eighty long days to reach his destination – twice what it should have if the roads had been properly patrolled or if any semblance of order had existed. But order was already a thing of the past in the ragged remains of the Empire. It was three years since the Rhine frontier had collapsed, and tens of thousands of Germanic barbarians had crossed the frozen river in a single night, avoiding the heavily defended bridges. And, in the months that it had taken Ambrosius to reach the man he would call 'Master', he had seen with his own eyes just how far the western provinces had been reduced. He had crossed Gaul, where the invaders and Roman infighting had destroyed everything outside the walled cities; Christian preachers spoke to hungry crowds by the roadside about the End and those who had food or arms hoarded them obsessively. He had met refugees escaping from the south of the Pyrenees, for the Hispanic Peninsula had also been overrun by the northern savages; private militias had been raised to guard the estates of the wealthy, those, at least, who had not been executed after the battles between Roman factions. While in Britain ... It would simply take too long and be too painful to recount the trials of his homeland in that time. And when asked, by officials or the curious who heard his effete, clean British Latin, he answered only that the citizens in the island waited and prayed for the Emperor's intervention.

However, it was only when he had shown his credentials and the seal on the letters to the guards on the mountain passes leading over the Alps that his questions had been reciprocated by the information that he so desperately needed – some clue as to where and how he would find the Emperor. His Imperial Highness was, said the equestrian in charge, planning to travel to Trier. And he would certainly, this officer added without any hint of sympathy, be glad to hear news from the rebel island. But the lone traveller, despite being an official messenger, was given no escort and only cursory advice on how to reach his destination with the urgent letters he carried. For ten further days Ambrosius rode to the north, keeping his business to himself. The barbarian invaders, he discovered from sentries on town walls, had even spilt over into Italy and an army of Goths had passed towards the south, swearing to sack Rome itself. Negotiations were said to be under way, representatives of the Emperor offering the invaders rich land on which to settle within the Empire: a desperate strategy. But the enemy knew that they had the upper hand and their king spoke publicly of replacing the Roman Empire, or what was left of it, with a Gothic empire of his own. All this, as the worst snowstorms in living memory whipped the countryside and those unlucky enough to be found travelling over it.

Ambrosius rode north, his horse struggling through the blizzards, before learning that the Emperor's plans had changed and that he had headed back towards Rome, the endangered city. The young man followed the rumour south – desperate, for he had promised the Council of Britain to be back in the island by the middle of January, their next meeting – losing his exhausted mount on the northern Italian plain. But, after misfortune, some fortune. It was an hour later, as he struggled through the snow, now looking only for shelter, that Ambrosius came upon the outriders of the Emperor's Household, the elite cavalry that formed the Imperial guard, and begged, his knees sunk in the white drifts, to be taken immediately to Honorius, Lord of Rome. Who was he? He was Ambrosius, son of Gratian Atrebates from the island of Britain and he brought with him news of much importance. Yes, yes, news from the rebel island had arrived at last.

The guards had insisted that he wait, in the kneeling position, a blade held hovering near his throat. And when instructions came for him to approach the Imperial quarters, his eyes had closed in the horrible cold and his legs refused to work. Now, beyond caring and almost beyond feeling, he was dragged by unseen hands towards a place where many voices echoed and in which he could even hear laughter. After that, he passed out entirely and came to only hours later, lying on a broken camp bed. They had stripped him naked to remove the wet clothes and dried him to drive out the fever that had started to break over his body. The letters that he had tied to the inside of his waist with the last of his gold in a leather wallet were gone; he thumped his chest, for he had sworn to defend them with his life. And they had placed half a dozen horse blankets on top of him that he threw off, stumbling to his feet. Needless to say, he could hardly walk and was helped back to bed by an attendant, falling in and out of a nightmarish sleep for two days. Again and again in that time, his hands moved to the place where the letters had been kept on his long journey. His bloodshot eyes rolled and his face twitched as he searched for them.

On the third day, in the morning, he was woken with snow rubbed into his face and was told to dress, some new, ill-fitting clothes being thrown onto the bed. Five minutes later he was helped to a nearby room and there realised that he was in an Italian villa that must have been appropriated by the Imperial party on its way south. And before him, imperturbable, sat a man in senatorial dress. The room was cold and Ambrosius had to fight to stop himself shivering as he was questioned – he was not invited to sit. Yes, he had brought the letters directly from the Council of Britain. Yes, of course, the letters were genuine. Yes, the Council wished to re-establish contact with the

Emperor, their Lord – the request was unanimous. 'And the revolt?' The revolt, answered Ambrosius, was over. All realised, even those who had been its reluctant supporters, that it had been a terrible, terrible mistake: the senator must understand that the civil authorities had been driven to it by the garrisons. But, there were now more important events afoot. The situation on the eastern coast was desperate. Saxon pirates had ceased raiding and actually begun to set up permanent bases there, claiming the land as their own. There were no longer enough troops in Britain to drive them back out – and the population, forbidden to use weapons for centuries, had formed derisory, ineffective corps. Even the coastal forts had been overwhelmed. Ambrosius himself had been sent to one, where the men guarding had been ambushed and slaughtered. Then, at the Colony [Colchester], the original seat of Roman rule in Britain, the Saxons had been audacious enough to attack the city walls, breaking through the east gate. The worst slaughter in the island since the times of Boudicca had followed.

But this patrician Roman was unconcerned and detached; he limited himself to nodding. And his response, when it came, was almost offensively measured. There were, he coldly pointed out, barbarians all over the Empire: Britain was hardly unique in that respect. And rest assured that the Emperor would restore order. But it was a question of priorities. Rome itself was under threat, as they spoke – they were waiting now for news. Rome, however, unlike Britain, had never rebelled and Rome had never sent its armies to Gaul to cause confusion there as Britain had. He pushed aside his chair and stood up. The interview was at an end. The Emperor was busy at the moment. However, if there was time afterwards, the Highest One might see a British subject, who begged to bow before His throne. Ambrosius should have protested, but he was too weak. He stepped backwards, his legs numb from the cold. Yet, the senator was not finished. He looked across at the young man: 'The Emperor also wanted to know whether you were the son of Gratian Atrebates.' He did not add 'the tyrant, the leader of the revolt', though that was in his voice. Ambrosius simply nodded and then turned and left the room. It would have been pointless to add more words. Any excuse, any explanation would have been misunderstood.

Another child of one of the leaders of the rebellion had been among the British soldiers who had gone to the Continent to fight against the Emperor. He had been arrested in Gaul, placed in a baggage train going into Italy. This miserable soul had then lived one miserable week, tied to the haunch of a donkey being dragged across the mountains, until the Imperial executioner had arrived and efficiently dispatched him. Ambrosius had known all along that meeting with the Emperor might, likewise, usher in his last days and had accepted this when the task of bringing the letters to the Imperial court had been given to him. But it was unpleasant to recall the senator's wilting gaze and the threatening, final question. And, trying to put these thoughts away, he passed through the corridors with guards on either side and slopped onto his bed. It was not long before there came into his tired mind, too clear and coherent to be a dream, but too fraught to be memory, images of those times when the rebellion had begun.

His father, Gratian, had at first opposed any disloyalty to the Emperor, as had almost all the civil authorities in Britain. It had been, as always, the army that had taken the lead, declaring the First Citizen a fool and an incompetent for allowing the barbarians to cross the Rhine; there was also the question of unpaid but promised bonuses. Then, in a fury of meetings and speeches, they had made a centurion, a certain Marcus on the Stone Wall, into a new Emperor, declaring their intention to bring the legions to the Continent and 'restore order', an ominous phrase. This Marcus, all had said, had been the worst kind of soldier: grasping, threatening, with no knowledge of politics and no understanding of moderation. The Woody City and the other British towns had tried to remain neutral – Ambrosius remembered his father's conversations with other leaders of the counties of southern Britain, held secretly in the villa, late into the evening. But so terrified had they been at the prospect of the soldiers leaving, denuding the island of its already inadequate defences – no one wanted a repeat of the terrible raids of thirty years before – that they had, in the end, entered into talks with the rebels and a price was, eventually, offered for their co-operation, not by Marcus but by his deputies.

Ambrosius was only seventeen at the time and had not been invited to the meeting – representatives of all fifteen British counties were present and the heads of the legions, Gratian heading the civic delegation. However, his father's nerves had showed that something more than simple negotiations were afoot. Then, two days later, the news came that Marcus was dead: he had been murdered by his own escort and Gratian had been declared the new British Emperor. In fact, Ambrosius had woken up to see a specially prepared bodyguard arriving at the door of the city house. And, once the family had been gathered together, the commander of this troop had undone the heavy parcel of purple robes that would be the symbol of Gratian's office, while another discreetly showed his new master the sack with Marcus' head in it. Of course, Ambrosius had not been privy to this secret and had lived only the wonder of that time. For how many seventeen-year-olds see their father shrouded in the Imperial purple, passing through the streets of their home town to the screams of the populace? It had been an extraordinary period and they had all talked of Gratian as the trumpet that heralded a new golden age.

But soldiers are impatient and it was the soldiers who had done for his father. Yes, the borders had been secured, the cities protected, trade that had slowed down in the aftermath of the rebellion had spluttered into life again: mosaics were commissioned, house plans made, roads laid . . . Yet, it was not enough. The legions could protect Britain, but what point was there in protecting Britain when the whole of Gaul still laboured under the ravages of currish barbarians? Britain must act not only to save itself, but also to save the Empire. Meetings and more meetings were held as this point was argued out and, from one of these meetings, Gratian had not returned.

The family had never been shown the body. And the next day, a soldier with the name of Constantine, a simple legionary, was proclaimed the new Emperor of Britain and had had the heavy and by now bloodstained purple cloak of office hung around his neck. His detractors said that he had been chosen not for his charisma, nor his ability, but because his name was that of the Emperor Constantine who had brought Christianity to the Romans. Certainly, he was intent on following in that other Constantine's footsteps to power. For, later that year, this new Constantine took the legions to Gaul 'to conquer back the Empire', leaving only skeleton garrisons behind. And, almost immediately, the barbarians attacked. Ambrosius, who had been shuffled away from the city to protect him from his father's killers, was moved again and then again, this time from the raiders who came deeper and deeper over the British plains and even into the hills.

A year passed and then six months, before the news that his father's murderer had been driven back on the Continent and then many of the British legions had changed sides. It was in those circumstances that the Council of Britain had met and it had been decided to send an urgent appeal to Rome. The letters had been written and Ambrosius, as heir of one of the most noble families in the island, had been chosen. It was only November when he crossed the icy seas to Gaul. But already the blinding snow was blowing across the Channel and his long journey towards Honorius had begun in glacial conditions. Another meeting of the Council of Britain was set for the middle of January; at all costs Ambrosius had to return by then with news.

Stuck for almost a week in this small room of a villa, in painful proximity to the Emperor, the hope and single aim of his mission, the Briton became increasingly frustrated. But he was treated well and his strength returned. Indeed, over the next two days he found that he was able to potter around and undertake simple tasks – he began a letter to his family. Then, on the fifth day, good news of a sort. The guard who had been placed in charge of his care told him that the Emperor had announced that the party would move on. And, while no interview had been granted, Ambrosius was to be allowed to travel with them. The Briton did not ask whether he was a prisoner. But it was clear that he was and his protests that he must return to Britain were politely ignored or deflected. In fact, that very afternoon the still-ailing man was helped onto a horse and placed in the colunm of Imperial hangers-on, with armed riders on either side of him. Escape would have been ridiculous under the circumstances: he was supposed to bring news back to his home and he still did not have that news. But, more importantly, it would have been impossible.

Ambrosius, in all the time he had been kept with the Imperial party, had still not seen the Emperor. But that day, trotting in the procession of troops and officials, he saw, at least, the Imperial litter carried by a team of eight slaves. And, as they travelled, he watched this contraption bob along in the snow and even, with undisguised curiosity, heard profanities issuing from within, as a carrier stumbled or as a scout rode by to bring important news from the campaign nearer Rome. With only this to distract him, and with some especially taciturn guards riding by his side, all might soon have become tedious beyond bearing. But, in the early evening, a hunter's moon out above them, and their destination, a series of villas on the distant hillside, alight with prepared fires and lanterns, something so far out of the ordinary happened that it woke the Briton from his stupor.

They were riding across a plain towards this, their final destination when, from out of the brush to the side, came the howls of wolves. None in the column stopped, or bothered to turn their heads, for wolves were common in this part of Italy and would never threaten a train of four hundred armed Romans. But the howls did not understand their indifference, seemed almost to be offended by it, and followed unseen, just out of sight, as if stalking this giant snake of men. Then, after half an hour of this lupine noise-making, equivalent shouts erupted from the Emperor's litter and, at the raising of His hand, all the line pulled up sharp. It was rapidly conveyed to the men around the Emperor, in words that Ambrosius could hear, that the wolves were annoying His Highness' sleep. There would be no more than two or three; let some riders go with spears and get rid of them. Yes, he knew they were close to the villa, but with these damn beasts there was a danger that the noise would continue all night! The order was understood. But in the ranks there was discomfort, for the wolf was, after all, the animal of Rome and hunting it seemed an unnecessary abuse of fortune. Had it not been the wolf that had suckled the founders of the city, Romulus and Remus?

Then just at that point, as a party of reluctant guards was leaving the circle of light around the Emperor, for torches had been brought from all sides, something almost supernatural happened, something that none who witnessed it had ever seen before or would ever forget. The wolves – there were only two of them, for all the racket they had made – did not wait to be attacked but instead slipped out of the bushes and, with rage, bounded towards the hunters. The men on horseback had been chosen specially for their suicidal bravery in serving the Throne of the Emperor. But as they saw these animals, which usually show fear of mankind, now charging a small army, they pushed their panicking horses away and, for a moment, the Emperor himself was exposed. Indeed, it was only the courage of one, who hurled himself from his mount and managed to slash at the ribcage of the leading wolf, that brought the soldiers back to their senses. And even then they took a full minute to kill the furious beasts: the second, an ancient she-wolf with grey fur, was still fighting after five or six blades of steel had run their way through her.

The omen was appalling – the animal of Rome attacking the leader of Rome – and Ambrosius went as high as he could on his horse, kneeling on the saddle, to see the carcasses. But it was not over. It was about to get worse. One of the guards picked up the muzzle of the dead male, gingerly, because for the animal to have acted so peculiarly there was a danger that it was rabid. However, he saw something there that disturbed him and, calling for space, stretched the beast out: 'It has an object caught in its mouth,' he shouted. Then, handed a knife, he cut at its throat, eventually pulling the mystery from out of the creature's airway. For some moments all stared. Ambrosius had moved forwards now with his escort, as both captive and guards desperately wanted to see; and the shadow of the Emperor himself was visible, bending out of his litter. All held their breath as the chief of the party washed this mess of blood and wolf saliva with snow and then lifted it up. It was a man's hand, severed by wolf teeth, some poor traveller who had not had any guards and whom the wolf's hunger had driven to attack. No one spoke. But everyone asked themselves the same question: in the thousand years of Rome's history had there ever been such an evil omen?

As the shock wore off, the train slowly fell back into order. The hand was thrown down in the snow, for it served no one, and the column moved again towards the heights where they would spend that night. But the men could hardly help speaking of what this meant: Rome was under siege, Gaul and Spain occupied and then this? Four hundred years before, the young Claudius, later the Emperor who had conquered Britain, had been given a divine sign when an eagle had dropped a wolf cub into his lap, the proof of his Imperial destiny. However, for the Emperor to be attacked by wolves, one with a human hand in its mouth! What could that mean but terrible and unmitigated disaster? Ambrosius reflected that the last three years had been terrible enough. It was difficult to see things getting much worse. And he was tempted to reason with the men who rode alongside him. The animals had been starved in winter, one had had a hand stuck in its throat and had been driven wild with the pain of it into attacking other humans. But the mood of the riders was too perturbed to reason with. And, when they finally arrived at the outhouses, Ambrosius was escorted roughly to a room and locked within. Across the courtyard instructions were shouted; the Emperor, much shocked by what he had seen, wanted to talk to his advisers immediately. The curse placed on Rome had, somehow, to be warded off.

That night a little of the fever that had previously burnt Ambrosius returned. He felt unwell and the coverings were insufficient. However, the morning after, he woke refreshed and walked out into the compound – his door had been mysteriously unlocked at dawn – realising that something wonderful had happened. He breathed the Italian air and looked, curiously, over the white landscape. What had not even seemed possible the day before was now under way. The sun had become strong and the snow had started to melt back from the valley sides. Until midday he ambled around aimlessly, crossing and re-crossing the paths in the villa's gardens. In fact, it would not have been difficult for him to slip away. But he owed it to the Council to bring back some news from the Emperor and he determined, once more, to wait until he had seen the Master of Rome himself. True, that could be days away and he would miss the meeting of the Council of Britain – by now that was, in any case, all but inevitable. Yet, in one way or the other, he would get a promise or an assurance to help his countrymen. Then, almost as if his prayers had been answered, just as the sun reached its pinnacle in the sky, a man whom Ambrosius had never seen before came across the yard and summoned him. The Emperor's response was ready: his decision on Britain had been communicated and put into writing that very morning.

Ambrosius marched in step between two servants towards the villa's reception area, where the meeting was to take place. Yet he was disappointed, for there he found no throne or Emperor. Instead, at a long table, he saw only one man: it was the same senator who had addressed him in his initial interview the week before. They exchanged some useless greetings, tarried politely over the change of weather and talked of the defence of Rome in such friendly terms that Ambrosius, at first, thought that the man wished to help him. But as soon as the Briton asked whether he might not see His Excellency

Honorius in person, he was savagely told to sit: the Emperor was far too busy with the present crisis to be attending personally to the vanity of the sons of tyrants. However, the hard voice continued, in the meeting of the night before and that morning – for it had covered many hours – important decisions had been made concerning the defence of Britain and letters had been written.

The senator gestured to an overlapping row of seventeen sealed letters on the table: 'Our scribes finished copying only now. The letters are identical. They are addressed to the heads of the fifteen British counties in the fifteen capitals, there is also a letter to those in control of the garrisons that remain in the island and the last, of course, to the head of the Council of Britain; Vortigern I believe his name is.' Ambrosius nodded and risked a smile: 'You cannot imagine how much this will mean to the people of Britain! Is there an indication of when help will arrive, when the legions will return to secure our island?' The senator hushed the young man with an upheld, barely patient hand. 'The letters are clear. The best you can do is to return, as quickly as possible, to your own land and make sure that the relevant authorities receive them.' Ambrosius again offered his thanks and asked for them to be extended to his lord the Emperor. Could the senator give no clue to their content? Again the senator, who had slept little the night before, shook his head. 'They are not the concern of the messenger. I can tell you only that with these letters the barbarians in Britain will no longer be a problem for the Empire.' Then, after reiterating that the messages should reach the rightful authorities as soon as possible, he dismissed Ambrosius from the room. The Briton bowed twice, almost the happy courtier. He would, he stated, leave that very hour, if the Roman state could afford to lend him a horse. Then, to himself, he swore that, even were he to finish the journey a starved corpse, he would still arrive in his homeland in time for the Council of Britain.

If it had taken Ambrosius eighty days to reach the Emperor in Italy, owing to the shocking state of the roads and the raiders and invaders still racing up and down the country out of control, then the return journey took only half that time. A harsh winter had led to an early and unprecedented spring, so already in January the buds were pushing into bloom, the ice and snow disappearing from all but the highest peaks, the trees and fields a virgin green. There were still barbarians everywhere. But, for the most part, they had taken to signing contracts with the Romans and settling next to cities or on wealthy expropriated estates: the invasions had been legalised. And, across the burnt-out remains of the Empire, there was an optimism that Ambrosius, the previous year, had not felt. The populace talked of the Emperor Honorius as the one who had restored the ancient laws – a contrast to the way in which he had been vilified in the months before. True, Rome was still at risk: the legions had not yet faced off the huge Gothic army that had awoken hungry and angry, like a hibernating bear, after wintering in central Italy. It was true too that the omen of the wolves had leaked out and become exaggerated, for Rumour grows and speeds as she moves. In the tale, there were now two hands, the right hand in the stomach of the she-wolf, the left hand in the stomach of the male; Ambrosius marvelled that for all he rode quickly, this news was always before him. Yet these things did not seem to matter, for despite it all, there was a sense that something like sanity was coming back, that the Empire had turned the corner.

Concerning Britain, though, Ambrosius heard only bad news. The Gaels and the Picts had attacked once more, it was said, and there was talk of further atrocities on the part of the Saxons in the Fens and in the Cornerland. But at least there Ambrosius would be able to bring some help to his desperate countrymen. He had, originally, considered taking the road to the north and crossing from the Channel ports to Londinium. But in the end, remembering his oath to arrive in time for the Council, he rode to the mouth of the Loire – to the place where all those years ago his grandsire Commius had left the Continent for his own journeys into unknown lands with the tribune Volusenus – determined to seek out a British merchant ship. It proved difficult. He had had to search and beg for two days, tramping uselessly around the Roman port, before finding a trader from Eboracum [York], who agreed to take him on the promise of ample rewards from the Council.

Then the journey, of course, proved a horrible one. Ships rarely set out prior to April and, as they headed north, they had to stay close to the coast, putting in whenever the wind provoked the waves to even a moderate height. And, all the time, the days were passing. It took six to reach the Channel. It would have been best, of course, to pass up the Thames, directly to Londinium, where the Council of Britain was to meet. But they had heard that the river was unsafe, for the Saxons had set up encampments there, driving the natives out. So instead they disembarked at one of the shore forts in the Cornerland and Ambrosius found an official who confirmed that the Council had just started. The man also knew something of Ambrosius and his mission. And, on hearing the young Briton's news, blessed first the Emperor and then Rome and then pulled together a party of guards to help the son of Gratian ride through to Britain's greatest city.

The party did not wait for the morning. There was no time. They rode through the night and arrived at dawn the next day. What he heard from his bodyguard in the dark hours surprised and dismayed Ambrosius; he had not imagined that the situation in the island could have deteriorated so badly in the few months since he had left in search of Roman help. The Woody City had declared its independence from the rest of Britannia and had begun to build defensive ditches around the town – a representative had been sent to the Council of Britain, but was refusing to vote. The county of Dumnonia had evacuated the city of Isca [Exeter] and settled on the heights nearby, better to defend itself from the Gaels. There were whispers too that, near Eboracum, the Pennine tribes had caused as much trouble as the invaders. The Stone Wall had been almost entirely abandoned. And Londinium had protected its boundaries with Saxons whom it had bribed to change sides.

The escort had a first-hand encounter with these as they rode towards the outskirts of the city: glowering Germans, their hair combed back with greased butter, smelling of the stables and the rain. Offer them a penny more than the gold that the Britons were paying and they would, without scruple, turn their weapons on the city that they were protecting. They held Ambrosius up for the best part of three hours and it was only the British guards who had come with him who prevented the barbarians searching, indeed ransacking, the bags where the precious letters had been secreted. Then, finally, as the sun rose higher and the news that the messenger had returned from the Emperor got through, an escort was sent from within the walls with instructions to bring Ambrosius into the city immediately, as the second day's meeting had just begun.

Ambrosius crossed the bridge and was received, at the threshold of Londinium, by several men known to him from the days of his father's rule. They saw a triumphant face and walked beside him, congratulating him on having saved Britain. Then, moving rapidly through the empty streets – the island's first city had been depopulated by the recent attacks, for little food reached her walls – the young messenger and his companions soon got to the forum and there Ambrosius looked up at the high windows of the room where the Council was meeting. They must, surely, have been told that the messenger had returned by now. They must be waiting. And certainly, the guards stepped aside as Ambrosius appeared and he continued alone trotting upstairs, half running, half walking down long corridors. Then, as he came to the final stretch of passageway, the door at the end opened and a secretary looked out, whispering back into the room. A moment later the head of the Council, Vortigern, appeared. This man, a Briton from the hills of Cambria, who had been elected chief in the absence of the Emperor's authority, came over, wasting no smiles or greetings and waited while Ambrosius unhooked the bag in which the letters had been placed. Usually a patient man, he scowled as Gratian's son fiddled and tried to extract the missives until, his patience at an end, he grabbed the sack from Ambrosius' hands and upturned it, pouring the letters onto the table and rapidly picking out his own.

Vortigern snapped the seal, read the words once, then as the letter had been written in the celestial script of the Imperial court – famous for being difficult to decipher – he read it again. Then, he read it a third time because he could not believe what he was reading. In the background he heard young Ambrosius receiving the thanks and the congratulations of members of the Council. Since the noise distracted him Vortigern rose, shut the door between himself and the crowded room and sat at the table where the letters were spread out, reading the words of the Emperor's scribes for a fourth and final time. Ambrosius Atrebates had been wrong. It was a solution he had brought. But for the Empire, not for Britain. For the Roman island, for the Chief of the Council, for all those gathered in the next room it was death.

Vortigern started to recite the iron phrases idiotically. He did not need to look at the words. He had seen them four times and he would never be able to forget them. 'The Emperor Honorius, for the good and security of his possessions in Gaul, Italy and Spain, renounces the Imperial claim over Britain. All British counties and British garrisons are to fall to their own defences. They are forthwith independent.' Of course, Vortigern knew that for Rome it was a not unintelligent choice. Britain had always cost a great deal to defend and why expend effort to win it back when the same effort could be better spent on the wealthier provinces to the south? But undefended, unprotected, unprepared there would be nothing for the Britons to do, save retreat and surrender in the face of the barbarian storm that would break, with ever more violence, on their shores. For the Gaels, for the Picts, for the Saxons and a myriad of other tribes from beyond the borders of civilisation this was a beginning – dominion in a new land. But even then, before the apocalypse had started to crawl out from between the bars of the gates of Hell, Vortigern knew that for his people it was an end. Imagine then, for a moment, the burden of this man, the only in the island to know its fate, as he started to walk towards the laughing, happy room to communicate the Emperor's decision.

~~~ Historical Background ~~~

The end of Roman Britain came in a series of events so hopelessly interlaced and confusing that it is unlikely that even well-informed contemporaries always understood what was happening. On 31 December 406, hordes of Germanic invaders crossed the frozen Rhine and overran Gaul. In Britain, shortly before or shortly after, and possibly as a reaction to this invasion, the garrison there chose one of their own men, a certain Marcus, as a new Emperor thus starting a civil war. Then, only a matter of months later, Marcus was killed by his fellow-soldiers and replaced by Gratian, a city councillor. Then again, after a short delay, one Constantine replaced Gratian (who was done away with) and took the British garrison to the Continent. There, after a series of minor victories against the barbarian invaders, who by now had poured into Spain, he sent his faithful lieutenant Gerontius across the Pyrenees to assure the loyalty of Hispania. However, Gerontius, once arrived, confusingly declared war against Constantine, effectively adding a third side to the civil war. It took a further two or three years for the Emperor Honorius – who legend says had an encounter with wolves sometime after 400 – to put down Gerontius and Constantine's revolt and restore some semblance of order to Gaul and Spain. But before then Italy was tipping into crisis and in 410 Rome itself was sacked.

It should be clear, even from this very general description, that the western Empire had fallen into irretrievable crisis: and though Roman government on the Continent stumbled on for another half-century and more, it was effectively doomed by the events of those years. For Britain these events were more immediately fatal: *c.*410 Honorius renounced Imperial control over the island in a letter to the Roman authorities that remained there. Ambrosius was the name of a British leader from (probably) the mid fifth century, who led his people to victory at the Battle of Mount Badon. His father seems – on the evidence of a sixth-century British writer, Gildas – to have been one of the three tyrants noted above, perhaps Gratian, who was a civilian and likely British. Vortigern, 'Lord of Britain,' appears in later British-Celtic legend and may be alluded to by the same Gildas.

EPILOGUE

Evacuation, 430 AD

It is two decades since Ambrosius came back to Britain and, in that time, there has not been a year that was not worse than the one that went before. It is six months since I began to write the history of my family and, in this time, our present has tapered out to a pointed end. The news arrived at daybreak. The news that Vortigern, the Protector of Britain – the ruler who governs us now that Rome is no more – has negotiated the surrender of the territory around the Woody City to the Saxons. All must leave quickly, otherwise no safety can be guaranteed. It is a cruel joke, of course. As if we have been living in safety for the past years. The settlements overrun, human blood pouring through the streets of towns and villages like the juice from a hellish winepress. Our people massacred or, worse still, made into the slaves of the savages from across the sea. In truth, all our rulers have done is to legislate the final disintegration of our civilisation: giving a timetable and some polite order to the unspeakable. The only mystery that remains is our destination. Will we be settled in the west among barbarian Celtic cousins, who cannot read or even speak our language, the Latin tongue? Or will we be taken to the boats and the new British colonies springing up on the edge of Gaul [Brittany], where so many of our fleeing compatriots have gone in the last years? Or, perhaps, we will be overtaken by the hated Saxon on the road: two or three hundred sheep left to as many packs of wolves, and end buried in the bellies of beasts and of birds.

And so it is that this morning our little family, what is left of it, gathers around and my son passes me the treasures from out of the trunk where we keep our heirlooms. We have only an hour before the evacuation begins and the sorting has to be done quickly. Here is the scrap of parchment on which Trifosa's certificate of slavery was written; I place it into the hands of a niece who will wrap it around the silver spoons, given by my brother Gratian to his wife when he received the purple cloak of Imperial office. The sword that Lucius Artorius Castus carried with him into battle against the Picts has rusted past the point of use. Its blade would snap off on so much as touching one of the enemy. It is broken and discarded, with regret, into the mud. There is a coin minted with Tincomarus' head that I put in the pouch on my belt as a keepsake; for we, like he, are destined to exile. The golden torque of Commius, worn by Togidubnus on his return to the island, we almost weep over; but it must be done. We need the money. My younger brother walks to a merchant and begs a price from him. The knuckle bone, said to be a relic of our martyr ancestor Iamcilla, might be sold later on. I give it into the outstretched hand of a nephew. A brooch has a tie of hair around it: the hair, my father told me, of the Greek who was decapitated by Catuarus in the kitchens of the palace of Togidubnus. I never believed him. It is at most a century or two old, and a trinket without worth. I hurl it into the long grass. And here are the first pages from Silvius' 'Poem of My Escape'. They will be good for packing some valuable; I pass them to my wife to tear up. And so it goes on, until the slaughter of our past is complete.

NOTES

Reading and Writing Roman Britain

In print there are two conduits by which the history of Roman Britain is communicated to the present. The first, the various historical works written about the Roman province: for example, Sheppard Frere's *Britannia*; the outdated, yet always readable *Roman Britain* of R. G. Collingwood; or Anthony Birley's *The People of Roman Britain*, a kind of *Yellow Pages* for the population of the island in the centuries of occupation. In fact, for all that the Roman province of Britain was one of the most marginal in the poorer western half of the Empire – perhaps *the* most marginal – it is today among the best-studied. This is partly because antiquarian interest began in Britain earlier than in much of the rest of Europe; and partly because British scholars have put together, over the last century, a remarkable series of tools, reference guides, archaeological programmes and collections. There is actually a very real sense in which we know more about Roman Britain than we do about, for instance, Roman northern Italy.

A second conduit has been fiction. Indeed, Roman Britain is perhaps the only period of British history for which the reading public owes its knowledge more to novels – Kipling and his successors, Henry Treece and Rosemary Sutcliffe – than to textbooks. Why this should be is not easy to say. An exotic atmosphere where the quality of day-to-day life matters more than the relatively sparse 'big events', perhaps? The crowding of these 'big events' at, as is typical in the history of provinces, the beginning and end of their association with an empire, leaving a fertile, uninhabited series of centuries in the middle? Or even the strange relation of Britain's present to the Roman past alluded to in the Preface? Whatever the reason might be it is, in any case, notable that historians of Roman Britain have also been attracted to fiction to set out their vision of Britannia. Two recent examples include the scholar Lindsay Allason-Jones, who in 2000 published a novel *Roman Woman: Everyday Life in Hadrian's Britain*, describing the adventures of a Romano-British girl, Senovara. And Martin Henig, arguably the most interesting writer working on Roman Britain today, who in 2002 inserted in *The Heirs of King Verica: Culture and Politics in Roman Britain* a series of fictional interludes.

This rich cross-fertilisation of history and fiction was the starting point for *Farewell Britannia*. The intention was that of telling the story of the Roman island through a family saga: the family's fortunes following that of the province in a genealogical version of 'the pathetic fallacy'. This saga was intended to showcase life and happenings in that era and throughout its writing I benefited from the extra-ordinarily fine literature put together on the province over the last century, see further the notes below. Each story has hiding behind it a Roman-British event or episode or an object that has survived from those centuries. I used the names of real individuals who lived at the time corresponding to the story. And these characters, often, had something to do with the occurrences that are described; so, for example, Commius in Chapter One was, truly, a Gaulish prince who went to Britain as Caesar's ambassador and after ruled over a tribe there; Artorius Castus, in Chapter Eight, really was in charge of Iranic auxiliary cavalry in the second century and it has been suggested that he rode out against the wild northern Britons when they invaded the province; a British king named Tincomarus – Chapter Two – did come to the Romans as an exile *c*. 9 AD . . .

At other times fiction was allowed to prowl on a longer leash. So, we know that a semitic Salmanes and a Roman Cocceius lived near each other on the Antonine Wall in the mid second century; we know too, from a legal digest, that Cocceius was the owner of a slave girl who was sent to a salt-workings and was later returned to him. But by calling this anonymous girl Trifosa we are filling in gaps: we do not know her name – Trifosa was recorded in the case of another British slave. And by making theirs into a romance (of sorts), as I do in Chapter Seven, I am simply taking liberties – albeit liberties hemmed around with contemporary details.

Then there are times when the leash on the beast that is fiction snaps. The adventures, for example, of Gratian among the Irish are 'inspired' (one can hardly say based) on the finds of some Roman coins at Newgrange in Ireland. My interpretation is just one of several to be offered; others include the idea that merchants or Gaels buried the coins at 'the Temple of the Sun'; while Gratian is a Romano-Briton recorded from the early fifth century and here shown at the outset of his career. The plot of Chapter Fourteen then has nothing to do with recorded events. But the scenario is credible: the Romans benefited from remarkable intelligence services with spies and ambassadors in enemy provinces. And, most importantly, the details given there about the Barbarian Conspiracy – which really happened – are supported by our few written references and several burnt-out villas on the Severn. Indeed, throughout this work I have used archaeological, historical or linguistic sources relating to Roman Britain or classical civilisation more generally.

The one sustained fiction in the book is that many of the characters mentioned (principally the hero or heroine of each chapter) are part of the Atrebates family. Now, Commius and Tincomarus and perhaps Togidubnus and Catuarus, in the first four chapters, were part of the same line; but there is little evidence that any of the other characters mentioned had ties of blood. I took to this conceit simply because a Roman *Forsyte Saga* seemed a more efficient way of tying together the Romano-British centuries than, say, an account of a village or a legion. A family does better justice to the most important Romano-British theme: the marriage of the indigenous and the foreign and its development over time. Both Celtic and Roman societies placed the family at their centre; indeed, the March of the Ancestors from the Introduction is borrowed from a particularly beautiful passage in

Plutarch. A family also allowed glimpses into different geographical locations and different strata of society. Admittedly, by giving the family the surname the Atrebates I offended against good historical taste. The Romans had no surnames as we understand them. But 'Atrebates' was the name of the Gaulish tribe that the historical Commius came from and that seems to have straddled the Channel in the first century BC and it was also the name of a British tribe that Commius' sons ruled. Tribal names were not normally used in Roman naming – there are a few examples – but Romano-Britons certainly showed a consciousness of their tribal origins in inscriptions.

The idea, meanwhile, of describing Britannia from the perspective of a villa owner, looking back from after the painful destruction of his Roman world, was not so much a fiction as a provocation. Historians accept that there was little continuity between the Late Empire and the Early Middle Ages in Britain. However, there has also been, in the last generation, a reluctance to allow for the agony that this change would have caused those who lived through it: something I tried, instead, to stress. A simple illustration of this tendency is the way historians count and describe the barbarian Saxons who overturned Roman civilisation in much of the island. The Victorians talked of hundreds of thousands or even millions arriving in Britain from the Germanic north and upending the province in a veritable *Sturm und Drang*. Today, on the other hand, historians muse, without any appreciable new evidence – though genetics will eventually bring results here – of a couple of thousand 'migrants'. But the truth is that, even if we accept peaceful or minimalist models for the turnaround in life *c*.410 and the two or three decades that followed, the change from a Roman province to a fragmented, tribal commonwealth would have been world-shattering: the collapse of the Romano-British moneyed economy; the introduction of human sacrifice by warriors from across the sea; the disappearance of pottery and glass as the workshops closed; the abandonment of the cities ... Historians will naturally explain these events as the evidence and their inclinations and prejudices require. But one needs little imagination to understand that those who came through this collapse must have suffered enormously, as humanity always does in periods of rapid, disintegrating change.

Now, there is no need to beg pardon for dramatising what was a dramatic period. But purists and sticklers for terminology are owed, at the very least, an explanation and perhaps an apology, for other parts of this book. For example, I refer to the Picts as early as 184 AD, whereas the first written reference to this people comes more than a century later in 297 AD; before that archaeologists solemnly tell us that we must speak of the 'proto-Picts'. I use the word 'Celtic' with abandon, notwithstanding recent gambits to remove it from history, because, in early chapters, it is a useful way of stressing a reality: the closeness of 'Celtic' Gaul and 'Celtic' Britain. I have enjoyed using later 'Celtic' sources to suggest the home-grown legends of the Romano-British; for, in the last generation, the work of Dr John Koch has shown that some of the medieval legends of the British date back, in one form or another, to this period. I have not placed muzzles on the Romans, preventing them, as a minority of modern academics would wish, from using words such as 'savage' and 'barbarian': words that, however uncomfortable for us, were fundamental in Roman life. I refer always to Britain or Britannia, never 'the Britains' as became normal after the province was divided in the second century: to modern ears 'the Britains' sounds peculiar and this administrative event hardly seemed worth the effort needed to explain it. For similar reasons I continue to refer to the 'Governor' of Britain even after the most powerful Roman in the island had become, instead, the *Vicarius*.

I have tried to respect the chronology of the various objects mentioned, though in a couple of cases I have bent this chronology to its limits; for example, the dating of the Water Newton silver in Chapter Ten. Notably, there have been omissions that those interested in the period will inevitably spot. As the focus of the book was on Britain, essentially a product of the early Empire, I left the transition from

Republic to Principate to one side. Likewise I did not, in later chapters, refer to the division of the Empire under Diocletian and Constantine's sons. Then, most painfully, Agricola, Constantine (for the most part) and Magnus Maximus were sacrificed for reasons of space and because of the risk of repetition. I trust that the reader will judge these to be venal sins committed in, rather than against, the name of history.

Chapter One: Discovering Britain

Curiosities

• The Gaulish Celt Commius went to Britain to bring messages from Caesar to the Celtic tribes there. Celtic tribes did, in fact, sometimes straddle the English Channel in the pre-Roman centuries. One example of this is Commius' tribe the Atrebates, based both in Gaul and Britain. Another is the Parisi, found both on the Seine and in what is today East Yorkshire, regions that interestingly had similar burial customs. The name of the French capital comes from this tribe.

• Hostility between the Celts and their Mediterranean neighbours was pronounced in antiquity. One of several insults the Greeks and Romans deployed for the northerners was 'trouser-wearer', a phrase that might seem innocuous today, but represented an important difference for the 'toga-wearers' of the south.

• Volusenus' reference to 'red people' is a nod to a peculiar episode. In about 70 BC a boatload of a mysterious people were washed up on the shores of Gaul. The Romans, contrary to modern myths, believed that the world was not flat but a globe; and so when these sailors of an unknown race appeared in their territory they made the Columbus-like mistake of calling them 'Indians', thinking that they had been washed across from India on the other side of the world. It has been suggested, very tentatively, that they were, instead, Amerindians. Of course, a crossing of the Atlantic is not entirely impossible in this period – though it would have been a one-way, historically irrelevant, storm-driven, rather unfortunate affair. Certainly, we know that, in the Early Modern period, Eskimos were sometimes washed up in Europe: William H. Babcock, 'Eskimo Long Distance Voyages', *American Anthropologist* 15 (1913), pp. 138–41.

• There may have been other early Roman contacts with Britain. One account describes Romans shadowing a Punic tin merchant to try and discover the island and being tricked by their guides onto sandbanks: Strabo, *Geography*, 3, 5.

Details

For Caesar's instructions for scouting see *The Gaulish Wars*, 4, 21; for the Carthaginians and the tin trade and Britain see R. Penhallurick, *Tin in Antiquity* (Seaby, 1991); for Roman fear of the ocean in general see David Braund, *Ruling Roman Britain: Kings, Queens, Governors and Emperors from Julius Caesar to Agricola* (Routledge, 1996), pp. 10–23; for Albion see Pliny, *Natural History*, 4, 102; for Thule (usually taken as Iceland) see V. H. de P. Cassidy, 'The Voyage of an Island', *Speculum* 38 (1963), pp. 595–602; Scandia or Scandinavia, as we would say, is judged by Germanic philologists to have meant the 'Dangerous Place', perhaps because of its rocky coasts – it was believed to be an island in this period; Ireland was known as the Holy Island, for which see Avienus, *Ora Maritima*, 50 (J. Soubiran, *Aviénus: Les Phénomènes d'Aratos*, CUF, 1981); and its inhabitants also had a reputation for cannibalism: Strabo, *Geography*, 5, 4, 4; for the Little Pigs (the Orkneys) see A. L. F. Rivet and C. Smith, *The Place-Names of Roman Britain* (Book Club, 1981), pp. 433–4; for Gaulish druids going to Britain see *Gaulish Wars*, 6, 13; for the Greek man blown out into the ocean, Pausanius, *Description of Greece*, 1, 66; for the 'red people', Geoffrey Ashe, *The Quest for America* (Praeger, 1971), pp. 90–92; for the sea mist and the 'sea lung' (a jellyfish?), Christina Roseman, *Pytheas of Massilia, On the Ocean: Text, Translation and Commentary* (Ares Publishing, 1994), p. 125; for the wickerwork boats, Pliny, *Natural History*, 4, 104; for Volusenus refusing to leave the boat while scouting the southern coast, Caesar, *Gaulish Wars*, 4,21.

Chapter Two: A Briton in Rome

Curiosities

• In the first paragraph of the chapter, some of the more distant contacts of the Romans are mentioned including the Indians, the Ethiopians and, perhaps most interestingly, the Chinese or 'Seres' as the Romans called them. Several bold and difficult-to-believe theories about Roman legionaries turning up in China have been suggested over the last fifty years, starting with the writings of an Oxford Professor of Chinese, Homer Hasenphlug Dubs and including, more recently, David Harris' *Black Horse Odyssey: Search for the Lost City of Rome in China* (Wakefield Press, 1991). Whatever we think of these extravagant claims the Romans were, however, certainly in indirect contact with the Chinese, for many centuries their sole source of silk.

• A fundamental division throughout European history, perhaps *the* fundamental division, has been that between the wine drinkers of the south and the beer drinkers of the north. As in this chapter, the beer drinkers have, over the centuries, regularly been accused by the wine drinkers of over-drinking and drunkenness. There may be some truth in this, but the northerners have also evolved rules to limit their alcoholic excesses. The Celts, for example, fined warriors who developed pot bellies: Strabo, *Geography*, 4, 4, 6.

• The tallness of the Gauls and the Britons seems to have brought out a veritable Napoleon complex in the shorter Romans. It has even been suggested that tallness, typical of the northern Gauls and Britons, acted as a kind of 'colour bar' in the Empire – a racial characteristic that was discriminated against; far more than, say, skin colour, which did not generally excite comment. Certainly, Britons were one of the least successful ethnic groups, rarely being promoted to important positions.

Details

For Cicero and the visiting druid (Diviciacus) see Cicero, *On Diviniation*, 1, 41; for the Celts' love of drink see Athenaeus, *The Deipnosophists*, 4, 36; for the large size of the Gauls and Britons see A. N. Sherwin-White, *Racial Prejudice in Imperial Rome* (CUP, 1967), pp. 57-8; for head-hunting and the hanging of heads off manes and doors see Diodorus Siculus, *History*, 5, 29; for British tattoos and woad, Caesar, *Gaulish Wars*, 5, 14; for lime-bleached hair, Diodorus Siculus, *History*, 5, 28; for 'Great Tench' (that is far from certain), C. E. A. Cheesman, 'Tincomarus Commi Filius', *Britannia* 29 (1998), pp. 309-14, at 313; for Rome's night-time carts – wheeled traffic was only allowed after dark – Jérôme Carcopino, *Daily Life in Ancient Rome* (Penguin, 1975), pp. 61-2; for Celtic dining habits, including Tincomarus' dislike of olive oil, his habit of sitting on the floor with straw, and a passion for fish and vinegar, Athenaeus, *The Deipnosophists*, 4, 36; for the king's Celtic insistence that only the greatest warrior should take the first portion of meat, Athenaeus, *The Deipnosophists*, 4, 40, a custom attested later in medieval Ireland; for British 'wife-swapping', Caesar, *Gaulish Wars,* 5, 14; for the geography of the tribal federations see Barri Jones and David Mattingly, *An Atlas of Roman Britain* (Oxbow, 1990), p. 45; for chariots see the notes for Chapter Three; for the later biography of Commius see the notes for Chapter One and Caesar, *Gaulish Wars* 8, 23 and 8, 48, and Frontinus, *Stratagems*, 2, 13 (though Volusenus was not said to be involved in this); for Tincomarus' confused 'mythic' reminisces of Caesar's invasion, John Koch, 'A Welsh window on the Iron age: Manawydan, Mandubracios', *Cambridge Medieval Celtic Studies* 14 (1987), pp. 17–52.

Chapter Three: Invasion

Curiosities

• We know that elephants were used in Britain in the campaign though they are associated by Dio Cassius with the Emperor Claudius, who arrived only towards its end. It is surely one of the great tragedies of antique writing that no first-hand account of the Britons' reaction to this animal survives. The best we have is to be found in Polyaenus, *Stratagems*, 8, 23, 5 who declared, dubiously, that Julius Caesar had used an elephant in his adventures in the island. He says, though, only that the Britons 'were struck with terror at the sight of a beast that was enormous and that they had never seen before'.

• The use of the chariot slowly died out in the early centuries BC in Europe and Asia. And the British, along with the Irish and Persians, were among the last to use it. However, it should be said that the British chariot of our imagination, with its scythed, deadly wheels, is based on an error, namely Pomponius Mela's confusion with the Persian chariot: *De Chorographia*, 3, 6, 52. Archaeology and all historical sources, with the lonely exception of Pomponius, know nothing of scythes on British chariots.

• Roman siege weapons were particularly intimidating to peoples who had not yet mastered the art of artillery and their power became legendary. We have, for example, from the Jewish Wars, references to a pregnant woman being hit and her child thrown from the womb, not to mention enemies being decapitated and their heads propelled long distances through the air.

Details

For Roman fear of the ocean and the refusal to board the invasion ships see Dio Cassius, *Roman History*, 60, 19; for a credible estimate of the size of the invasion (on which our numbers are based) see Gerald Grainge, *The Roman Invasions of Britain* (Tempus, 2005), pp. 128-9; for the omen, Dio Cassius, *Roman History*, 60, 19; for Caligula's invasion, R.W. Davies, 'The Abortive Invasion of Britain by Gaius', *Historia* 15 (1966), pp. 124–8; for Sentius Saturninus, a senatorial commander involved in the invasion, Eutropius, 7, 13: and the Bodunni, Dio Cassius, *Roman History*, 60, 20, an unknown tribal grouping – often equated (optimistically) with the Dobunni; for 'Caesar's mistake', *Gaulish Wars*, 5, 17; for northern nudity or near-nudity in battle, Diodorus Siculus, *History*, 5, 30 and Polybius, *History*, 2, 28; for challenges and duels, S. P. Oaldey, 'Single Combat in the Roman Republic', *The Classical Quarterly* 35 (1985), pp. 392–410.

For the silent Roman march that unnerved the louder, more vocal barbarians of northern Europe, see Goldsworthy, *The Roman Army*, pp. 196–7; for hand-to-hand fighting, which in its pushing and banging of shields seemed to have resembled a rugby scrum of two or three minutes' duration, Goldsworthy, *The Roman Army at War: 100 BC – 100 AD* (Clarendon Press, 1996), pp. 224–7; for elephants, Dio Cassius, *History*, 60, 21; for the swimmers (described as 'Celts', though most historians believe they were the non-Celtic Batvians), Dio Cassius, *History*, 60, 20; for listening with a tube of wood, Julius Africanus, *Variegated Girdles*, 2, 12; for the chariot see Caesar, *Gaulish Wars*, 4, 33 and 5, 15; for the effective use of Roman siege weapons against British forts see the archaeological evidence relating to Hod Hill, I. Richmond, *Hod Hill: Excavations carried out between 1951 and 1958* (The British Museum, 1968), vol. II, p. 73.

Chapter Four: Boudicca's Revolt

Curiosities

- The threefold death (or the triple death) is referred to in medieval Irish tales and found archaeologically in the bog bodies that sometimes turn up in Britain and Ireland – including Lindow Man (Cheshire), contemporary with and perhaps connected to the revolt. The ritual had a range of varying, but consistently unpleasant features including the ritual cutting-off of nipples and the painting of the victim. Archaeologists suggest that the sacrificed one often volunteered himself for the good of the community.

• There has long been controversy about how to spell the name of the rebel queen, but almost no attention paid as to how her name would have been pronounced. Kenneth Jackson, the celebrated Celtic philologist, in 'Queen Boudicca?', *Britannia* 10 (1979), p.255 notes that the British Celts would have called her 'Bow<u>dee</u>ka', Jackson's sensible rendering of 'popular' phonetics, with the stress very much on the second syllable.

• The most famous example of the orgy of British violence in the revolt is the head of Claudius, sawn from the statue of the temple at Colchester. It was fished out of the Alde (Suffolk) by a surprised schoolboy in the first years of the twentieth century. It had probably been left there as a ritual sacrifice to the waterway. Also on the subject of ritual deposition, Catuarus, on crossing the Thames, is made to respect the custom of the region and throws a 'sacrifice' of some coins into the water. Even before the Romans arrived in Britain the native population had cast in discarded heads and swords to the gods of the Thames. Nor has this practice altogether died out. Archaeologists recently found some peculiar 'Roman' statues there that, it eventually transpired, were modern Hindu statuettes hurled into the waters after a religious ceremony.

Details

For the revolt generally see Richard Hingley and Christina Unwin, *Boudica: Iron Age Warrior Queen* (Hambledon and London, 2005), pp. 41–107; for Togidubnus and 'the Kingdom' (part of the old Atrebates territory) see Martin Henig, *The Heirs of King Verica: Culture and Politics in Roman Britain* (Tempus, 2002), p. 69; for Catuarus, Henig, *The Heirs*, pp. 48–51; for the triple death see Miranda Green, *Exploring the World of the Druids* (Thames and Hudson, 1997), p. 80; for the hare (let loose, in fact, from Boudicca's skirt), Dio Cassius, *History*, 62, 1; for Andate (or perhaps Andraste), the goddess favoured in the uprising, Dio Cassius, *History*, 62, 1; for London Bridge and objects thrown in the river see Gustav Milne,

'Further Evidence for Roman London Bridge?', *Britannia* 13 (1982), pp. 271–6; for the bar outside the Temple of Isis in Londinium (we have an amphora with the address scratched onto it), M. Taylor and R.G. Collingwood, 'Roman Britain in 1923', *Journal of Roman Studies* 12 (1922), pp. 240–87 at p. 283; for the confused omens relating to that city, Tacitus, *Annals*, 14, 31; for the villa owner named Faustinus from this region see A. L. F. Rivet and C. Smith, *The Place-Names of Roman Britain* (Book Club, 1981), p. 499; for the mistreatment of the Iceni, including the flogging of Boudicca and the rape of her daughters, Tacitus, *Annals*, 14, 31; for Seneca and his 'investments', Dio Cassius, *History*, 62, 2.

For the proposed abandonment of Britain, see Suetonius, *Lives*, 'Nero', 18 – a policy shelved after the revolt; for Celtic social organisation (clans, septs etc.) see Alex Woolf, 'Romancing the Celts: a Segmentary Approach to Acculturation Cultural Identity in the Roman Empire', *Cultural Identity in the Roman Empire*, ed. R. Laurence and J. Berry (Routledge, 1998), pp. 111–24; for the horse and boar clans see the theory of D.F. Allen, 'The Coins of the Iceni', *Britannia* 1 (1970), pp. 1–33 at pp. 14–15; for British destruction generally see Hingley and Unwin, *Boudica*, pp. 83–96; for Romano-British pragmatism and treachery in the revolt see Tacitus, *Annals*, 14, 32; for the attack on Colchester and the Temple of Claudius (the site of the last stand), not to mention the destruction of the relief legion, Tacitus, *Annals* 14, 32; for atrocities on both sides (cut-off breasts, etc.), Dio Cassius, *History*, 62, 7 and Tacitus, *Annals*, 14, 33; for the head of Claudius see George Macdonald, 'Note on Some Fragments of Imperial Statues and of a Statuette of Victory', *Journal of Roman Studies* 16 (1926), pp. 1–20 at pp. 3–4.

Chapter Five: Wife on the Frontier

Curiosities

• The birthday invitation from Claudia to Sulpicia is something of a record-breaker. It is the earliest text certainly written by a woman's hand to have survived in Britain and, to the best of our knowledge, the earliest from anywhere in Europe.

• The description of a civilian settlement outside the gates of the Roman fort corresponds to practice throughout the Empire. *Canabae*, as these settlements are usually called, included shops, but also households where soldiers' partners would live: in this period marriage was forbidden to legionaries, who would have to wait until retirement before tying the knot after twenty-five years of service.

• There are some comments in the chapter about recent Roman innovations in the British diet. The Romans, in fact, introduced olive oil to Britain. They were probably the first to cultivate the grape in the island and to export wine on a large scale. (Wine imports prior to the Romans were rare and high-status. The relatively few examples we know of would not have been enough to give even one Celtic chieftain cirrhosis of the liver.) They introduced edible snails, which, though endangered, still survive here. They also introduced various fruits and vegetables that seem so British that it is difficult to imagine the island without them: the apple, the parsnip, the plum, the carrot, cabbage – a Roman favourite – celery, the walnut, the mulberry and oats.

Details

The most accessible guide for the Vindolanda tablets is by Alan K. Bowman and entitled *Life and Letters of the Roman Frontier* (British Museum Press, 2003); for the British attitude to lightning, Plutarch, *On the Disuse of Oracles*, 419e; for Aelius and Claudia Bowman, *Life*, pp. 48–9; for fourteen as an acceptable age for a girl to marry see J. Balsdon, *Roman Women: their History and their Habits* (Barnes and Noble, 1983), p. 173, though perhaps the average was a little older, Brent D. Shaw, 'The Age of Roman Girls at Marriage: Some Reconsiderations', *Journal of Roman Studies* 77 (1987), pp. 30–46; for the Governor and patronage, Bowman, *Life*, pp. 24-5; for Flavius and Sulpicia, Bowman, *Life*, pp. 20–21; for Claudia's birthday invitation, Bowman, *Life*, pp. 71–2; for highly prized British dogs see, among several sources, Strabo, *Geography*, 4, 5, 2; for Brigionius see Bowman, *Life*, p. 22 and p. 25; for the merchant and the centurion, Bowman, *Life*, p. 46; for the information on the kitchen and food see Joan Alcock, *Food in Roman Britain* (Tempus, 2001); for flamingo, not mentioned by Alcock, I have adapted the recipe of Apicius – the Delia Smith of the ancient world – to Britain; for goose as a taboo bird see Caesar, *Gaulish Wars*, 5, 12; for blue British women see a little-known passage of Pliny, *Natural History*, 22, 2: 'with glastum the wives of the Britons and their daughters-in-law, cover their body … walking naked with a colour like that of the Ethiopians'.

Chapter Six: At the Waters of Sulis

Curiosities

• The sculpted head from Bath that almost crushes the young Magnius is arguably the most famous work of Romano-British art; it is found on the front cover of many books concerning Roman Britain and Bath. John Hind has argued that it is the head of the giant Typhoeus who personified geothermal activity and that the 'snakes coming out of the head' are actually subterranean steam. This is beyond proof but extremely interesting given Bath's hot springs. Other suggestions, meanwhile, include a transvestite portrait of the goddess Sulis or a depiction of Ocean. This striking work may also have been responsible for the later legend of Bladud, the 'Flying King' of Bath who surfaces in medieval times: the snakes and wings coming from the head suggesting a flying being.

• Romano-Britons, perhaps more than other members of the Empire, threw offerings into the waters for their gods. At Bath an extraordinary range of objects have been found including an ivory amulet of breasts, various cups and bowls and as many as twenty thousand bronze, silver and gold coins.

• The fourth-century historian Ammianus Marcellinus notes that it was normal in polite Roman society to ask which bath another frequented: the Roman equivalent of two Englishmen speaking about the weather?

Details

For the name Magnius see R.G. Collingwood and R.P. Wright, *The Roman Inscriptions of Britain, Volume I: Inscriptions on Stone* (OUP, 1965), p. 54. For Bath generally see Barry Cunliffe, *Roman Bath Discovered* (Routledge, 2000), pp. 63–6; for discussion of the probably late-first-century Gorgon head see John Hind, 'Whose Head on the Bath Temple-Pediment?', *Britannia* 27 (1997), pp. 358–60; for the idea that it was painted, Collingwood, *Roman Britain* (Clarendon Press, 1932), p. 115; for the flying king, A.T. Fear, 'The Flying King of Bath', *Folklore* 103 (1992), pp. 222–4. Many of the details about baths are taken from Garrett G. Fagan, *Bathing in Public in the Roman World* (Michigan University Press, 2002): including animal bones floating around (p. 33); sex in baths (pp. 34–6); dirty baths (p. 183); and mixed bathing (though some baths preferred to segregate), pp. 24–9. The description of bath noise is adapted, instead, from Seneca's fifty-sixth letter. Bath's status as a Temple Bath may have meant that normal habits were moderated or not followed.

Chapter Seven: On the Turf Wall

Curiosities

• Britannia, mentioned in the chapter, was a creation of the Roman period, but was very different from our trident-wielding Victorian Amazon. When the Roman poet Claudian described her she was a tattooed titan dressed in furs – a biker Britannia: 'Next spoke Britannia clothed in the furs of a Caledonian beast, her cheeks tattooed, and a blue cloak, rivalling the ocean swell, sweeping across her feet.'

• Roman law stated that a slave who had murdered or attempted the murder of a master would cause the slaying of the entire slave household, innocent or guilty. Whatever the pragmatic basis of this rule, it sometimes created manifestly unjust situations. Tacitus, for example, tells us of the murder of one master by a slave that led to all four hundred of the slave household – including children – being crucified and that also excited public protests and debates in the Senate.

Details

For Cocceius' home on the Black Sea, E. Birley, *Roman Britain and the Roman Army* (Wilson, 1953), pp. 87–103; for Trifosa as a slave's name see Anthony Birley, *The People of Roman Britain* (Batsford, 1979), p. 147; for the signal system on the Wall see D. Wooliscroft, 'Signalling and the Design of the Antonine Wall', *Britannia* 27 (1996), pp. 153–77; for soldiers' hunting activities, there is a shrine at Bollihope Moor in the north of England that records legionaries hunting and 'bagging' native boar, Collingwood and Wright, *The Roman Inscriptions of Britain* (OUP, 1965), no. 1041; for Trifosa's boar legend see the later British-Celtic legend 'Culhwch ac Olwen' in *The Mabinogion*, trans. Gwyn Jones and Thomas Jones (Everyman, 1974), pp. 95–136 at pp. 131–5; for chalked feet and slaves from abroad, Pliny, *Natural History*, 35, 17; for exposed children being taken up as slaves see the notes for Chapter Nine; for suicide and epilepsy as excellent reasons not to buy a slave, Cicero, *De Officiis*. 3, 17; for long-serving slaves being too clever by half see, *inter alia*, Martial, *Epigrams*, 1, 42; for the parchment around the neck – the *titulus* – that acted as a guarantee, Gellius, *Attic Nights*, 4, 2; for slaves as the sexual playthings of masters, Peter Brown, *The Body and Society: Men, Women and Sexual Renunciation in Early Christianity* (Columbia University Press, 1988), p. 23.

Salmanes' stories are adapted from the Babylonian collection of rabbi tales that are antique in date and often contain stories about the Roman Empire; for the Jew Tax and the story of Jews being made to eat pork in Alexandria, H. I. Bell, 'Anti-Semitism in Alexandria', *Journal of Roman Studies* 31 (1941), pp. 1–18 at p. 8; for Jewish men being humiliated by having to show their circumcised genitals, Suetonius, *Emperors*, Domitian 12, 2; for households of slaves being killed for the murder by one slave of a master see Tacitus, *Annals*, 14, 42; for the description of the salt-workings, Apuleius, *Golden Ass*, 9, 2 – Apuleius, though, it should be noted, is actually describing the conditions in a state bakery.

Chapter Eight: Defending the North

Curiosities

• Over the years there have been literally hundreds of candidates for the figure of 'the real King Arthur'. So much so that one book on the subject is entitled: *Will the Real King Arthur Stand Up?* Among these, one of the most credible is the hero of the present chapter. Artorius' Arthurian credentials begin with his name: Artorius is almost certainly the original form of 'Arthur' – the only time that it is recorded in Roman Britain. But Artorius also had other Arthurian traits. He defended Britain against invaders as the great king did; he was in charge of a body of 'knights' – Sarmatian horse-men; he also, like the legend, invaded the Continent from Britain on a military mission from Rome, he undertook an operation in Armorica (Gaul). The first person to make the Artorius-Arthur connection was an American scholar, Kemp Malone, who noted the vague similarities in the 1920s: 'Artorius', *Modern Philology* 22 (1924–25), pp. 367–74. However, in recent years supporters of a Roman Arthur have flocked to the standard. The Celticist Oliver Padel, for example, the greatest living authority on Arthur, in an article 'The Nature of Arthur', *Cambrian Medieval Celtic Studies* 27 (1994), pp. 1–31 at p. 31, while sceptical about the once and future king's historical origins, stated that, of the candidates available, Artorius was among the most convincing.

A whole book was published on the topic with the wonderful name *From Scythia to Camelot: A Radical Reassessment of the Legends of King Arthur, the Knights of the Round Table, and the Holy Grail* – authors C. Littleton and Linda Malcor (Garland Publishing, 2000) – pushing the idea that many elements of the Arthurian legend had their roots in Iranian folklore and that they were brought to Britain by Artorius' Sarmatian cavalry, the Sarmatians being an Iranian steppe people. This book in turn had various spin-offs including a film and two articles, one in the first and one in the second issue of the online journal *Heroic Age* by Linda Malcor. The second article goes so far as to suggest that a ninth-century list of battles associated with Arthur were actually the battles that Artorius fought against the Picts in the campaign described here. The most serious objection to Artorius as Arthur is that the chronology is apparently wrong. Arthur is normally situated in the sixth century, fighting the Anglo-Saxon invaders. However, there are other British and Irish examples of legendary figures being displaced through the centuries by the enthusiastic application of legend and the evidence for a sixth-century Arthur is, in any case, minimal.

• The Picts are one of Europe's most interesting peoples. There is a strong case to be made that they were a non-Indo-European people, that is a people from a period of migrations thousands of years prior to the Celts. Certainly their language (what little remains) is difficult to parallel in Europe – connections have been alleged with Basque and even Berber. They also seem to have retained a system of matriliny, that is the descent of nobility was decided by the female not the male line. The name 'Pict' is itself also curious. Various interpretations have been offered, but the most probable is that Pict comes from Latin meaning 'the painted one'. The Picts disappear from history in the ninth and tenth centuries as Viking raids in the north of Britain turn to full-scale invasions.

• The Sarmatians, after surrendering to the Empire on the Danube, were brought to Britain, at the other end of the Empire. This was a typical Imperial strategy to take unstable barbarians as far away from their homes as possible so that escape or rebellion was pointless. Indeed, any Picts absorbed into the Roman fighting machine would have likely ended up on the frontiers of Persia or the edges of the Atlas Mountains.

Details

For the Picts the best guide remains F. Wainwright (ed.), *The Problem of the Picts* (Nelson, 1955): it should be noted that 'Pict' is, strictly speaking, anachronistic here as the word, used to describe the inhabitants of the Highlands, only seems to have come into use in the late third century; it was, in any case, first attested then. However, I have deployed it for convenience, to give a sense of continuity between this and later chapters. For signalling see D.J. Wooliscroft, 'Signalling and the design of Hadrian's Wall', *Archaeologia Aeliana* 17 (1989), pp. 5–205; for the Pictish harpoon see *Gildas, The Ruin of Britain and Other Documents* (Phillimore, 1978), p. 23; for trees being used in an ambush by barbarian enemies of Rome see Livy, *History*, 23, 24; for the Sarmatians in Britain – 5,500 originally – see Dio Cassius, *History*, 71, 16; for the square on the ice see Dio Cassius, *History*, 72.7 – that may have been the work of Artorius who was a centurion in the legion at this time, as suggested by Linda Malcor in an article in the online journal *Heroic Age*.

I describe in this chapter, for the first time, the *arcani*: Roman spies working beyond the frontier. For many years, there has been a controversy over whether the correct term is *arcani* or *areani* – the latter perhaps the more commonly used. However, twenty-five years ago W. Seyfarth, 'Review', *Gnomon* 53 (1981), p. 452 argued persuasively for *arcani*. For more on this group see the notes for Chapter Fourteen.

Chapter Nine: Scandal at the Villa

Curiosities

• Children who were exposed were often picked up by passers-by and brought up as slaves. In Egypt, where infanticide was especially common, there was even a naming element, 'Kopr'-, that meant 'taken from the dung pile' and referred to those who had been rescued in this way.

• The first writers to speak out against the custom of infanticide in the Empire were, interestingly enough, Christians. However, the motives they gave were not always ones that would be familiar to a pro-lifer today. The second-century Christian apologist Justin, for example, criticises infanticide because of the risk that it would lead to incest. The danger for Justin was that a discarded child would be taken up by a passer-by and brought up, as often happened, to be sold as a slave to a brothel. There was then the danger that a member of the original family would visit the brothel and unknowingly have carnal relations with a close relative.

Details

For an outstanding survey on infanticide see W. Harris, 'Child-Exposure in the Roman Empire', *Journal of Roman Studies* 84 (1994), pp. 1–22; for the names of Tammonius and Victor see Anthony Birley, *The People of Roman Britain* (Batsford, 1979), pp. 119–20; for the name of Calgacus see Tacitus, *Agricola*, 29–38; 'the three tools' of the Roman estate owner come from Terentius Varro; for the bath at Silchester and the abortions see George C. Boon, *Silchester: the Roman Town of Calleva* (David and Charles, 1974), p. 61 ('Several skull-bones of very young babies were nevertheless recovered from a drain at the public baths; and although it would be highly speculative to account for their presence there is little alternative to supposing that a person could be found at the baths to dispose of unwanted babies').

For slaves and their position in the family generally see Keith Hopkins, 'Novel Evidence for Roman Slavery', *Past and Present* 138 (1993), pp. 3–27; for the *bacaudae* (or *bagaudae*) – it is sometimes suggested that the Celtic word for war, 'cad', is found there, hence 'the warriors' – see E.A. Thompson, 'Peasant Revolts in Late Roman Gaul and Spain,' *Past and Present* 2 (1952), pp. 11–23 (note that the evidence for British *bacaudae* is indirect); families did sell children into slavery and there may be some cases from Britain, Birley, *The People*, p. 147; for British wolves in this period see J. E. Harting, *British Animals Extinct within Historic Times* (Trübner and Co., 1880), pp. 115–26 and Derek Yalden, *The History of British Mammals* (Poyser, 1999), p. 116. For Augulus see the next chapter.

Chapter Ten: A Persecution of Christians

Curiosities

• One of the most surprising facts about Roman Christianity for modern readers is the insults and slanders that were cast at Christian heads by pagan neighbours. Christians were, for example, said to be cannibals – probably because of the eating of Christ's body and the drinking of His blood in mass; sexual innuendo associated with Christian worship may have been based on a misunderstanding of the Christian sign of peace, given by a kiss; the claim that Christians were donkey-worshippers is perhaps partly related to Christ riding into Jerusalem on the back of that animal, but the donkey was also a symbol of the slave – a memorable early graffito, the earliest surviving anti-Christian image, shows a donkey nailed to a cross. Finally, there was the claim that Christians were atheists, a bizarre one for a modern reader. But Christians, in denying the traditional gods of the Empire, were seen as being impious.

• British Christianity had a reputation even from the earliest times of being somewhat eccentric. This was accentuated in later centuries with the creation of the so-called Celtic Church. But even the Water Newton treasure hoard gives us clues of forms of worship that contemporary Continentals may have found strange, perhaps even unacceptable. There are in that hoard, for example, plaques of prayers and petitions with the names of petitioners that had been previously pinned to the church altar, a practice used in paganism but not attested anywhere else in the Christian world.

• The easily visited amphitheatre at Silchester is one of the most atmospheric Romano-British sites – more atmospheric in some ways than the remains of the town and its walls; it would have accommodated between three and four thousand. The ancient 'container of death' is now grown over with trees and grass.

Details

Augulus was possibly a British martyr from this period: see Anthony Birley, *The People of Roman Britain* (Batsford, 1979), pp. 152–3; for Christians eating kosher meat see the narrative of the Martyrs of Lyon; for the Water Newton treasure and the names of Iamcilla, Publianus and Innocentia see Charles Thomas, *Christianity in Roman Britain to* AD *500* (Batsford, 1981), pp. 113–22 – note that here I have stretched the traditional chronology to its limits, the silverware might date back to the late third or early fourth century but it was buried *c.*350; for the insults and allegations thrown at the heads of Christianity, their burning of Rome is found in Tacitus, *Annals*, 15, 44, while the sexual innuendo is found in the Roman writer Minucius Felix, *Octavius* 9; for the difficulties and decisions that the martyr must make see

W. Frend, *Martyrdom and Persecution in the Early Church* (Blackwell, 1965), essentially an extended essay on these questions; for the general narrative taken from the *acta* of Perpetua see now Joyce Salisbury, *Perpetua's Passion: The Death and Memory of a Young Roman Woman* (Routledge, 1997); for 'mythological deaths' see K.M. Coleman, 'Fatal Charades: Roman Executions Staged as Mythical Enactments', *Journal of Roman Studies* 80 (1990), pp. 44–73; Lucius the British gladiator – the only recorded – is found in Birley, *The People*, p. 121; for Caledonian bears see Martial, *Liber de Spectaculis*, 15 and for the British bear in general, J. E. Harting, *British Animals Extinct within Historic Times* (Trübner and Co., 1880), pp. 11–32.

Chapter Eleven: Reunion

Curiosities

• Helena's most famous biographer was Evelyn Waugh, who in a novel of the same name described her life from a youth spent in Roman Britain to the discovery of the true Cross on a pilgrimage to Jerusalem. The evidence that she was, in fact, British is based on late and very uncertain sources, though it was held as a simple truth by the medieval British Celts. One legend, even, claims that she was the daughter of King Cole of the nursery rhyme.

Details

For Publianus see the notes for the last chapter; for 'The Dream of Macsen Wledig' (the tale included in this chapter) see *The Mabinogion*, trans. Gwyn Jones and Thomas Jones (Everyman, 1974), pp. 79–88; for the reliability of this legend for history see John Matthews, 'Macsen, Maximus, and Constantine', *Welsh History Review* 11 (1983), pp. 431–49.

Chapter Twelve: The Police State

Curiosities

• None of Silvius' poetry survives. Yet we have the insulting series of epigrams written about Silvius surnamed, it seems, Bonus or 'the Good', by a Gaulish contemporary, Ausonius. I include them here in a charming sixteenth-century Scots translation by George Buchanan, *Rerum Scoticarum Historia* (1582):

> Tis Silvus Bonus whom my disticks blame; But Britto Bonus were his
>   proper name
> Silvius is good. What Silvius? The Britain. Silvius no Britton is, or a bad
>   one
> Silvius Bonus, a Britan or Britton, How he degen'rates from good
>   denizon
> No Britton's good: if Silvius 'gin to be Simple, simple and good do not
>   agree
> Silvius is Bonus, yet a Britton still. 'Tis plainer phrase to say, the Britton's
>   ill
> O Silvius, bonny Britton but bad man: Britton and good together joyn
>   who can?

It tells us a lot about the reputation of Britons in the Empire that Ausonius thought it hilarious that a Briton was nicknamed 'good' – to his mind a contradiction in terms.

• London is perhaps the only long-lasting achievement of the Romans within Britain. Before the Romans arrived in the island the Thames was a border between two British tribes, and so unsafe. Under Roman rule, when such borders became purely administrative, and were no longer fought over, a settlement quickly grew up where the banks of the river narrowed. It seems, though, not to have been a planned city – its streets were, as noted in this chapter, unusually winding – and its governmental status, despite being the largest settlement in the island, is still not properly understood. Meanwhile, the south bank of the city was a sprawling and disorganised settlement outside the official boundaries. This has led to the suggestion that it was a somewhat lawless area.

• The story of Bran or 'Raven' appears in a later British-Celtic legend, but one that certainly had roots in the Roman period and perhaps went back even further, as the Celticist John Koch has demonstrated. What is particularly curious about it, and what has not been previously noted, is the parallel between the head-burying and the modern myth that Britain will only survive while the ravens dwell in the Tower of London. In the

British-Celtic legend, Britain will not be invaded while Bran's head remains in the White Hill (the site of the Tower) and Bran means 'raven' in Celtic. How one explains this extraordinary coincidence and the yawning centuries between is not at all clear.

Details

For a discussion of postmen as secret police see A.D. Lee, *Information and Frontiers: Roman Foreign Relations in Late Antiquity* (CUP, 1993), pp. 172–4 – it should be noted that not all scholars agree that they served both roles; for 'Paul the Chain' and the purges associated with him see Ammianus Marcellinus, *History*, 14, 5; for Silvius the Good, see Ausonius, *Epigrams*, 118; for Roman Londinium and the details given here about it see John Morris, *Londinium: London in the Roman Empire* (Weidenfeld & Nicolson, 1982); for a later fourth-century cathedral perhaps for the city see Ken Dark, *Britain and the End of the Roman Empire* (Tempus, 2000), p. 51, who almost certainly dates the building too late; for the White Hill and Bran see *The Mabinogion*, trans. Gwyn Jones and Thomas Jones (Everyman, 1974), pp. 38–40 and John Koch, 'Bran, Brennos: An Instance of Early Gallo-Brittonic History and Mythology', *Cambridge Medieval Celtic Studies* 20 (1990), pp. 1–20.

Chapter Thirteen: To the Temple of Dreams

Curiosities

• The ring mentioned in this chapter, known today as the Vyne Ring, was possibly the inspiration for Tolkien's 'One Ring to Rule them All'. Tolkien worked with Mortimer Wheeler on his digs at Lydney Park in the late 1920s, looking at linguistic questions for the great archaeologist: he would have learnt of the 'cursed' ring then and, it has been suggested, it was here that the first seeds of his epic were sown.

• There seems to have been the belief in ancient times that dream treatments were best carried out at locations where metals lie in the ground. Certainly, the most famous 'hospital of dreams', the Temple of Aesclepius on the Greek Island of Cos, has a mineral-rich soil. It may not then be an accident that the temple at Lydney was built on the wreck of an old iron mine.

• The god Nodens is one of the most interesting Celtic divinities of Britain, associated with cures, dreaming, the sea, dogs – the licking of dogs was credited with healing – and perhaps the Severn Bore and the hunt. What is most curious about him though, is that he survived into modern times as the father of the Welsh spirit of the underworld Gwynn ap Nudd (Gwynn, son of Nudd, i.e. Nodens). He also had the dubious honour of being pulled into the horror fiction of H. P. Lovecraft as an otherworld entity.

Details

For the evidence relating to Senicianus and Silvanus see R. Goodchild, *Antiquity* 27 'Note' (1953), pp. 100–5; for the shrine of Nodens, P.J. Casey and B. Hoffmann, 'The excavations at the Roman Temple in Lydney Park, Glos.', *Antiquaries Journal* 79 (1999), pp. 81–143 – in this chapter I have favoured an early if controversial chronology; for Victorinus the Interpreter of Dreams, R. P. Wright, 'A Revised Restoration on the Mosaic Pavement found in the Temple at Lydney Park, Gloucestershire', *Britannia* 16 (1985), pp. 248–9; for Nodens see George Boon, 'A Roman Sculpture Rehabilitated: the Pagans Hill Dog', *Britannia* 20 (1989), pp. 201–17. The magic associated with dreaming and love has been quarried from various antique occult sources gathered in Daniel Ogden, *Magic, Witchcraft and Ghosts in Greek and Roman Worlds: A Sourcebook* (OUP, 2002), with the exception of the druidic ox hide, for which see Miranda J. Green, *Exploring the World of the Druids* (Thames and Hudson, 1997), p. 130 – a similar ritual was also associated with Irish poets in search of inspiration; for the interaction of Christian and pagan in Britain in this period see generally Dorothy Watts, *Christian and Pagan in Roman Britain* (Routledge, 1991); for Christian destruction of temples see Ken Dark, *Civitas to Kingdom: British Political Continuity 300–800* (Leicester University Press, 1994), pp. 55–64.

Chapter Fourteen: The Barbarian Conspiracy

Curiosities

• The Latin word 'Scottus' has a long and interesting history. It seems to have been used at first solely for Irish raiders. However, with time it came to mean all Gaels and crops up in 'Scotland', 'Scottish' etc., the name of the most famous Irish colony that was founded by the Gaels in the early centuries AD.

• Nipple-sucking is recorded for Ireland in the fifth century as a way of sealing a protective friendship between men; to the best of our knowledge women did not give or take the nipple. What is perhaps most curious about this custom is the fact that it is attested in only two places: ancient Ireland and ancient Egypt.

• Patricius in the chapter is based on the young St Patrick, patron saint of Ireland (a Romano-Briton), who, as a teenager, was seized from his family's villa in Britain 'with so many thousands' and taken to Ireland. He later escaped back to Britain and then organised a mission into the land of his captivity.

• Newgrange was a prehistoric shrine, built about 3200 BC. But it was still believed to be holy in the Christian period. Indeed, a medieval Irish tale describes how the Irish hero Angus won this monument from his father, the god Dagda, by playing tricks with the sun. This is especially curious as Newgrange was designed and built to take the sun into the central chamber at the summer solstice. However, the front entrance collapsed about a thousand years after its construction and, from then onwards, no one would have been able to enter or test this for themselves. The association with the sun must then have been a folk memory that survived over several millennia, to the time the story was written in about the eighth century. John Carey, 'Time, Memory, and the Boyne Necropolis', *Proceedings of the Harvard Celtic Colloquium* 11 (1993), pp. 24–36.

Details

For Gratian see Orosius, *Against the Pagans*, 7, 40, 4; for the barbarian attacks and the betrayal of the *arcani*, Ammianus, *History*, 27, 8 and for discussion A.D. Lee, *Information and Frontiers: Roman Foreign Relations in Late Antiquity* (CUP, 1993), p. 179 – for the correct form of this word see notes to Chapter Eight; for Irish raids on the Severn that left behind extraordinary archaeological evidence – bodies down wells, for example – see Keith Branigan, *The Roman Villa in South-West Britain* (Moonraker, 1976), pp. 94–7; for young Patricius see *St Patrick: His Writings and Muirchu's Life*, trans. A.B.E. Hood (Philimore, 1978), 1; for nipple-sucking. Bernard Maier,

'Suggere mammellas: a Pagan Irish Custom and its Affinities' in *Celtic Connections: Proceedings of the 10th International Congress of Celtic Studies*, ed. Ronald Black (Tuckwell, 1999), pp. 152–61. For the lines slashed on wood or ogham, an Irish alphabet, possibly already in use by the fourth century, see Damian McManus, *A Guide to Ogam* (Maynooth Monographs, 1991); for Roman coins ritually buried at Newgrange, Vittorio Di Martino, *Roman Ireland* (Collins Press, 2003), pp. 118–19 and the discussion in Charles Thomas, *Christianity in Roman Britain to AD 500* (Batsford, 1981), pp. 296–7 who suggests these coins were left by Roman merchants; for the king of all Ireland generally (in this period possibly a myth), Thomas Charles-Edwards, *Early Christian Ireland* (Cambridge, 2000), pp. 469–521; for Irish settlement in Wales under the supervision of the Empire see Philip Rance, 'Attacotti, Déisi and Magnus Maximus: The Case for Irish Federates in Late Roman Britain', *Britannia* 32 (2001), pp. 243–70; for possible evidence for a Roman eye doctor in Ireland, Di Martino, *Roman Ireland*, pp. 98–100.

Chapter Fifteen: The End of Roman Britain

Curiosities

• As will have been gathered from this book, revolts were frequent in the Roman Empire and especially in Britain, described as being 'fertile in tyrants' by St Jerome. Britain rebelled regularly because it had, along with the Rhine frontier, one of the largest concentrations of troops in the Empire (about ten per cent of the Roman army) and it was the legionaries who were the only ones in a position to rebel in a serious and sustained fashion. What is curious about late Imperial revolts is that they apparently never involved secession. The typical model was that a garrison would choose one of its men as Emperor and this Emperor would then attempt to unseat the 'false' Emperor. Of all the many revolts that started in Britain, we have no evidence that any ever began with the intention of declaring independence for the island – though see the next point. Rather, the island was a springboard for the conquest of the whole of the Roman territories.

• The biggest debate about Britain in this period is whether, as I have suggested here, the Empire threw Britain to the wolves or, as others claim, Britain decided enough was enough and declared independence. An underexploited piece of evidence suggests it was, in fact, the former. The *Narratio de imperatoribus domus Valentinianae et Theodosianae*, an early/mid-fifth-century text, records 'the loss of Britain for ever'. No Roman writer would have written 'for ever' unless Britain had had its new non-Imperial position constitutionalised and that suggests that British independence was a Roman decision. Certainly, Britain continued to try and win aid from Rome, including a mid-fifth-century embassy that went to Roman authorities in Gaul to ask for assistance.

Details

For the confused and confusing events concerning the end of Roman Britain see Chris Snyder, *An Age of Tyrants: Britain and the Britons, AD 400–600* (Sutton, 1998), pp. 18–25; for Ambrosius see *Gildas, The Ruin of Britain and Other Documents* (Phillimore, 1978), 25; for the sacking of Colchester see 'Christopher Snyder, *Sub Roman Britain (AD 40–600)* (BAR, 1996), pp. 15–16; for an unusual take on the early-fifth-century wolf story including a dobermann see Adrienne Mayor, 'Ambiguous Guardians: The Omen of the Wolves', *Journal of Folklore Research* 29 (1992), pp. 255–68; for the letters of Honorius sent to the British counties *c*.410, telling them to defend themselves, E.A. Thompson, 'Zosimus 6.10.2 and the letters of Honorius', *Classical Quarterly* 32 (1982), pp. 445–62. For the building of dykes at Silchester see Snyder, *Sub Roman Britain*, pp. 41–2; for barbarian mercenaries around London as guards, Ken Dark, *Britain and the End of the Roman Empire* (Tempus, 2000), pp. 97–103; for the use of and the retreat to hilltop strongholds and the general abandonment of towns, *Gildas*, 24.

In this chapter I talk of the 'counties' of Britain. This is a translation – perhaps an inadequate one – of the Latin word *civitas*, the basic territorial unit of the Empire. This word should translate 'city state' or 'city district', a portion of land based around a city. But this is inapt for Britain, where the balance between town and country remained very much tipped towards the latter, so I have used the more rural 'county', though the territory of the *civitates* tended to be somewhat bigger than their modern British equivalents.